Mihai Duguleană · Marcello Carrozzino
Matjaž Gams · Iulian Tanea (Eds.)

VR Technologies in Cultural Heritage

First International Conference, VRTCH 2018
Brasov, Romania, May 29–30, 2018
Revised Selected Papers

Editors
Mihai Duguleană
Transylvania University of Braşov
Brasov, Romania

Matjaž Gams
Jožef Stefan Institute
Ljubljana, Slovenia

Marcello Carrozzino
Sant'Anna School of Advanced Studies
Pisa, Italy

Iulian Tanea
E-nformation
Bucharest, Romania

https://doi.org/10.1007/978-3-030-05819-7

Preface

This volume contains the papers from the First International Conference on VR Technologies in Cultural Heritage (VRTCH 2018). The event was organized under the project eHERITAGE (Expanding the Research and Innovation Capacity in Cultural Heritage Virtual Reality Applications), which is a Coordination and Support action that addresses the challenges described in the topic H2020-TWINN-2015 of the H2020 Work Program.

The coordinator of the eHERITAGE project is the Transilvania University of Brasov, a public research-oriented higher education institution that has been participating in a wide variety of nationally and internationally funded research projects. The supporting partners involved in the eHERITAGE project are Jožef Stefan Institute and Scuola Superiore Sant'Anna di Pisa. The Jožef Stefan Institute is the most important research institute in Slovenia, ranked among the top 50 research centers in Europe with respect to European involvement. Scuola Superiore Sant'Anna di Pisa is a public university that holds a unique position within the Italian higher education system. It is active in the fields of experimental sciences and social sciences and currently aims at developing graduate programs where rigorous traditional courses are combined with opportunities for research, service learning, internships, and entrepreneurship.

Not coincidentally, VRTCH 2018 was organized in 2018, which is the European Year of Cultural Heritage. As a sign of integration within this initiative, VRTCH 2018 received the label of the European Year of Cultural Heritage from the EU.

Conserving and promoting cultural heritage is a challenging task. When preserving cultural heritage through means of virtual reality, researchers deal with a wide array of techniques and methods. From Web-based virtual assistants to photogrammetry, there are thousands of studies out there tackling multiple areas of interest, throughout various channels of communication. The First International Conference on VR Technologies in Cultural Heritage (VRTCH 2018) tried to cluster some of the latest trends in these areas. The selected papers come from researchers based in several countries including Italy, Greece, Turkey, Portugal, and Romania. The highly diversified audience gave us the opportunity to achieve a good level of understanding of the mutual needs, requirements, and technical means available in this field of research.

The topics included in the first edition of this event include the following fields connected to cultural heritage: data acquisition and modeling, visualization and audio methods, sensors and actuators, data management, restoration and digitization, and cultural tourism. All the accepted papers were peer reviewed by three qualified reviewers chosen from our Scientific Committee based on their qualifications and experience.

The proceedings editors wish to thank the dedicated Scientific Committee members and all the other reviewers for their contributions. We also thank Springer for their trust and for publishing the proceedings of VRTCH 2018.

July 2018

Mihai Duguleană
Marcello Carrozzino
Matjaž Gams

Organization

Scientific Committee

Erik Malcolm Champion	Curtin University, Australia
Marinos Ioannides	Cyprus University of Technology, Cyprus
Enrica Salvatori	University of Pisa, Italy
Pavlos Chatzigrigoriou	Syros, Greece
Radu-Daniel Vatavu	Stefan cel Mare of Suceava University, Romania
Florin Stelian Gîrbacia	Transilvania University of Brasov, Romania
Yiorgos Chrysanthou	University of Cyprus, Cyprus
Fotis Liarokapis	Masaryk University, Czech Republic
Sara de Freitas	Murdoch University, Australia
Daniel Pletinckx	Visual Dimension bvba, Belgium
Krzysztof Walczak	Poznań University of Economics and Business, Poland
Raffaele De Amicis	Oregon State University, USA
Dorin Mircea Popovici	Ovidius University of Constanta, Romania
Alexandra Angeletaki	Norwegian University of Science and Technology, Norway
Federico Avanzini	University of Milano, Italy
Bruno Simoes	Vimcotech, Spain
Alfredo Liverani	University of Bologna, Italy
Ioan Dziţac	Agora University, Romania
Nicolae Ispas	Transilvania University of Brasov, Romania
Anghel Chiru	Transilvania University of Brasov, Romania
Adrian Soica	Transilvania University of Brasov, Romania
Claudiu Pozna	Transilvania University of Brasov, Romania
Sorin Moraru	Transilvania University of Brasov, Romania
Paul Borza	Transilvania University of Brasov, Romania
Florin Nechita	Transilvania University of Brasov, Romania
Laurentiu Mihail Ivanovici	Transilvania University of Brasov, Romania
Mircea Nastasoiu	Transilvania University of Brasov, Romania
Stelian Tarulescu	Transilvania University of Brasov, Romania
Sebastian Radu	Transilvania University of Brasov, Romania
Bogdan Cornel Benea	Transilvania University of Brasov, Romania
Corneliu Cofaru	Transilvania University of Brasov, Romania
Dinu Covaciu	Transilvania University of Brasov, Romania
Dragos Sorin Dima	Transilvania University of Brasov, Romania
Hunor Erdelyi	Siemens Industry Software N.V., Belgium
Angel Huminic	Transilvania University of Brasov, Romania
Gheorghe Alexandru Radu	Transilvania University of Brasov, Romania
Radu Tarulescu	Transilvania University of Brasov, Romania

Janos Timar	Transilvania University of Brasov, Romania
George Radu Toganel	Transilvania University of Brasov, Romania
Daniel Trusca	Transilvania University of Brasov, Romania
Raffaello Brondi	Scuola Superiore Sant'Anna Pisa, Italy
Chiara Evangelista	Scuola Superiore Sant'Anna Pisa, Italy
Franco Tecchia	Scuola Superiore Sant'Anna Pisa, Italy
Julien Jenvrin	IIT, Italy
Cătălin Ciobanu	Amsterdam University, The Netherlands
Bogdan Filipič	Jožef Stefan Institute Ljubljana, Slovenia
Adrian Budala	Transilvania University of Brasov, Romania
Cristian-Ioan Leahu	Transilvania University of Brasov, Romania
Teodora Girbacia	Transilvania University of Brasov, Romania
Adrian Stavar	Electrobit, Romania
Alina Panfir	UiPath, Romania
Alexandra Covaci	nChain, UK
Adrian Iulian Dumitru	Benchmark Electronics, Romania
Ioana Firastrau	Transilvania University of Brasov, Romania

Organizing Committee

Riccardo Galdieri	Scuola Superiore Sant'Anna Pisa, Italy
Aleš Tavčar	Jožef Stefan Institute Ljubljana, Slovenia
Marcello Carrozzino	Scuola Superiore Sant'Anna Pisa, Italy
Matjaz Gams	Jožef Stefan Institute Ljubljana, Slovenia
Mihai Duguleană	Transilvania University of Brasov, Romania
Andreea Beraru	Transilvania University of Brasov, Romania
Eugen Butilă	Transilvania University of Brasov, Romania

Local Committee

Cristian Cezar Postelnicu	Transilvania University of Brasov, Romania
Florin Gîrbacia	Transilvania University of Brasov, Romania
Daniel Voinea	Transilvania University of Brasov, Romania
Răzvan Boboc	Transilvania University of Brasov, Romania
Gheorghe Mogan	Transilvania University of Brasov, Romania
Silviu Butnariu	Transilvania University of Brasov, Romania
Csaba Antonya	Transilvania University of Brasov, Romania
Octavian Machidon	Transilvania University of Brasov, Romania

Contents

Sensors and Actuators

Data Management

Restoration and Digitization

Cultural Tourism

Data Acquisition and Modelling

Application of Fourier-Transform Infrared Spectroscopy (FTIR) for the Study of Cultural Heritage Artifacts

Valentin Raditoiu[1], Irina Elena Chican[1(✉)], Alina Raditoiu[1], Irina Fierascu[1], Radu Claudiu Fierascu[1], and Petronela Fotea[2]

[1] The National Institute for Research and Development in Chemistry and Petrochemistry - ICECHIM, 202 Spl. Independentei, 060021 Bucharest, Romania
irina_chican@yahoo.com
[2] Romanian Peasant Museum, 3 Kiseleff Str., 011341 Bucharest, Romania

Abstract. Analysis of cultural heritage artifacts represents a very important first step in any restoration/conservation attempt. Fourier-Transform Infrared Spectroscopy - Attenuated Total Reflectance (FTIR-ATR) technique can be successfully applied for the study of a wide range of historical artifacts (several papers describing the application of FTIR for the analysis of historical metals, paper, ceramic, fabrics, etc.). The present paper aims to present the application of FTIR-ATR for the characterization of historical fibers. The analyzed artifact represents a traditional pillowcase originating from Moldavia historical region, from the end of the XIXth century – beginning of the XXth century, belonging to a private collection. The technique offers some advantages because relatively small samples are directly analyzed after they are pressed against the surface of the diamond crystal without damaging the samples. Identification of fiber type enables sometimes to approximate the age of an artifact, the climate type or the trade routes and manufacturing process used. The artifact is formed of two major components: the support textile fiber and the colored fibers. The most encountered materials traditionally used for such objects are wool, flax and hemp. While wool is easily identified in the FTIR spectra due to its sharp and intense characteristic peaks, in the case of cellulosic fibers and especially for differentiation between flax and hemp fibers it was necessary to calculate the average values of the band intensity ratios I_{1595}/I_{1105} and I_{1595}/I_{2900}.

Keywords: Historical textiles · FTIR-ATR spectroscopy · Colored textile Lignin

1 Introduction

The FTIR spectroscopy represents a valuable tool for the analysis of different types of historical artifacts due to its sensitivity, specificity and non-destructive character [1]. The technique can be successfully applied for characterization of metallic artifacts (such as iron [2] or bronze objects [3]), paper artifacts [4, 5], ancient ceramics [6] or historical textiles [7, 8]. Chemical changes because of materials ageing can be observed

M. Duguleană et al. (Eds.): VRTCH 2018, CCIS 904, pp. 3–9, 2019.
https://doi.org/10.1007/978-3-030-05819-7_1

and sometimes quantified using FTIR spectroscopy, which is important especially for art conservation efforts [9]. The identification of fibers originating from different natural materials: cotton, silk, wool, hemp, flax is of crucial importance to choose appropriate treatment and conservation strategies for textile artifacts, but also to ensure their proper exhibition [10, 11]. Moreover, specific knowledge of fiber type enables sometimes the approximate dating of an artifact, the type of climate a place had or the trade routes at a particular time together with information about the manufacturing process [11].

Analysis by FTIR in the field of historical textiles related to Romanian traditional fabrics can provide useful information regarding the type and origin of textile materials and dyes. It is well established that in Romania for the textile support mainly two types of cellulosic fibers were used (flax and hemp) and only one type of protein fiber (wool) [12]. Therefore, the range is relatively limited, making the investigation much easier from this point of view.

The first objective of conservation or reconstruction of textile artifacts is to determine the constitution of the fibers and this task is usually accomplished by performing FTIR spectra of different materials from different sources and regions and comparing with the spectra of artifacts [13].

2 Experimental

2.1 Textile Material

The analyzed textile artifact represents a traditional pillowcase originating from Moldavia historical region, manufactured at the end of the XIXth century – beginning of the XXth century (Fig. 1). From the large artifact, several smaller samples were obtained, representing both the support material and the colored fibers (Fig. 2). All the samples were analyzed as they were obtained from the original artifact (see Fig. 1).

Fig. 1. The textile artifact studied (Color figure online)

Fig. 2. Different collected samples from the artefact – the support material and the different colored samples (Color figure online)

2.2 Analytical Method

The FTIR spectra were recorded on a FTIR 6300 instrument from Jasco Inc., Japan, equipped with a Specac Golden Gate ATR which is fitted with a diamond crystal and an interaction angle of 45°. All the spectra recorded in the range 4000–400 cm^{-1} were averaged over 32 scans at a resolution of 4 cm^{-1}. All the recorded data was processed with Spectra Manager II software from Jasco Inc., Japan.

3 Results and Discussion

In the field of natural dyes used as coloring materials, the major issue is related to the amount applied on the surface of the fiber, which is frequently situated bellow the detection limit in the infrared spectroscopy [14]. Thus, it is difficult to determine structural characteristics of the dyes directly from FTIR-ATR spectra of dyed textiles.

As it can be observed from the spectra of the samples obtained from a traditional pillowcase from Moldova historical region, the signals are specific to the textile support without interferences due to the presence of different dyes onto the surface of the fibers. The superimposed spectra of the colored fibers showed strong bands corresponding to amide I and amide II, situated at 1634 and 1511 cm^{-1}, together with several other intense characteristic bands (1390 cm^{-1} – CH_3 symmetrical deformation and 1055 cm^{-1} – asymmetrical stretch C-O-C and C-N stretch), confirming that the textile support is wool in all the cases (Fig. 3).

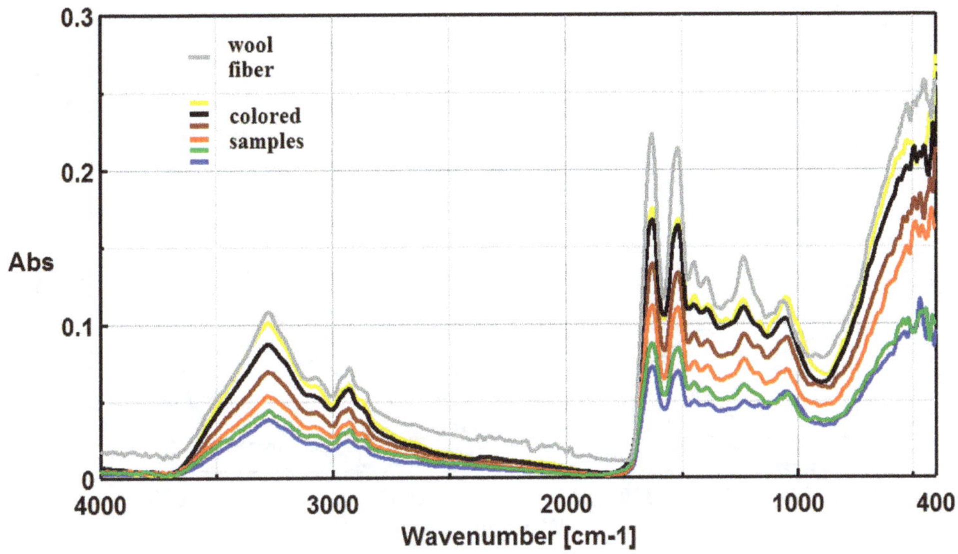

Fig. 3. FTIR-ATR spectra of colored samples from the textile artifact (Color figure online)

Spectra of cotton, flax and hemp recorded and compared with the white sample, which represents the artifact main material demonstrated similarities, as the main component of these fibers is cellulose and the other major component (hemicellulose) is a polysaccharide too. However, in deep analysis of the spectra showed certain differences, which can be used to differentiate them due to the lignin content (Table 1).

Table 1. The composition of some cellulosic fibers [15]

Fibers	Cellulose (%)	Hemicelluloses (%)	Lignin (%)
Cotton	82.7	5.7	0.0
Flax	64.1	16.7	2.0
Hemp	67.0	16.1	3.3

As it was already established, the fibers can be differentiated from one another by calculating ratios between intensities of the infrared absorption bands at about 2900, 1595 and 1105 cm^{-1}. These bands are associated with the C-H stretching vibration (used as a measure of the overall organic content), the C=C in plane aromatic vibrations (due to the lignin content) and the C-O-C glycosidic ether band (due to the cellulose content) [16].

The FTIR-ATR spectrum of the white sample, which is the main material of the artifact, reveals the presence of the characteristic peaks corresponding to cellulose and lignin and apparently may be hemp or flax (Fig. 4). The shape of the sample spectrum is closed to the flax spectrum, but for a reliable result the analysis of the intensity ratios must be calculated.

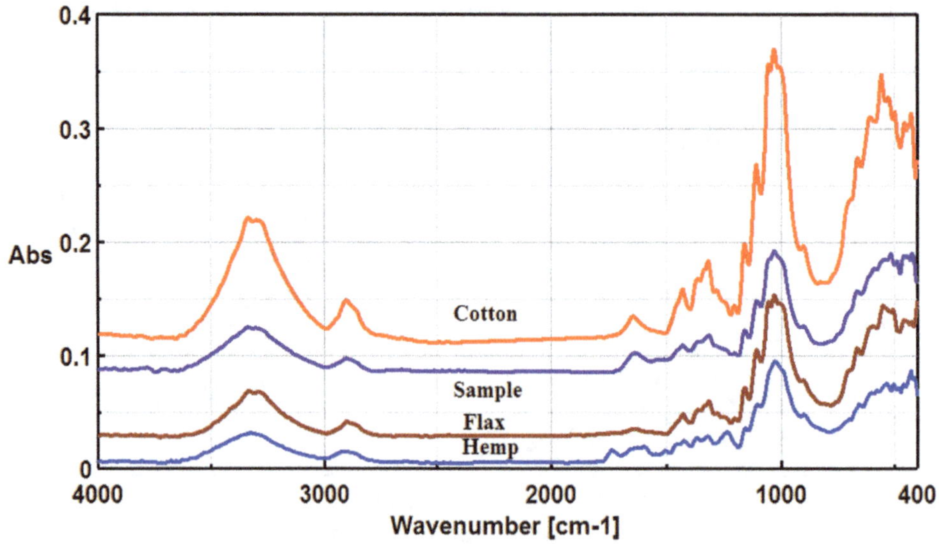

Fig. 4. FTIR-ATR spectra of possible textile fibers for the textile artifact main material

The average values of the band intensity ratios R_1 (I_{1595}/I_{1105}) and R_2 (I_{1595}/I_{2900}) were calculated for three types of pure cellulosic fibers (cotton, hemp and flax) and for the support sample (Table 2).

Table 2. The band intensity ratios R_1 (I_{1595}/I_{1105}) and R_2 (I_{1595}/I_{2900})

Fibers	R_1 (I_{1595}/I_{1105})	R_2 (I_{1595}/I_{2900})
Cotton	0.33	0.11
Flax	0.38	0.09
Hemp	0.83	0.27
Sample	0.41	0.10

As it can be observed, the results obtained for the band intensity ratios do not follow exactly the composition of the fibers due to the overlapping of the bands in the regions where the measurements are made. An important task to be solved seems to be drying the samples before the measurements, because the water bending at about 1640 cm^{-1} artificially increased the band of lignin at 1595 cm^{-1}. The deconvolution of the spectra does not solve the issue and if the measurement conditions remained unchanged, the results are consistent and the method can be used without restrictions to determine differences between cellulosic fibers. Valuable results that elucidate this kind of sensible difference probably can be obtained by performing polarized ATR-FTIR measurements [17]. As there is a great similarity among flax and hemp fibers, usually besides FT-IR spectroscopy it is necessary to perform investigations by complementary techniques, such as: the twist test, fiber diameter measurements, general microscopic observation, SEM analysis and polarized ATR spectroscopy completed whenever is possible with chemical tests (phloroglucionol reaction; Herzberg reagent, Schweitzer's reagent).

4 Conclusions

Despite minor differences between different types of cellulosic fibers, FTIR-ATR technique proved to be a useful tool in order to distinguish them on the basis of some of their structural features.

Comparison between spectra of different cellulosic fibers, in terms of intensity ratios can lead to valuable results which allow differentiation even in the case of problematic species such as flax and hemp.

The fabric artifact studied by us is a traditional pillowcase originating from Moldavia historical region, from the end of the XIXth century – beginning of the XXth century, belonging to a private collection. The obtained results prove that it is formed of two types of fibers: the support textile fiber, identified as flax, and the colored fibbers, identified as wool fibers dyed with natural colorants. In order to analyze the natural colorants, present at the surface of the fibers, further investigations should be made and probably correlations with complementary techniques are necessary (such as extraction of the pigments and their analysis using High-performance liquid chromatography, SEM analysis etc.).

Acknowledgments. The authors gratefully acknowledge the financial support obtained through the project SoVaReX, Contract No. 10PS/2017, from the Sectorial Program – Romanian Ministry of Research and Innovation.

References

1. Peets, P., Leito, I., Pelt, J., Vahur, S.: Identification and classification of textile fibres using ATR-FT-IR spectroscopy with chemometric methods. Spectrochim. Acta Part A Molec. Biomolec. Spectrosc. **173**, 175–181 (2017)
2. Ramesh Kumar, A.V., Balasubramaniam, R.: Corrosion product analysis of corrosion resistant ancient Indian iron. Corros. Sci. **39**(6), 1169–1178 (1998)
3. Ion, R.M., et al.: Combined spectral analysis (EDXRF, ICP-AES, XRD, FTIR) for characterization of bronze roman mirror. Met. Int. **13**(5), 61–65 (2008)
4. Fierascu, R.C., Avramescu, S.M., Vasilievici, G., Fierascu, I., Paunescu, A.: Thermal and spectroscopic investigation of Romanian historical documents from the nineteenth and twentieth century. J. Therm. Anal. Calorim. **123**(2), 1309–1318 (2016)
5. Fierascu, I., et al.: Micro-analytical and microbiological investigation of selected book papers from the nineteenth century. J. Therm. Anal. Calorim. **129**(3), 1377–1387 (2017)
6. Ion, R.M., et al.: Thermal and mineralogical investigations of historical ceramic: a case study. J. Therm. Anal. Calorim. **104**(2), 487–493 (2011)
7. Akyuz, T., Akyuz, S., Balci, K., Gulec, A.: Investigations of historical textiles from the Imperial Pavilion (Hunkar Kasri) of the new mosque Eminonu-Istanbul (Turkey) by multiple analytical techniques. J. Cult. Herit. **25**, 180–184 (2017)
8. Mai, H., Yang, Y., Jiang, H., Wang, B., Wang, C.: Investigating the materials and manufacture of Jinzi: the lining of Futou (Chinese traditional male headwear) from the Astana Cemeteries, Xinjiang, China. J. Cult. Herit. **27**, 116–124 (2017)
9. Higgitt, C., Harris, S., Cartwright, C., Cruickshank, P.: Assessing the potential of historic archaeological collections: a pilot study of the British Museum's Swiss lake dwelling textiles. Br. Museum Techn. Res. Bull. **5**, 81–94 (2011)

10. Kavkler, K., Demsar, A.: Application of FTIR and Raman spectroscopy to qualitative analysis of structural changes in cellulosic fibres. Tekstilec **55**(1), 19–31 (2012)
11. Chae, J.: Observation and analysis for identifying materials of textile objects. In: Conservation of Papers and Textiles, pp. 262–279. National Research Institute of Cultural Heritage, Daejeon (2011)
12. Olaru, A., Geba, M., Vlad, A.M., Ciovica, S.: Metallic accessories on ethnographic textiles deterioration problems. Eur. J. Sci. Theol. **9**(3), 177–186 (2013)
13. Zemaityte, R., Jonaitiene, V., Milasius, R., Stanys, S., Ulozaite, R.: Analysis and identification of fibre constitution of archaeological textiles. Mater. Sci. (Medziagotyra) **12**(3), 258–261 (2006)
14. De Luca, E., Bruni, S., Sali, D., Guglielmi, V., Belloni, P.: In situ nondestructive identification of natural dyes in ancient textiles by reflection fourier transform mid-infrared (FT-MIR) spectroscopy. Appl. Spectrosc. **69**(2), 222–229 (2015)
15. Lewin, M., Pearce, E.M.: Handbook of Fiber Chemistry, 2nd edn. Marcel Dekker, Inc., New York (1998)
16. Garside, P., Wyeth, P.: Characterisation of plant fibres By infra-red spectroscopy. Polym. Prepr. **41**(2), 1792–1793 (2000)
17. Garside, P., Wyeth, P.: identification of cellulosic fibres by FTIR Spectroscopy. Differentiation of flax and hemp by polarized ATR-FTIR. Stud. Conserv. **51**, 205–211 (2006)

Digital Scanning and Non-destructive Techniques for Size Recovering and Rehabilitating the Structural Performance of Traditional Stuccoes

Rodica-Mariana Ion[1,2(✉)], Valentin Gurgu[3], Ioan Alin Bucurica[3], Sofia Teodorescu[3], Ioana Daniela Dulama[3], Raluca Maria Stirbescu[3], and Anca Gheboianu[3]

[1] National Institute of Research and Development for Chemistry and Petrochemistry – ICECHIM, 202 Splaiul Independentei, 060021 Bucharest, Romania
rodica_ion2000@yahoo.co.uk
[2] Faculty of Materials Engineering and Mechanics, Valahia University of Targoviste, 13 Sinaia Alley, 130004 Targoviste, Romania
[3] Institute of Multidisciplinary Research for Science and Technology, Valahia University of Targoviste, 13 Sinaia Aleea, 130004 Targoviste, Romania

Abstract. Nowadays, there is a lack of knowledge regarding the traditional construction technology used in many of some important monuments in Romania. To address this limitation and to assist in their conservation and restoration, this study documents the existing condition of different historic structures. Methods and applications for 3D scanning, image scanning and no-contact and non-destructive methods are applied in this paper for structural analysis of the stuccoes from a patrimony building (Fântaneanu House, Slatina). To record and document the condition of this house, the laser scanning is used in order to identify the initial size and shape of some damaged parts of the monument. Advancement in diagnosis methods (spectral and microscopic analytical methods) for the conservation/restoration of this patrimony building.

Keywords: Patrimony · Stucco · 3D scanning

1 Introduction

In conservation and restoration procedures applied to different monuments from cultural heritage, is absolutely necessary to obey some rules, as follows:

- selection and characterization of historical materials (stones, mortars, bricks, plasters, pigments, binders, concrete, plastics);
- preparation of model substrates;
- simulation of their degradation in the presence of different external agents;
- *in situ* assessment of the materials (destructive and non-destructive testing);

M. Duguleană et al. (Eds.): VRTCH 2018, CCIS 904, pp. 10–18, 2019.
https://doi.org/10.1007/978-3-030-05819-7_2

- identification of the cleaning materials and protective coatings;
- application and characterization of new materials correlated with environmental impact study, strengthening frescoes and basoreliefs with various consolidants;
- developing a methodology for testing the effectiveness of consolidation [1].

Known from more than 15 years, the three-dimensional scanning (3D scanning) method is a process that uses a contact or non-contact digitizing probe to capture the objects form and recreate them in a virtual workspace through a very dense network of points (xyz) as a 3D graph representation. There are known two types of 3D scanning, as follows: contact mode, which refers to the mechanical contact of the surfaces, and non-contact mode (without mechanical contact) which use optical sources, laser or a combination of the reproduction of the scanned surface. The best equipment is the 3D contact scanner, based on the controlled direction of the laser beam, followed by a measuring the distance of each point, the shape of objects, buildings and landscapes. The laser beam is that it can penetrate even the smallest cracks of the surface [2].

Materials that can be scanned with laser include: stone, ceramics, glass, metal, wood, plastic, rubber and clay. The tracks are measured by laser 3D scanning then they are compared to the projected model (CAD file) using a specialized software.

Methods and applications of 3D scanning method with image scanning correlated with non-contact and non-destructive investigation methods are applied in this paper for structural analysis of the stuccoes from a patrimony building (Fântaneanu House, Slatina). The laser scanning is used in order to identify the initial size and shape of some damaged parts of the monument, and some analytical methods (FTIR, SEM-EDS, MO) have been used for the diagnosis of this patrimony building.

2 Experimental Part

The used equipment is EXAscan Portable 3D Laser Scanner is a Mobile 3D Laser scanner, Portable 3D Metrology equipment, Creaform Exascan.

It could scan pieces of different sizes, with different geometries: 25,000 measurements/s, resolution of 0.2 mm, accuracy of up to 0.040 mm (0.0016 in.), depth of field: ±150 mm (±6 in.), volumetric accuracy (with MaxSHOT 3D) of minimum 0.020 mm + 0.025 mm/m (0.0008 in. + 0.0003 in./ft, VXelements software, Catia V5, V6, 3D X-Element CD software, portable 3D Laser Scanner.

2.1 Scan the Object

After the parameterization, the object to be scanned is placed at the center of the reference points and the scan operation takes place, which involves scanning the surface of the object with the laser on the scanner. The result of the operation is a cloud of points. The program analyzes the points and joins them, so the final result being the scanned object in electronic format (digitized).

2.2 Analytical Investigation Equipment

Fourier transformed infrared spectroscopy (ATR-FTIR) has been recorded with a Vertex 80 spectrometer (Bruker Optik GMBH, Germania) in the range of 4000–400 cm^{-1}, equipped with DRIFT accessory.

The optical microscopy was performed with a Novex trinocular microscope (at different magnifications) and by a Primo Star ZEISS optical microscope that offers the possibility to investigate the samples in transmitted light at a magnification between 4X and 100X. The equipment had attached a digital video camera (Axiocam 105) which, by the microscope software, allowed real-time data acquisition.

The Scanning Electron Microscopy with Energy Dispersive Spectroscopy (SEM-EDS) results were obtained by a SU-70 (Hitachi, Japan) microscope, used for characterization of micro- and nanomaterials qualitative and quantitative analysis of samples and composition of the structure for a sample surface, respectively.

2.3 Samples

The prelevated samples have been taken firstly for 3D scanning (Fig. 1) and secondly for analytical investigation (Fig. 2).

Fig. 1. The aspect of the stucco sample

Fig. 2. The multilayer conserved stucco

3 Results and Discussion

3.1 Scan the Object and Results Processing

After the parametrization, the object to be scanned was placed at the center of the reference points and the scan operation takes place, which involves scanning the surface of the object with the scanner laser [3]. A network of points was obtained. The program allowed joining the points and a scanned object in electronic format (digitized) has been obtained. The processing was done using the "Digitized Shape Editor" module in the Catia program. A series of operations were performed to remove unusable surfaces and for the symmetrical reconstruction the mirroring operation was applied. After the scanner was configured, the reference points were scanned. They have the role of keeping the scanned object in a fixed position in 3D space [4, 5]. The next step involved parameterizing the scanning procedure, namely choosing the resolution, optimizing the dot network, optimizing the limits, optimizing the precision, automatically filling the holes and removing the isolated surfaces. The file containing the digitized object was saved and processed in the CATIA program [5]. A series of operations were performed to remove unusable surfaces and for the symmetrical reconstruction the mirroring operation was applied, Fig. 3.

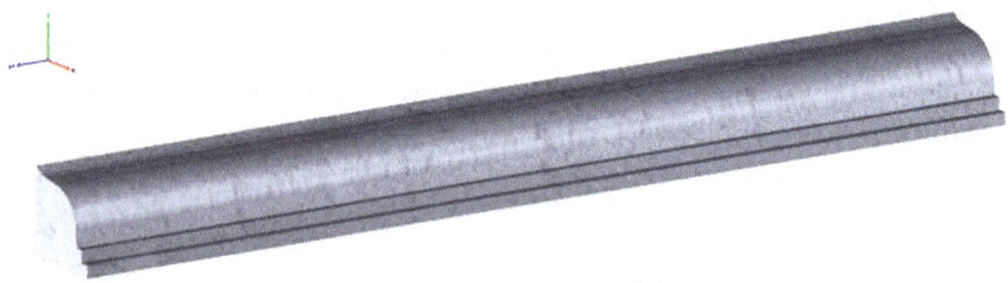

Fig. 3. The aspect of the stucco after 3D scanning

As could be observed, this program analyzes the points and joins them, so the final result being the scanned object in electronic format (digitized), by "Digitized Shape Editor" module in the Catia program [6, 7]. The not useful surfaces have been removed and for the symmetrical reconstruction the mirroring operation was applied.

After digitalization a detailed examination and investigation have been applied by using different multidisciplinary techniques applied for identification of the structure, composition and morphology of different heritage samples [8, 9], as follows: Scanning Electron Microscopy with Energy Dispersive Spectroscopy (SEM-EDS), Optical microscopy and Fourier Transformed Infrared spectroscopy (FTIR), only mentioning few of them.

By scanning electron microscopy was possible to identify 7 successive layers of various compositions, Fig. 4.

From the SEM investigations of the whole sample, some results have been obtained: seven layers of various materials, some of the layers without a perfect connection to each other due to the incompatibility of materials or degradation induced by the passage of time and the action of external agents: moisture, freeze-thaw, light or even improper restoration operations with negative effects. These data could be correlated with other chemical techniques, for example FTIR.

The FTIR spectral data of the MIR-region of the stucco's layers samples show only little variation and generally a high absorbance (strong signal) at wavenumbers between 500 and 1500 cm^{-1}. This region of the spectrum is characteristic for CO

Fig. 4. SEM images of the analyzed stucco mortar

bonds, such as those originating from carbonates or carboxyl-groups of limestone. The most rich sulphate layers show the most intense band of 1700–1600 cm^{-1}, and an increase of this band can be observed for the most degraded layer. Practically all layers show calcium sulphate, more intense as the most damaged, a sign that the degradation took time over each layer of plaster without cleaning the previous layer, Fig. 5.

Within the recorded spectra of all seven clay samples presented a weak absorbance centered on 3600–3700 cm^{-1} which can be attributed to hydroxyl vibrations.

According with the spectral data for both category of samples it can be concluded that the chemical composition of the layers are is quite similar (hydroxyl, carbonyl and SiO_4 groups) [10–14].

FTIR spectral data are in well compliance with EDS and SEM, Fig. 6.

Based on the partial results obtained, we assume that the masonry is made of carbonate stone, the plaster applied on the wall of the house is mostly of lime with the most likely binders of different nature (glue, clay, sand, etc.).

The green color identified at one of the layers is due to a natural green pigment that varies in shades and color compositions. The “green earth” pigment is a mixture of Fe, Mg, Al, K (mainly minerals such as celadonite and glauconite) [15].

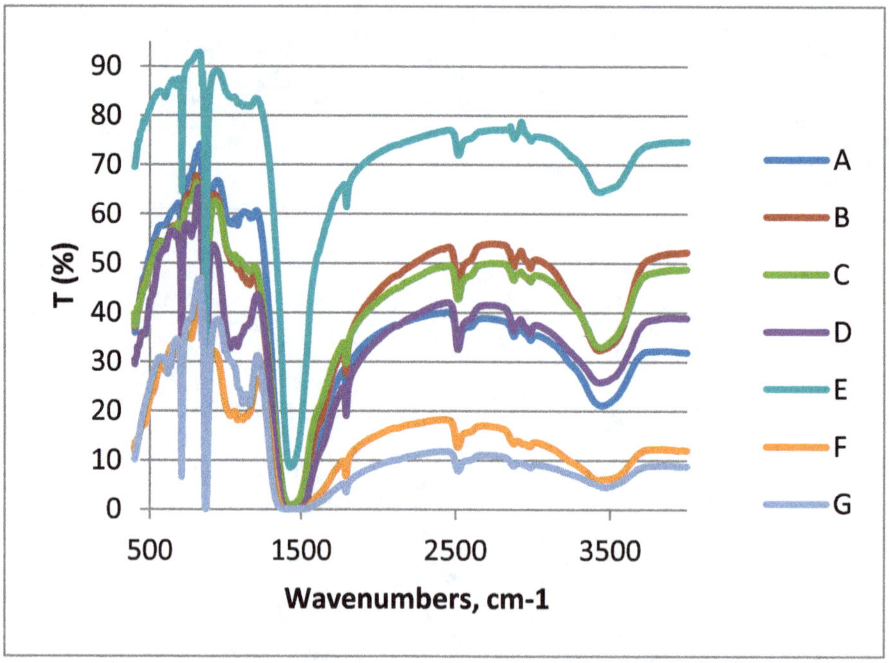

Fig. 5. FTIR spectra of the stucco's layers

The SEM images led to the following conclusions: the masonry layers from stucco sample present a lamellar structure, with a granular structure with lamellar inclusions as well. The first layer (the oldest one) shows a damaged structure, mostly due to the second layer applied, entirely based on gypsum, the most aggressive agent for masonries in general. The second layer shows a structure of aluminosilicates responsible for implosion, Fig. 6.

The presence of gypsum is major diminished in all the subsequent layers, and as other mortar layers have been applied over time, new elements specific to building materials that have emerged over time, such as barium sulfide or zinc or even chromium, as a component of some pigments (PG17 for example) [16].

EDS results (Fig. 7) have shown that with the exception of the layers I and II, where are predominant lime and gypsum, in all the other layers, C (40–60%), O (20–25%), Zn (30–50%) are the major constituents of the stucco's masonry sample, but also have been recorded elements as: Ca (0.14–3%), Mg (1.23–1.61%), Ti (1–3.23%).

From elemental analysis through EDS, we can observe the presence of calcium, which leads us to the conclusion that the plaster is lime-based, and in some layers, especially those rich in zinc, a green dye may have been used, Fig. 6.

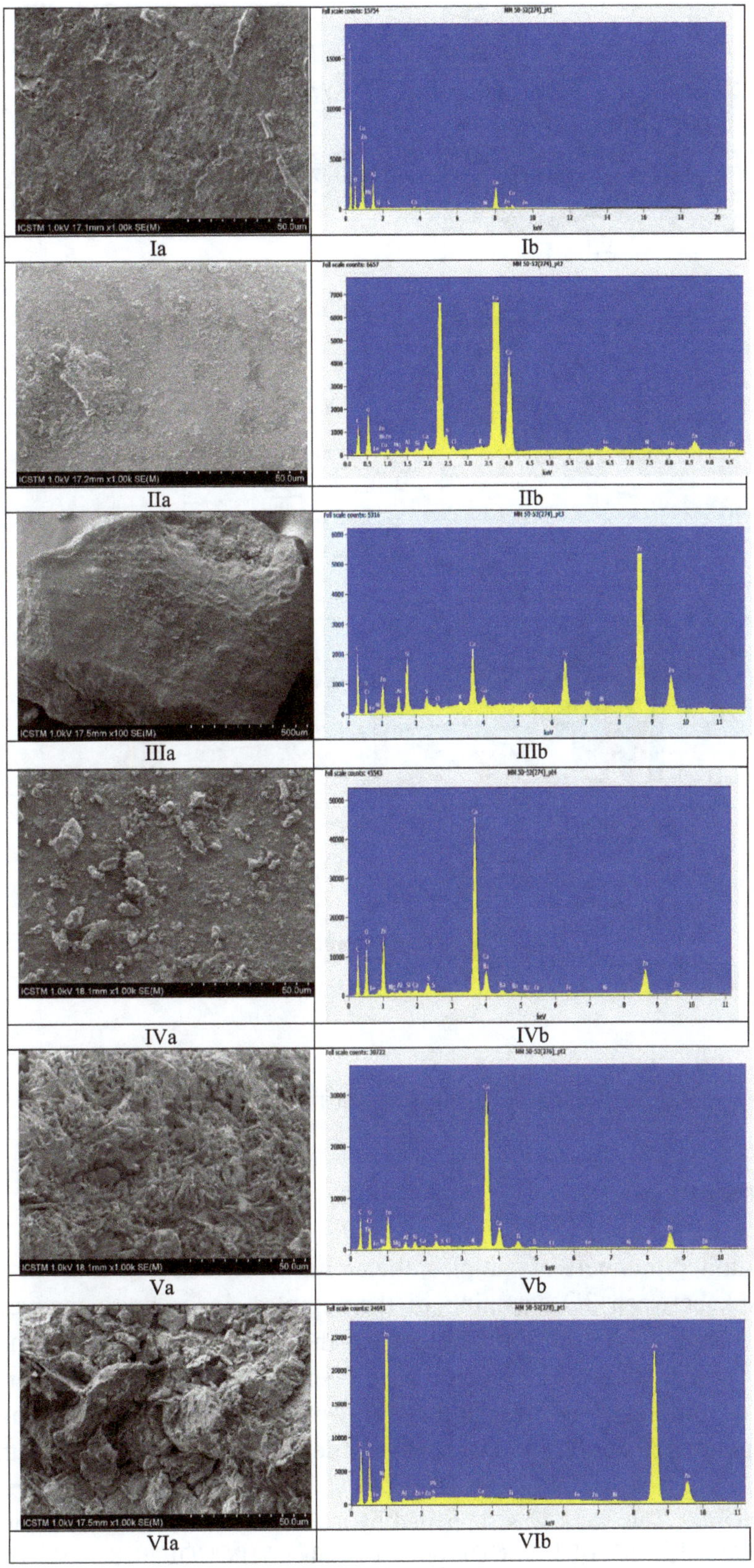

Fig. 6. The SEM images (left) and EDS diagrams for the studied samples (Color figure online)

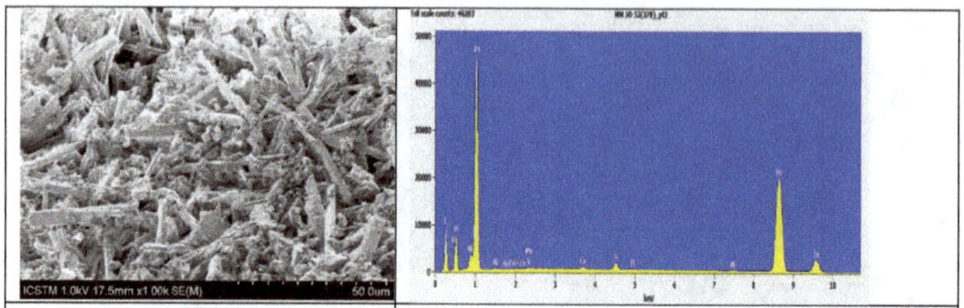

VII

Fig. 6. (*continued*)

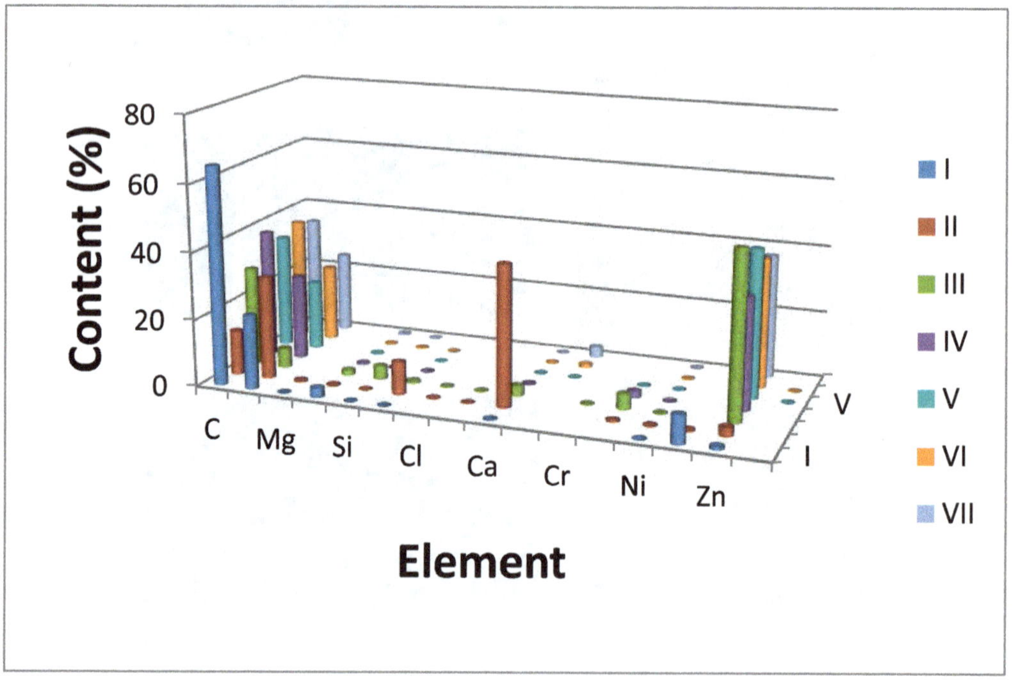

Fig. 7. The elements distribution from the stucco's layers

4 Conclusions

Despite the limited numbers of samples, the archaeometric results indicate that there is a obvious link between 3D scanning of the samples, in order to recover the initial shape, and to analyze the successive layers of the masonry applied in time.

Some of the local clay sources could have been considered the suitable raw material used for the restoration procedures in time. However, further determinations performed on a larger number of samples are needed in order to confirm this state of the research.

Acknowledgments. This work was supported by a grant of the Romanian National Authority for Scientific Research, MCI-UEFISCDI, project number 51PCCDI/2018.

References

1. Ion, R.-M., Teodorescu, S., Bucurica, I.A., Ion, M.-L., Turcanu-Carutiu, D.: Restoration and preservation of cultural heritage monuments. digital presentation and practical solutions. Digit. Present. Preserv. Cult. Sci. Herit. **6**, 107–116 (2016)
2. Ion, R.M., et al.: 3D-reconstruction of the complex stuccoes from patrimony buildings. Digit. Present. Preserv. Cult. Sci. Herit. **7**, 107–112 (2017)
3. Addison, A.C., Alonzo, C.: The vanishing virtual: safeguarding heritage's endangered digital record. In: Kvan, T., Kalay, Y. (eds.) Proceedings of New Heritage: Beyond Verisimilitude, pp. 36–48. University of Hong Kong (2006)
4. Bosche, F., Haas, C.: Automated retrieval of 3D CAD model objects in construction range images. Autom. Constr. **17**(4), 499–512 (2008)
5. Datta, S.: Digital reconstructions and the geometry of temple fragments. In: The Proceedings of the 2007 International Conference on Digital Applications in Cultural Heritage, Taiwan, pp. 443–452 (2001)
6. Fontana, R., Greco, M., Materazzi, M., Pampaloni, E., Pezzati, L., et al.: Three-dimensional modelling of statues: the Minerva of Arezzo. J. Cult. Herit. **3**(4), 325–331 (2002)
7. Pieraccini, M., Guidi, G., Atzeni, C.: 3D digitizing of cultural heritage. J. Cult. Herit. **2**(1), 63–70 (2001)
8. Shih, N.J., Wang, H.J., Lin, C.Y., Liau, C.Y.: 3D scan for the digital preservation of a historical temple in Taiwan. Adv. Eng. Softw. **38**(7), 501–512 (2007)
9. Franzini, M., Leoni, L., Lezzerini, M.: A procedure for determining the chemical composition of binder and aggregate in ancient mortars: its application to mortars from some medieval buildings in Pisa. J. Cult. Herit. **1**, 365–373 (2000)
10. Franzini, M., Leoni, L., Lezzerini, M., Sartori, M.: The mortar of the B Leaning Tower of Pisa: the product of a medieval technique for preparing high-strength mortars. Eur. J. Min. **12**, 1151–1163 (2000)
11. Moropoulou, A., Bakolas, A., Bisbikou, K.: Investigation of the technology of historic mortars. J. Cult. Herit. **1**, 45–58 (2000)
12. Jordá, J.D., et al.: Mineralogical analysis of ceramic tiles by FTIR: a quantitative attempt. App. Clay Sci. **115**, 1–8 (2015)
13. De Benedetto, G.E., Laviano, R., Sabbatini, L., Zambonin, P.G.: Infrared spectroscopy in the mineralogical characterization of ancient pottery. J. Cult. Herit. **3**(3), 177–186 (2002)
14. Chukanov, N.V.: Infrared Spectra of Mineral Species, vol. 1. Springer, Dordrecht (2014). https://doi.org/10.1007/978-94-007-7128-4
15. Antonelli, F., et al.: Multianalytical approach to diagnosis and conservation of building materials: the case of Punta Troia Castle in Marettimo (Aegadian Islands—Sicily, Italy). App. Phys. A **122**(4), 1–10 (2016)
16. Bruno, P., et al.: Chemical–physical and mineralogical investigation on ancient mortars from the archaeological site of Monte Sannace (Bari-Southern Italy). Thermochim. Acta **418**, 131–141 (2004)

Proposal for an Automated Form Finder System to Deduce the Authentic Morphology of Siirt Cas Houses

Mehmet Gökhan Berk(✉)

Yildiz Technical University, Istanbul, Turkey
mgokhanberk@gmail.com

Abstract. This paper aims to summarize the steps taken towards the development of a semi-automated system in an attempt to create computer modeling of the original morphology of the individual buildings and respective urban texture for the so called "cas" houses which are the characteristic traditional buildings of the Siirt Province in Turkey. For the purpose of developing the proposed system, the architectural space forming methods that are closely related with the structural composition of the buildings where loose stones are joined with a strong and quick drying mortar are observed. It has been detected that cas houses are in fact built in time through an incremental expansion approach making use of repeating rectangular cells in horizontal plane coming side to side, and upper floor plans are developed almost identically to ground floor layout. The rhythmic layout of the façade elements such as doors and windows, cut rectangular pyramidal form of the buildings and specific elements such as stair covering vaults and underpasses are both enriching the building form and enabling easier detection of the original morphology of the buildings. The proposed form finding system is based on the principle of processing the approximately measured outer boundaries of the existing buildings to deduce internal spaces' sizes and layout which are in fact the sole sources causing the exterior building form for cas houses.

Keywords: Siirt cas houses · Heritage modeling · Automated plan generation

1 Introduction

Architectural heritage at relatively less developed regions is under high risk of decay, deterioration and extinction mainly due to the owners' inadequate resources for maintenance, inadequate or lacking funding for conservation initiatives as well as due to poor awareness about the heritage value of such buildings. Interventions to this kind of buildings mainly aim to maintain and/or improve the buildings for daily practical needs or for expectations of adaptation to changing lifestyles without much sensitivity towards the original and authentic characteristics and generally results in degeneration and loss of valuable information with regards to regional, traditional and historical aspects. For such buildings it is not unusual to see that the original details are removed and the general form of the buildings is obscured during renovations and other interventions, thus the main heritage character is lost or concealed.

M. Duguleană et al. (Eds.): VRTCH 2018, CCIS 904, pp. 20–32, 2019.
https://doi.org/10.1007/978-3-030-05819-7_3

It is extremely difficult, almost impossible to bring back value, or further preserve such spoiled and degenerated buildings and reinstate the built environment to its original state, however much can be done by exploring the most appropriate methods, systems and intervention rules through fictionalizing the future they are destined to, with conservatory planning decisions that value the inherent authentic characteristics. This kind of interventions need to consider numerous parameters including but not limited to social environment, economical value, urban movements, population and other demographic aspects besides the local architectural, spatial, structural and planning decisions and initiatives.

Two extreme opposed intervention logics at such situations are towards either gentrification of this kind of buildings and neighborhoods, or towards urban regeneration through a totally changed character. It is obvious that more elaborated mechanisms are needed in search of a more accurate approach ensuring coherence of physical built environment with social needs, open to improvement and development through still preserving the authenticity and heritage value of buildings and respective neighborhood.

Clearing the extrinsic interventions, conservation and restoring the original and authentic form of historical buildings and neighborhoods is a complex process even on drawings and virtual models. Contemporary digital technologies are providing large opportunities for exploring, inducing and modelling the original form of buildings with heritage value and respective physical built environment. It is now possible to build three dimensional models of the historical neighborhoods at a given moment in time although this kind of studies can be quite difficult, time, resource and effort consuming due to the complexity of the buildings and respective physical environment as well as due to the considerable need for background information to be extracted from documentary and photo archives.

The amount of manual work may be remarkably reduced in parallel to recent advances in technology such as three dimensional scanning devices, and advanced modelling software but the large number of information and point sets created still require a considerable effort for evaluating and processing the acquired data. This fact imposes a need for automatic and/or intelligent methods and systems for registering, merging, abstracting and processing in defined ways of large range of data sets. It is also possible to employ this kind of intelligent systems to predict missing information to deduce not only geometrical but also other types of information that might explain the shaping of the built environment either by human behavior or by other forces.

This paper aims to investigate possibilities for developing systems capable of modelling authentic forms of the urban texture and individual buildings through use of generative computer-aided systems which are supposed to make use of the inherent grammar of the concerned historical buildings and urban texture.

2 Computer-Aided Form Generating Systems

2.1 Broad Overview of the Form Generating Systems

Use of the generative computer aided systems for form finding process in architectural design has been a considerably researched topic since a few decades. In essence these systems are based on computer processed algorithms which are according to Rajaraman, specifications of a sequence of instructions to be carried out in order to solve a given problem. Instructions are telling what tasks are to be performed and the algorithm serves as a codification of the problem through a series of finite, consistent and rational steps [1].

Procedural modeling is a computer-aided generative system that can be simply defined to be content production by means of a procedure or a program. It is making use of a wide variety of techniques that can produce a specific type of content based on a set of input parameters in a defined degree of automatization. The procedural modelling has been an active subject especially in the videogames industry with capacity to produce complex virtual environments including road networks and urban settings. It is also applied in various areas such as modeling of plants, landscape, terrain, buildings, urban areas, road networks, rivers, or art creation. With the use of procedural modelling, considerable amount of resource of man skilled labor can be drastically reduced and expertise and knowledge dependent efforts can be concentrated on elaborating automatically created models by adding and altering particularities and details that might make them closer to expected results [2].

Many procedural models are essentially generative representations either of processes inspired by nature, such as plant development, or of man-centered processes, such as building design or urban developments. Due to the stochastic nature of the methods employed by procedural modeling a wide variety of results can be created from one set of input parameters [2]. This gives the procedural modelling its potential to reduce the amount of modeling effort required to create digital content. The use of the "procedural modelling" approach in the fields of architecture, urban planning and archaeology is generally based on the notions of "shape grammar" or "style grammars" approaches and has great potential as well in the field of architectural heritage modelling as it enables to cope with complexities and difficulties specific to this field.

Shape grammars are applications in which shapes are presented as design descriptions and transformed according to a rule based formalism [3]. Generation process can be modeled on the transformations of shapes. A shape grammar contains vocabulary, a set of shape rules and an initial shape. Form alternatives can be generated by applying the shape rules recursively to the initial shape. Stiny is considered the inventor and one of the pioneers of the shape grammar approach in architectural form generating through computer processed systems [4]. Eloy and Duarte provide a comprehensive background and examples of the shape grammar principles applied to building design [5]. Shape grammars are used in the field of vernacular housing by Flemming for Queen Anne Houses [6], Cagdas explored Turkish traditional housing patterns [7] and Colakoglu has made use of the shape grammar principles for translating the Turkish traditional house patterns and components to contemporary housing context [8].

Yong et al. describe a method to create a style in the form of Southeast Chinese vernacular houses using an extended shape grammar. The grammar used is hierarchically planned which is starting at city level, then producing streets, housing blocks, roads, and in further productions houses with components such as gates, windows, walls, and roofs. Through a number of controlling rules (defining component ratio constraints etc.), the validity of the buildings can be evaluated. Applying of this grammar system enables generation of a typical traditional Southeast Chinese town. The success of the system is closely related with the inherent grammar (building style) of these towns which are very rigidly structured [9].

An ontology based solution for procedural generation of ancient structures, specifically the so called "domus" roman houses configured by rectangular floor plans has been exemplified by Adao [10]. This approach implements a working methodology that relies on an abstract ontological specification for buildings, foreseeing the possibility of extension to other architectonic styles. Ontologies can be defined to be knowledge structures capable of describing a system, namely the relations between its parts. They have been successfully applied in different solutions that require the use of virtual models and environments. Ontology based procedural modelling is concerned with the rapidly and faithful visualization of virtual structures disregarding imperceptible details. The entire generation process relies in a set of definition and restriction rules to achieve the virtual building.

2.2 Proposed Form Finding Methodology

A methodology inspired by the computer-aided form generation systems is proposed in this paper to induce a shape grammar based approach to generate forms of the traditional Siirt cas houses, mainly to distinguish and extricate the authentic building forms from additional components and/or to deduce missing parts. This system is mainly based on the consideration that the authentic forms of the buildings can be generated with use of the identified basic forms and shapes and their inherent rule-based incremental development/expansion pattern or grammar. The formalization of the form finding procedure shall enable modelling of the authentic building forms and urban texture with relatively less information through use of less precise measurement and broad visual analysis and description (Fig. 1).

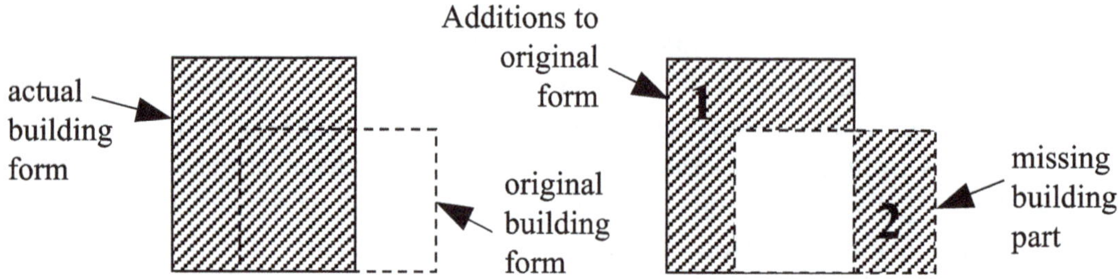

Fig. 1. The proposed methodology aims to deduce the original building form through identifying (1) the extrinsic additions to authentic form and (2) lost (missing) original building parts.

For this purpose, the extensively encountered room sizes and ratios of the rectangular shaped spaces' edge lengths forming the building plan have been identified and categorized to be compared with computer generated rectangular forms within building boundaries. Nonconforming shapes and layouts are eliminated. Eligible found building plans have been compared with pre-identified shapes to be able to judge the existence of additions or missing parts of the actual buildings.

3 Evaluation of Siirt Cas Houses

3.1 General Characteristics

"Cas" houses are without much doubt the most apparent and predominant traditional housing style of the Siirt Province and neighboring regions in South East Turkey. The name "cas" is originated from the name given to the mortar which is in fact a material produced through a process consisting of grinding, burning and processing the lime stone which is constituting the characteristic geological soil formation in the region.

Cas houses are typically two to three floor buildings in rectangular shapes, getting narrower upwards in the form of cut rectangular pyramid. The structural composition stands on loose and irregular stone walls erected with cas mortar; slabs are formed either with dome or vault shaped stone or with vertically placed round wooden beams covered again with a layer of cas mortar joined earth or stone. Same cas mortar is used for exterior façade plastering which is giving the yellowish white color to these houses.

The majority of the urban texture in the historical city center of the Siirt Province is constituted of cas houses although they are extremely modified and degenerated in actual situation. These buildings have lost their original form due to mainly to additions and modifications through use of clay or concrete bricks and reinforced concrete structural extensions and additional floors.

Apart from a number of examples in Siirt city center, relatively well preserved cas houses can be seen at East and North parts of the city, extensively at Tillo and Şirvan districts, less frequently in Pervari on the East side and Eruh on the South part and rarely in Baykan at Northwest and Kurtalan at the West side as the geological sub soil formation starts to change. Tillo District center and related villages probably contains the highest number of cas houses in good condition, namely in İkizbağlar (Tom), Dereyamaç (Fersaf), Çınarlısu (Hantrant) and Çatılı (Sinep) together with Halenze (Bağtepe) district on the road leading from Siirt to Tillo.

3.2 Typology of Cas Houses

The typology of a cas house basically relates to the derivation of a single cas mortar joined stone walled module in rectangular shape at plan and cut pyramidal form in three dimension. This modules are in fact spaces in the form of cells of 10 to 15 m^2 footprint area at an average inner height of around 3 m. The roof of the cells are covered with either vault shaped mortar joined stone or with wooden beams. Side walls of this cell has identical and rhythmic openings used either for doors or windows. The sizes of these openings vary around 60–80 cm in horizontal plane and the height of a window is in general double of its horizontal dimension. When the opening is a doorway, the transom of the door is at the same level of the top of the window. Some very much encountered plan forms are shown in Fig. 2 with typical cross sections. One edge of the typical cell measures generally around 450 cm and contains three openings used as door or window; whereas the other edges may have an average length varying from 250 cm to 600 cm.

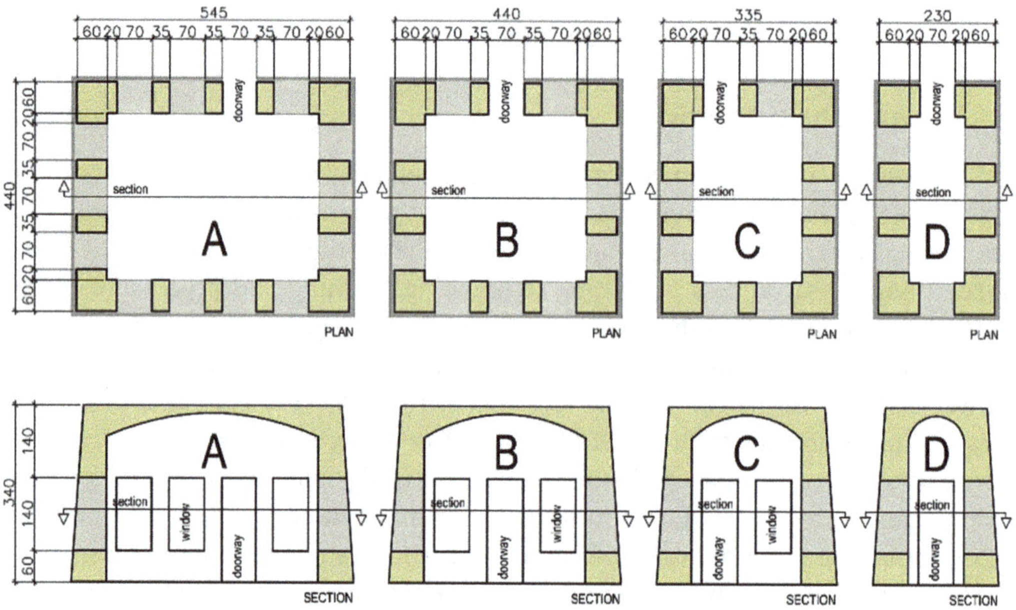

Fig. 2. Typical plans and sections of single floor cas house modules in different sizes varying according to the number of the façade openings.

Cas houses evolved in time through incremental enlarging on an expansion pattern. This incremental expansion of a cas house can be both in horizontal or vertical directions. In horizontal expansion the footprint of the building is enlarged through addition of rooms. Vertical expansion is by adding floors accessed through stairs built at the exterior of the initial cell. Both forms of expansions follow a set of rules originating from the specific geometrical character and structural properties of the houses.

It is possible to distinguish mainly two types of cas houses which are varying possibly according to the owners' economical wealth and status. Some houses are in the form of detached mansions generally isolated from other houses, surrounded with a garden and in a regular square or rectangular form at two or three floor levels. Remaining samples of these houses are relatively well preserved and generally keeping their integrity.

Others belonging to less wealthier population are in dense urban settings, mostly using each other's walls to form clusters also enabling protection from the effects of the hot and arid climate to form narrow and shady streets. These examples found in the old city center of the Siirt Province are extremely modified through addition of rooms, spaces or floors with reinforced concrete structures. The evaluated types of cas houses in this paper mainly relate to this second group.

Horizontal Development. Enlargement in horizontal plane is provided simply by joining other cells of same or different sizes to any direction to an existing cell. This kind of horizontal development of the cas houses is illustrated below. Regular dimensioning of the windows and doors facilitates enlargement by joining cells or in other words building new cells next to the existing ones (Fig. 3).

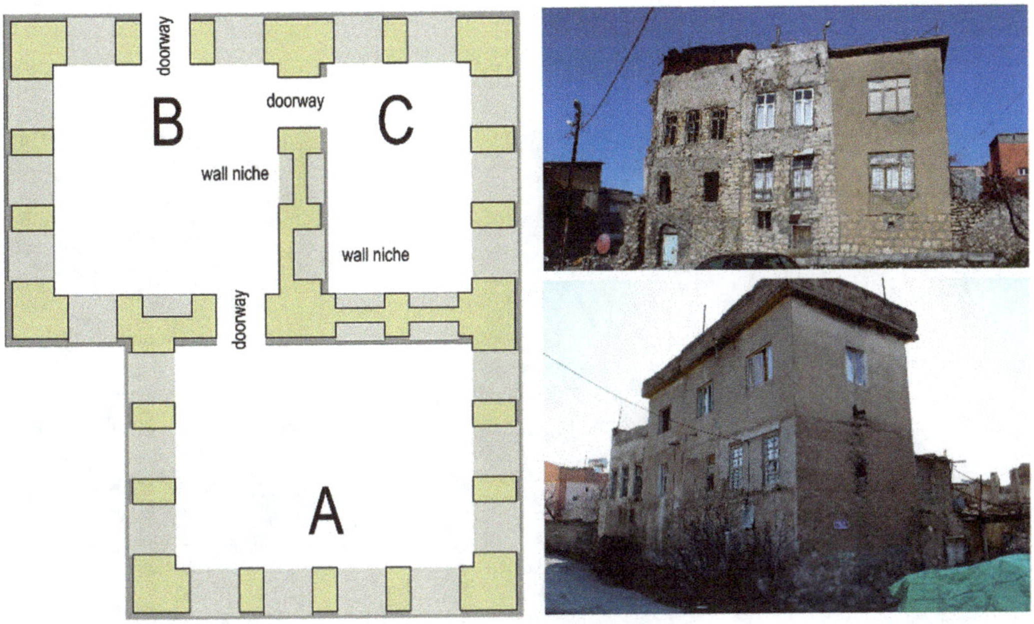

Fig. 3. Sample horizontal enlargement of the cas houses shown in schematic plans and in photos of the existing buildings.

In the internal arrangement after enlargement previously formed door or window openings are transformed to wall niches which are used in several ways such as cabinets, shelves or fire places (Fig. 4).

Fig. 4. Doors and windows transformed to wall niches used as shelves, cupboards or fire places.

Vertical Development. Increasing the number of floors for cas houses is made through continuing the outer walls vertically and adding another cell on top of the existing one. Access to upper floor is made with a stone stair built next to the outer wall, mostly L shaped using two sides of the cell. The stair is covered again by a stone vaulted tunnel in most of the cases. Due to this tunnel the stair becomes an indoor space and another level of stair can later be added when forming an additional level. In most of the cases the maximum number of floors in a cas house is three floors including the ground floor (Fig. 5).

Fig. 5. Doors and windows transformed to wall niches used as shelves, cupboards or fire places.

Another highly characteristic component of the cas houses are the underpass structures called “sabat”. This element is a tunnel like passage way covered by stone vault or by wooden beams used whenever a horizontal development of a cas house is likely to block an existing path. This type of an underpass is also quite useful to protect pedestrians from the effects of hot and arid climate of the region (Fig. 6).

3.3 Translating Cas House Typology to Shape Grammars

In relation with the typology analysis of cas houses summarized above, a shape grammar approach has been developed. Accordingly the initial shape in planar view is always a rectangular form defined as “A” identified by the length of the long and short edges named as “x” and “y”. The rule for enlargement with other (appendage) cells (rooms) identified as “B”, “C” etc. in alphabetical order is juxtaposing other similar rectangular forms to one edge of the initial shape which can be “up”, “down”, “left” or “right”. Derivation of appendages are identified with two parameters which are the “layout” and “alignment” with reference to a given initial or appendage shape.

Fig. 6. Stone vaulted underpass structures at ground floor of the cas houses are called "sabat" in the local language of the region.

Table 1. Shape grammar for cas houses.

Line no	Shape name	Edge lengths		Shape type	Reference	Layout	Align
		x	y				
01	A	400	300	Initial	Null	Null	Null
02	B	300	500	Appendage	A	Right (R)	Top (T)
03	C	600	400	Appendage	A	Down (D)	Right (R)
04	D	600	300	Appendage	B	Down (D)	Left (L)
05	Stair	600	300	Stair	C	Down (D)	Left (L)
06	Sabat	300	300	Sabat	D	Right (R)	Right (R)

Above given table derivate following building form when edge length values are entered as given as in the table (Fig. 7).

For multi-leveled buildings size and location of the stair can also be defined in the same table as shown in line 05. Whenever a path crosses the building, an underpass will be necessary to be placed in the building again with the same shape grammar table as illustrated in line number 06. The first floor of the building will in principle follow exactly the same units and layout in the ground floor due to the structural characteristics of the cas houses.

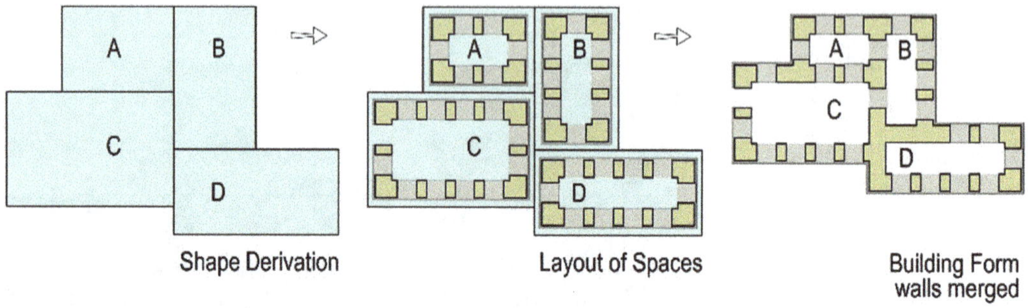

Fig. 7. Derivation of the size and layout of the cells and translation of the grammar to the building form in accordance with data given in Table 1.

4 Description of the Proposed Form Finding System

4.1 Identification of the Problem

The city center of the Siirt Province is formed of a dense urban texture almost wholly composed of cas houses degenerated through additions to existing buildings and/or demolishing of some parts of the authentic built environment. Identifying or modeling of the original form back in history is a quite complex task. The actual urban texture and some examples of modified traditional individual buildings are shown below (Figs. 8 and 9).

Fig. 8. Satellite view of the Siirt city center formed with buildings which are mostly originally composed of traditional cas houses [11].

Fig. 9. Some examples of the cas houses in Siirt city center which are lost their original and authentic form and properties.

Considering the complexity of the urban texture and the degree of modifications incorporated, a simplified way of form finding to deduce the original morphology of the built environment is proposed.

4.2 Form Finding System

The proposed system is based on the principle of plan layout generation composed of predefined existing space forms through processing the information obtained in the form of exterior foot print shape and size of the buildings and verification of generated plans for accuracy with existing other parameters to be received of the site. Consequent to the revealing of shape framing the outer (footprint) boundaries, the first step is the extension of all the lines at reflex angles until they cross a boundary line. This first step is labeled "angle extending". Resulting form is composed of rectangular tiles filling the outer boundaries. These tiles are enumerated as given in illustration below where eleven (11) tiles are produced. This method is similar to that employed by Camozzato et al. for their procedural floor plan generation from building sketches [12].

In the second step, the rectangular tiles are forming other larger rectangles with tiles next to them in an orthogonal manner at both x and y directions. Possibilities for tiles numbered from 1 to 4 are given within the 2nd frame of the figure below as examples. In the third level of the process the form finder searches alternatives for merging the tiles formed at the 2nd step with each other to produce larger rectangular forms. For each of the alternatives the outer boundaries are filled with other shapes which are not overlapping with previously produced rectangular shapes.

Upon derivation of all possible alternatives the nonconforming shapes in terms of dimensions and ratios with reference to predefined cas house room patterns are eliminated and marked as alien (shown with red color in Fig. 10).

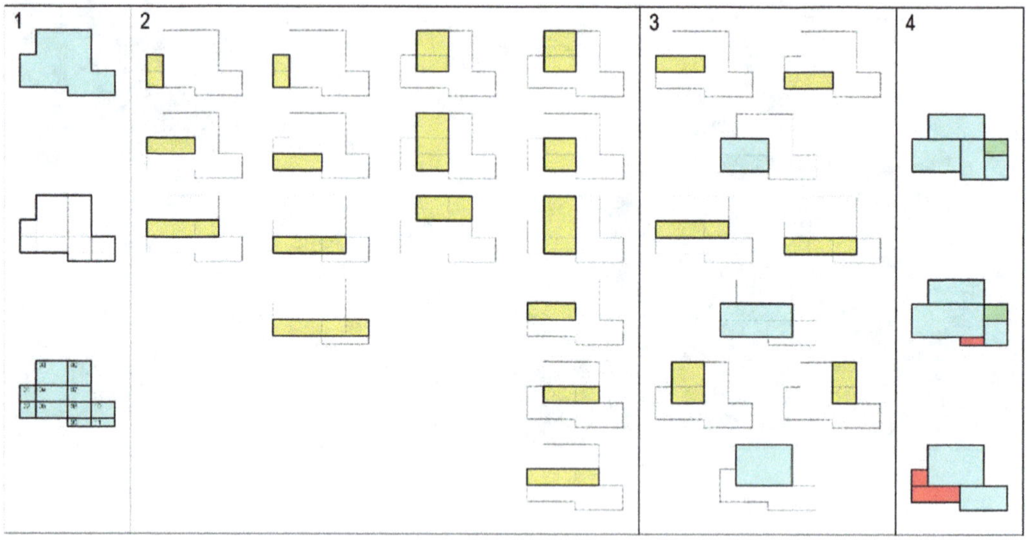

Fig. 10. Example of procedural form generation from a given outer boundary shape to deduce alien appendices to buildings. (Color figure online)

The process is also able to propose extensions (shown in green color in figure above) in order to establish similarity of a generated form with predefined forms. Those are interpreted as possibly missing parts of the authentic buildings.

4.3 Expected Results

The form generating system is expected to provide a number of plan alternatives generated through the information that relates to the outer boundary shape and approximate dimensions of the buildings that are revealed on site or through satellite maps. A portion of the generated alternatives are eliminated and some are marked with suspected unoriginal additions or suspected missing parts. Broad visual inspection of the real subject is expected to enable prompt revealing of the original composition of the house with considerably reduced time and effort consumption.

5 Conclusion

The mathematical modeling of cas houses aimed to enable an automated system helping the deduce the authentic form of the buildings and relevant urban texture. Considering the quantity and the complexity of the individual buildings and the physical environment they form, a need for an automated system to deduce the authentic morphology of the built environment is essential.

The inherent style and grammar of the Siirt cas houses have remarkable potential for the development of such a system due to their orthogonal and incremental expansion pattern. The system can be further developed to cover as well the other essential building elements such as entrance doors, windows, wall niches, stairs, underpasses etc. to respond to detailing needs of the modeling process. With study of adjacent buildings and other elements of the built environment an incremental modeling of the authentic urban texture can be obtained.

References

1. Rajamaran, V.: Computer Programming in C. Prentice Hall of India, New Delhi (2006)
2. Smelik, R.M., Tutenel, T., Bidarra, R., Benes, B.: A survey on procedural modeling for virtual worlds. Comput. Graph. Forum. http://hpcg.purdue.edu/bbenes/papers/Smelik14CGF.pdf. Accessed 26 Apr 2018
3. Ediz, O., Cagdas, G.: A computational architectural design approach based on fractals at early design phases. In: Dikbas, A., Scherer, R. (eds.) eWork and eBusiness in Architecture, Engineering and Construction, pp. 1055–1062. Taylor & Francis, Routledge (2004)
4. Stiny, G.: Introduction to shape and shape grammars. Environ. Plan. B **8**, 343–351 (1980)
5. Eloy, S., Duarte, J.P.: Inferring a shape grammar: translating designer's knowledge. Artif. Intell. Eng. Des. Anal. Manuf. **28**, 153–168 (2014)
6. Flemming, U.: More than the sum of parts: the grammar of Queen Anne houses. Environ. Plan. **14**, 323–350 (1987)
7. Çagdas, G.: A shape grammar: the language of traditional Turkish houses. Environ. Plan. **23** (5), 443–464 (1996)
8. Colakoglu, M.B.: Design by grammar: an interpretation and generation of vernacular hayat houses in contemporary context. Environ. Plan. **32**, 141–149 (2005)
9. Yong, L., Congfu, X., Zhigeng, P., Yunhe, P.: Semantic Modeling Project: building vernacular house of southeast China. In: VRCAI 2004: Proceedings of the ACM SIGGRAPH International Conference on Virtual Reality Continuum and its Applications in Industry, pp. 412–418. ACM, New York (2004)
10. Adao, T., Magalhaes, L., Peres, E.: Ontology-Based Procedural Modelling of Traversable Buildings Composed by Arbitrary Shapes. Springer, Cham (2016). https://doi.org/10.1007/978-3-319-42372-2
11. Yandex Maps. https://yandex.com.tr/harita/103878/siirt/. Accessed 27 Apr 2018
12. Camozzato, D., Dihi, L., Silvera, I., Marson, F., Musse, S.: Procedural floor plan generation from building sketches. Vis. Comput. Int. J. Comput. Graph. **31**(6–8), 753–763 (2015)

Towards Preserving Transylvanian Fortified Churches in Virtual Reality

Mihai Duguleana(✉) and Cristian Cezar Postelnicu

Transylvania University of Brasov, Brasov, Romania
mihai.duguleana@unitbv.ro

Abstract. A fortified church is a building which has a religious meaning, but also played a defensive role in times of war. Many fortified churches from countries such as Romania, Slovenia, Switzerland, Poland, France, Denmark, Portugal, Germany or Belarus featured thick walls and high battlements and embrasures. However, Middle Age fortified churches are different from castles and fortresses because they were designed to protect small communities. Transylvania hosts the highest number of fortified churches from Europe. In the medieval ages, more than 300 churches were built by the inhabitants of this area. This was the direct result of the constant invasions from the Ottomans and other nomad populations such as Tatars. Many of these edifices date since the 13th century, but some are in an advanced state of degradation, caused mainly by poor preservation measures and lack of interest from the local authorities.

This paper introduces a system which aims to increase the awareness about the fortified churches from a small area of Transylvania called "Țara Bârsei". Our focus is on the visual preservation of several of these monuments through the technique of photogrammetry, as well as the implementation of a stand which would attract the potential tourists. The key idea of our study is to influence them to visit several churches by placing next to each other in Virtual Reality both mainstream and low-profile objectives. We assess users' opinion about a holographic stand commanded by a mobile application which includes the 3D models, pictures and a short description of the fortified churches based on a modified HARUS questionnaire. Results show increased interest, directly resulted from the visualization technology.

Keywords: Transylvanian fortified churches · Cultural heritage Preservation

1 Introduction

A high concentration of fortified churches can be seen in places where there was a lot of hand-to-hand warfare, such as the Dordogne region of France, which was fought over by France and England in medieval times, and in Transylvania, which was the scene of Ottoman invasions. Some other places in Europe with fortified churches can be seen in Fig. 1.

Transylvania was called "the gate of Europe". This Romanian territory has the highest number of Saxon villages from Europe. These formed starting with the 12th century, after the Hungarians began to infuse the local population with German

M. Duguleană et al. (Eds.): VRTCH 2018, CCIS 904, pp. 34–45, 2019.
https://doi.org/10.1007/978-3-030-05819-7_4

Fig. 1. Europe's most prominent fortified churches.

colonists, in an effort to annex the territory. However, the Saxons blended well with the natives and some of the elements of their civilization managed impose over the older practices. One of these is their architecture. As the area was constantly under threat from Ottomans and Tatars, one of the most adopted elements is the fortification style. The common approach against invaders was the "high price for a small benefit" strategy. In most of the cases, raiding the churches was too hard to be worth the trouble. In fact some of the churches were never conquered. Such is the case of Prejmer Fortified Church, which featured thick walls and unique defensive systems such as the "Organ of death" (see Fig. 2).

A context information which is worth mentioning is the advanced degradation state of some of these fortified churches. The 7 Transylvanian villages with fortified churches which are listed in the UNESCO World Heritage index (Biertan, Câlnic, Dârjiu, Prejmer, Saschiz, Valea Viilor and Viscri) are at the moment well preserved and constantly taken care of. However, many others are on the verge of collapsing. If this happens, the consequences are so severe, the monument is probably lost forever (see the case of the Rotbav fortified church in Fig. 3).

A study from 2011 shows that although some of the UNESCO churches listed above are well-known, there are others which are also popular among the local population. These are Cisnădie, Cisnădioara, Agnita and Slimnic. However, not being listed in UNESCO index makes them virtually invisible to the foreign tourists, according to [2].

Fig. 2. Prejmer Fortified Church.

Fig. 3. Rotbav Fortified Church before and after collapsing in 2016.

Several researchers tried to find the possibilities of development of these areas, considering their rich cultural heritage. E.g. in [3], authors propose a set of long-term actions which they think it will act towards the preservation and the development of these settlements. However, some of these activities have been undergone in the past by local authorities and decisional factors, with little or no success. It is showed in [4] that the problems are more severe than what authorities initially thought. The Saxons, the population which maintained the fortified churches and the old village centers, have left Romania in the exodus which occurred right after the revolution from 1989. Many of the buildings are either uninhabited or were bought by new owners, which modernized them without considering the idea of preserving the past looks (materials, shapes and colors). Although this region is important on multiple levels (i.e. it hosts a unique habit [5]), the poor road infrastructure and the nonexistent regional strategy for tourism have contributed to the decay.

One idea which seem to catch was ecotourism [6]. However, ecotourism needs to be naturally sustained by an organic growth of visitors, resulted directly from a constant activity and a reasonable long-term preservation strategy, engaging enough to catch the interest of the newer generations of tourists, travelers and other stakeholders. Another idea which seemed to multiply the awareness effects was to ease the return of the Saxons, which are occasionally traveling to Romania to visit their homeland [7].

However, the amplitude of this phenomena is low, compared to the average numbers of tourists from the region. Even the most well-known fortified church from Transylvania, Viscri, is still struggling to implement a Western model of heritage management which will eventually allow better engagement with visitors, higher touristic rating and in the end, larger audience [8].

1.1 Types of Fortified Churches

According to [1] there are 3 types of fortified churches in Transylvania:

- Churches with fortified walls - the church itself is not a defensive structure, but it is surrounded by walls which fulfill this function. One good example is Prejmer Fortified Church (see Fig. 2).
- Fortified churches - the church's body is a defensive construction, and the outside fortifications are not present or if they are, they are not actually playing a defensive role. Large churches with thick walls such as Feldioara can be included here.
- Fortress churches - the fortified walls are provided with fortified storerooms for supplies and fortified with towers, bastions and warehouses, often being surrounded by a water channel. Fortress churches are related to notion of "citadel", but they differ because they were not permanently inhabited, but only in case of war and siege (see Fig. 4).

Fig. 4. Valea Viilor fortress church

Transylvanian fortified churches are fairly different from the ones built in the Western Europe, as their purpose was different. While Western Europe fortified churches belong to religious cults such as the Templars, or to the Catholic Church, and hosted only sacred relics and books, the Transylvanian fortified churches were supposed to offer protection against invaders for the tens of families for each of the villages which had them. Very often, each family had their own cellar in which they could store separately their belongings.

1.2 Study Objectives

This paper presents the main opportunities, limitations and challenges posed by applying the process of photogrammetry to some of the fortified churches from a small area of Transylvania called "Ţara Bârsei" from several points of view: technical, social and financial. Our study also proposes the development of a multi-language holographic stand which is able to output information about the fortified churches to visitors of a museum, gallery or any other kind of cultural heritage related exhibition. Making use of the holographic effect obtained from the reflection of the image outputted by flat monitor into a glass pyramid, the holographic stand can display various 3D models, animations and other types of visual effects. Thus, it is perfect to showcase the small yet very detailed 3D models of the churches from Tara Bârsei. In order to make to system more interactive, the physical device was coupled with a smartphone application which allows users to select their desired monument from a stylized historic map of the area (see Fig. 5). The application contains information on the most important fortified churches from Transylvania, which are both interesting touristic sites as well low marketed destinations.

Fig. 5. The holographic stand, the tablet and the main page of the application

Our final aims are to discover which the best means of digitally conserving these monuments, to implement a system which will enhance the visibility of less-known fortified churches from Transylvania and to assess the perception of the proposed implementation by the general public and by experts in the field of cultural heritage. On a side note, we wanted to build accurate 3D models for all the fortified churches from this region and to offer these for free to the cultural heritage enthusiasts, within an online repository. In order to accomplish these goals, we needed to interact with the representatives of the fortified churches, to ask permission to photograph and inspect the landmarks. Deriving from discussions with the curators, one idea which we hope to put in practice is to offer the developed system, the holostand presented in Fig. 5, to be displayed in the most visited churches from the regions, Prejmer and Harman, and perhaps, in the Bran castle. The purpose of this endeavor would be that tourists which are passing by would learn about the other churches and would want to also visit these, since all are very close one to the other. Although our study doesn't address the idea of a tour creation, the system proposed in this paper leaves tourists aware of the close proximity of similar landmarks, a piece of information which will help them decide on their next objective.

2 Methods and Materials

2.1 Photogrammetry

Photogrammetry is a technique which allows users to create 3D models from photos. We have used photogrammetry to build the 3D models presented in the holographic stand. The photogrammetry software used in most of the cases was Agisoft PhotoScan and Reality Capture. These programs allow users to import any kind of photo for the reconstruction phase. Thus, we have used several cameras, among which we can list Canon EOS 1300, Nikon D5300 and Samsung S8. In full compliance with this technique we notice that the higher resolution was used, the better were the results. Besides the photos taken from the surface level, use have used a drone (DJI Phantom 4 Pro) with 4K lenses to catch the looks of the roofs and of the crannies and nooks of the architectural elements from upper body of the monuments. Agisoft produces weaker results in terms of resemblance, but can accept a higher number of images, whereas Reality Capture is limited to 2500 (for a standard license).

Other software used in our study was Blender and Meshlab (for trimming the models to an acceptable number of polygons) and Unity (for constructing the 3D slow-revolving setup for the glass pyramid).

Doing the field work, we've discovered that a typical church needs at least 2000-3000 photos in order to get a good 3D model. There are cases where, because of the large dimensions of the monument, we've used approximately 10000 photos to build the 3D model.

The process of taking photos for photogrammetry is not trivial. The photos need to be focused well. Any defocused/blurry image can ruin the model. Cameras were adjusted to get the best exposure (the best ratio between ISO, aperture, shutter speed and zoom). After the photo shooting sessions, the pictures need to be sorted for eliminating all the ill-focused ones. Finally, using the .raw format may require more space, but also proves to be the best choice, especially in the preprocessing phase.

On a side note, the best time to take the pictures is when it is cloudy, because the sun light influences the resulted textures. Thus, posing a wall directly illuminated by the sun light outputs overexposed colors and diminishes the details of the surface.

Finally, computing the 3D model for medium quality may take even a week of continuous processing, using several connected servers.

In the post-processing phase, the surroundings which are not connected to the fortified church were cropped and the models were optimized to a smaller amount of polygons, in order to be ready for import in Unity.

2.2 3D Models

Our team computed 3D models for the following fortified churches: Prejmer, Harman, Vulcan, Sanpetru, Maierus and Feldioara. Additionally, Rotbav, the church which collapsed in 2016, was modelled in CAD and showcased on the stand. There are several other fortified churches for which we are in the process of obtaining the authorizations to photograph them. Our final aim is to offer these models for free on the portal of the eHeritage Project, in the repository section [9].

2.3 Holographic Stand

The holographic stand uses the classic principle of holography: the image emitted from a highly luminous 4K TV screen is reflected by a single-side reflexive glass mounted at an angle of 45°. Inside the glass construction, a white base lighten by a weak light source breaks the reflection sensation and creates the feeling of having the image reflected being inside the pyramid, instead of being on the surface of the glass. Thanks to the 3 reflections offered by the 3 sides of the pyramid, users can experience a greater sense of immersion.

The holographic stand undergone several changes since its initial concept presented in Fig. 6. The main improvement related to the shape of the glass pyramid. In order to increase the size of the holograms, instead of using a 4-face pyramid trunk, we have opted for using half of it. This translated in twice the space for the sides of the glass pyramid and also for the TV screen (instead of rendering 4 images, we need to render only 3). Other significant improvements are the exclusion of the Leap Motion device (as users can interact with the stand directly from the application installed on an Android tablet), the use of better and lighter materials (the first version was made from wood, while the second version was made from aluminum case and metal sheets sprayed in electrostatic field) and the use of castor wheels on the base, in order to make it mobile and easy to move. All these improvements we carried out at the recommendation of several museum custodians and gallery curators which explained us in detail the features of a museum-ready stand.

The system (in various versions) was presented at various events such the EU Open Day 2018 from Brussels, Belgium, AFCO 2018 from Brasov, Romania, Researchers Night from Brasov, Romania, Internet Festival 2017 from Pisa, Italy and the Lubec 2017 from Lucca, Italy.

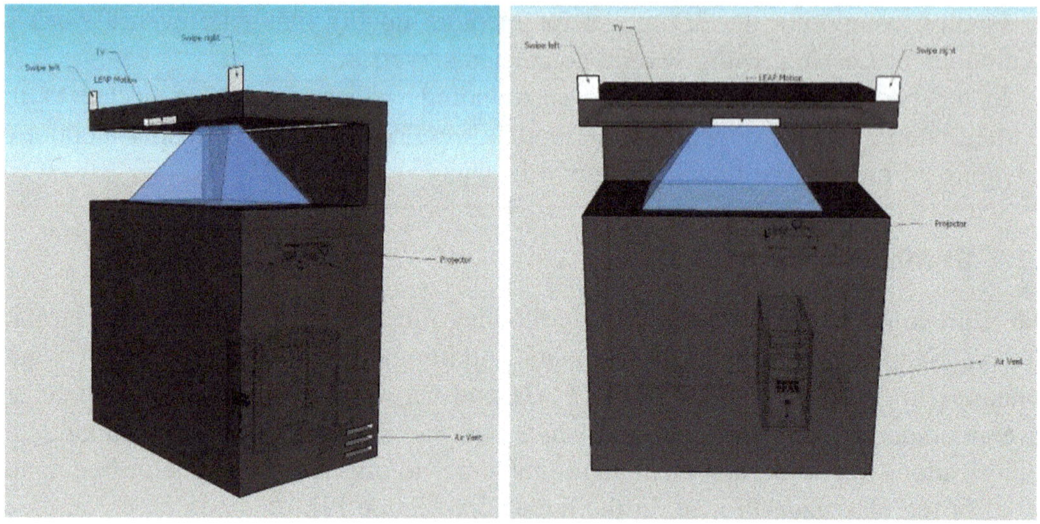

Fig. 6. The initial holographic stand prototype

3 Evaluation

14 people (11 males and 3 females) have taken the questionnaire presented in Table 1 during 2 separate events, AFCO 2018 and EU Open Day (although the stand was inspected by several hundreds, see Fig. 7). Most have never seen a holographic display and were thrilled about the experience. As it is the case with new technologies (e.g. the augmented reality (AR) applications for mobile phones [10]), people are attracted and excited partially due to the technology showcased and not necessarily because of the content. However, it was not the intention of this research to limit this phenomena – on the contrary, we wanted to capitalize the momentum offered by the holographic display which is something rarely seen by most people, and to build upon this in order to create some interest for the real objective of the study. As a results, many visitors from both events, even local people, became interested in visiting the fortified churches of Tara Barsei.

3.1 Questionnaire

Each participant was asked to fill in a modified version of the Handheld Augmented Reality Usability Scale questionnaire [11]. The HARUS questionnaire was developed to evaluate the comprehensibility and manipulability of AR applications for handheld devices. Since the system developed is not really an AR application, we have tweaked the questionnaire to cover the subject of our study, while preserving the statistical computation process behind it.

Thus, the first section, Personal Skills (Q1–Q3), was intended to create a baseline, derived from the degree of familiarity of the subjects with virtual reality and more particularly, with holography. The second section (Q4–Q11) aims to assess the usability of the holographic stand. Enjoyment (Q12–Q15) and Usefulness (Q16–Q19) derive directly from the HARUS design. Last but not least, the Empirical section tries to infer some common knowledge about the study itself, about the quality of the 3D

Table 1. Evaluation questionnaire

Personal skills	Q1: Have you used VR technologies before? Q2: Have you ever seen a hologram before? Q3: Are you familiar with the principles of holography?
Comprehensibility	Q4: I thought that using the system requires a lot of mental effort Q5: I thought the amount of information displayed on the screen of the tablet was appropriate Q6: I thought that the information displayed on screen of the tablet was difficult to read Q7: I felt that the system was responding fast enough Q8: I thought that the information displayed on screen of the tablet was confusing Q9: I thought the words and symbols on screen of the tablet were easy to read Q10: I felt that the quality of the 3D models was good Q11: I thought that the information displayed on screen was consistent
Enjoyment	Q12: I enjoyed using the system Q13: I found the system unpleasant Q14: I found the system exciting Q15: I found the system boring
Usefulness	Q16: By using the holographic stand, I was able understand the location of the fortified churches Q17: By using the holographic stand, I was more interested in visiting the fortified churches Q18: By using the holographic stand, I was able understand more about the history of "Tara Barsei" Q19: By using the holographic stand, I am more likely to visit fortified churches in the future
Empirical	Q20: Which 3D model was the most appealing? Q21: Which 3D model was the most unpleasant? Q22: Which fortified church would you be interesting in visiting the most in the near future?

models presented to the public and about their intentions in the near future. All of the questions from sections Comprehensibility, Enjoyment and Usefulness use a 7-point Likert scale, ranging from 1 – "strongly disagree", to 7 – "strongly agree". As a side note, in some cases, the 22 questions were perceived as too many by some of the respondents.

3.2 Results

The empirical questions were used to tweak features such as the luminosity of the light source inside the pyramid, or the luminosity and the position of the light source inside the scenario built in Unity. The 3D models were calibrated to cover all the screen allowed by the dimensions of the glass. All the answers from sections 2, 3 and 4 were

Fig. 7. The holographic stand at EU Open Day 2018, showcasing Prejmer fortified church

aggregated in order to obtain values for each of the 3 constructs: Comprehensibility, Enjoyment and Usefulness.

For each answer we inverted the results of the negatively stated items. After this action, we summed up all the values related to the specific construct and calculated the mean and the standard deviation. The obtained scores are mapped to a range of 0 to 100, in order to see easier the percentiles. The results for each construct are the following: Comprehensibility (M = 91.44; SD = 2.12), Enjoyment (M = 95.12; SD = 4.62) and Usefulness (M = 89.27; SD = 4.82). We infer that the respondents easily understood the way to use the system, enjoyed the stand even more, and found the content delivered to be very useful (Fig. 8).

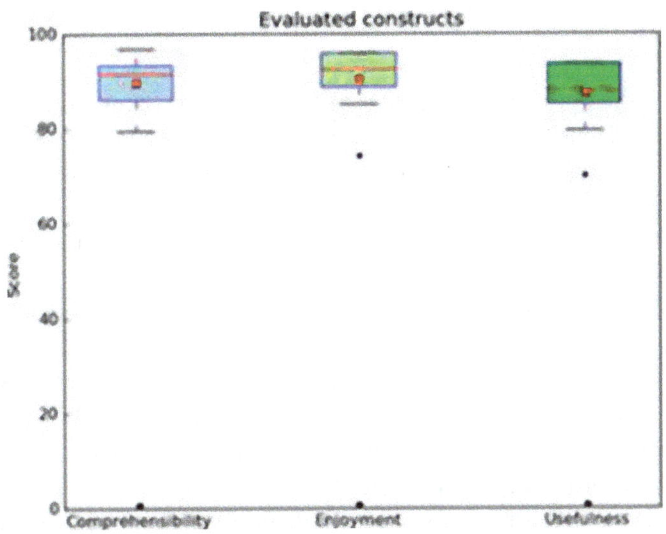

Fig. 8. Questionnaire results

4 Conclusions and Future Developments

As we initially thought, the system was very well received by all the participants of this study. Many praised the idea and the content, and even promised they will visit some of the fortified churches presented in the holographic stand, in the near future. However, there are still improvements to be made.

There are still 4 churches which need to be "photo-scanned" in order to obtain their 3D models and to put them in the application, not to mention the old city of Brasov, which we will most likely be represent by the fortress of Brasov. This means that additional 3D content needs to be developed.

Another way to develop the system is to add more interaction. Users like to interact with systems in a natural way. Using a mix between Leap Motion and the Andoird application installed on the tablet could prove worthy of investigating. Speaking of the application, one development which may have a greater impact would be to create an app which could be available to download for free on Google Play and IOS Marketplace, presenting the 3D models and historical facts about each of the monuments.

Other improvements related to the physical features of the holographic stand. We can improve the interior lighting of the glass pyramid, by investigating which light source is the best for holography (warm or cold) and which is the best light intensity. Last but not least, one of our future aims is to seal tight the stand and display it at several fortified churches from the area "Tara Barsei".

Acknowledgements. This paper is supported by European Union's Horizon 2020 research and innovation programme under grant agreement No 692103, project eHERITAGE (Expanding the Research and Innovation Capacity in Cultural Heritage Virtual Reality Applications).

References

1. Valentina, Ş.S.: The Fortified Churches from Transylvania – How Well Are They Known By The Romanian Citizens? European Integration–New Challenges, 1948 (2011)
2. Muresan, A.: The fortified church of Biertan (Transylvania). In: Visitor Management, pp. 26–45 (2000)
3. Gabor, D.I., et al.: Possibilities for rural tourism development around fortified churches. Lucrări Ştiinţifice Manag. Agricol **15**(4), 259 (2013)
4. Szaktilla, S.: The spirit of the Transylvanian fortified churches… The people have left, their buildings remain, pp. 1–10 (2008)
5. Akeroyd, J.R., Page, N.: The Saxon villages of southern Transylvania: conserving biodiversity in a historic landscape. In: Nature Conservation, pp. 199–210 (2006)
6. Iosif, D.: Ecotourism as a community industry: case study; Transylvanian Saxon communities with fortified churches. Cinq Cont. **1**(1), 17–28 (2011)
7. Iorio, M., Corsale, A.: Diaspora and tourism: Transylvanian Saxons visiting the homeland. Tour. Geogr. **15**(2), 198–232 (2013)
8. Corsale, A., Iorio, M.: Transylvanian Saxon culture as heritage: insights from Viscri, Romania. Geoforum **52**, 22–31 (2014)
9. eHeritage Project Repository. http://www.eheritage.org/category/repository/. Accessed 15 May 2018
10. Duguleana, M., Brodi, R., Girbacia, F., Postelnicu, C., Machidon, O., Carrozzino, M.: Time-travelling with mobile augmented reality: a case study on the Piazza dei Miracoli. In: Ioannides, M., et al. (eds.) EuroMed 2016, Part I. LNCS, vol. 10058, pp. 902–912. Springer, Cham (2016). https://doi.org/10.1007/978-3-319-48496-9_73
11. Santos, M.E.C., Polvi, J., Taketomi, T., Yamamoto, G., Sandor, C., Kato, H.: Toward standard usability questionnaires for handheld augmented reality. IEEE Comput. Graph. Appl. **35**(5), 66–75 (2015)

Evaluation of Using Mobile Devices for 3D Reconstruction of Cultural Heritage Artifacts

Răzvan Gabriel Boboc(✉), Florin Gîrbacia, Cristian Cezar Postelnicu, and Teodora Gîrbacia

Transilvania University of Brasov, 500036 Brasov, Romania
razvan.boboc@unitbv.ro

Abstract. This work aims to examine the reliability of smartphones that incorporate 3D depth sensors for 3D reconstruction of cultural heritage objects. The main focus is to compare the models generated with two image-based methods: photogrammetry and Tango Constructor application. The result are promising, showings that Tango-based method is an efficient way for 3D reconstruction of historical artifacts and is able to provide morphometric data comparable with photogrammetry-based data. The method can provide restorers a quick way to record vast amount of data, combined with sufficient accuracy and ease-of-use and this make it a potential alternative to conventional methods, like photogrammetry or laser scanning.

Keywords: 3D reconstruction · Mobile devices · Cultural heritage

1 Introduction

In the Cultural Heritage (CH) 3D reconstructed models provide an important support for procedures like historical reconstruction, analysis of artifacts and architecture, documentation of archaeological sites, preservation, marketing of museum etc. [1, 10]. The 3D models of cultural heritage objects are generated by using dedicated software graphical applications, image based methods of specialized sensors [2].

Many 3D digital models of cultural heritage objects like buildings, statues and historical places are developed using image based methods, active sensors like laser scanners, total stations or combination of them [2, 11, 13]. Although laser scanners are more accurate than image-based systems, the latter are preferred on the strength of their cost, ease-of-use and time saving. As mentioned in [11], some of the disadvantage of laser scanning are that many blind spots are generated and a great deal of time is required to obtain the data.

The possibility to reconstruct reliable 3D models by simply using consumer low cost devices is a great opportunity. Smartphones are widely used and offer the possibility to access a variety of applications for accomplishing a large number of tasks. Due to the development of camera features and the usage of multiple cameras, smartphones became a common device used for image acquiring.

In order to perform 3D reconstruction, the user can use a smartphone equipped with a depth sensor [4] or attach a depth sensor to the smartphone or simply make photos of

M. Duguleană et al. (Eds.): VRTCH 2018, CCIS 904, pp. 46–59, 2019.
https://doi.org/10.1007/978-3-030-05819-7_5

the target and upload the pictures on a cloud server and then run a web-based application to create the 3D reconstruction.

To obtain a high accuracy for the 3D reconstructed object, a set of the most representative selection frames is uploaded to the cloud where they are processed and the 3D model is obtain [15]. For volumetric 3D models of realistic scenes, like whole buildings, many agents using augmented reality smartphones collaborate through an online pose optimization [9]. In [7] multiple users with smartphones collaborate to provide the best frames for a 3D reconstruction pipeline that are uploaded on a cloud-based server and processed through a Structure form Motion (SfM) and Dense Image Matching (DIM) procedures.

Another method of reconstructing outdoor scenes of large proportions is by computing depth maps at interactive frame rates on the GPU of a Google Project Tango Tablet 4 through motion stereo [14]. In [16] is presented a comparison between the usage of Tango tablet and ZED camera in 3D reconstruction. The Tango tablet offers better accuracy of generated point clouds for outdoor environments and a lower value of the average error. The ZED camera per-forms better indoors because it has to be connected to a computer while scanning.

Because the lack of appropriate light source can be a disadvantage for 3D reconstruction using smartphones, in [6] was presented 3D structured light scanning that represents the combination between 3D reconstruction and the registration on Lenovo Yoga Tab 3 Pro to achieve a 3D point cloud model.

Due to the unfavorable environment conditions or object materials (e.g. poor lighting, shiny surface, homogenous textures), some authors proposed improved approaches for point cloud generation [14], but it is still room for new improvements of algorithms and used technology to overcome some limitations, like, for instance, transparent surfaces, that cannot be detected by the devices.

It should be noted that the point cloud's resolution depends on the user needs and the application in CH: the reconstructed 3D models can be used for documentation and analysis, for creating digital archives, for providing digital replicas for exhibitions and so on. Nevertheless, the quality of the resulted model should be as good as possible in all cases.

The aim of this research study is to investigate the accuracy of smartphones that incorporate 3D depth sensors for 3D reconstruction of cultural heritage artifacts compared with photogrammetry based approach. Using these techniques, two 3D measurements have been carried out and the goal was to analyze whether the first method, based on Google's Tango technology, is suitable to reproduce geometrical volumes of objects in CH preservation sector, using photogrammetry data as reference.

2 Android Applications (Apps) for 3D Reconstruction

Following is a brief overview of the 3D reconstruction Android apps available on the Google Play store with examples of their output. The most significant applications are presented, but it is not an exhaustive overview, there are many other applications that can be used for 3D scanning of objects.

2.1 Tango® Constructor

Tango Constructor [8, 19] allows users to scan their surroundings and visualize the reconstructed 3D textured mesh (Fig. 1) models directly on the mobile device. The processing of the 3D mesh is performed on the smartphone. The application enables export of the output using the OBJ format.

Fig. 1. Provence House 3D reconstructed using Tango Constructor [20]

2.2 Open Constructor for Tango

Open Constructor [21, 22] allows real time 3D reconstruction with textured models (Fig. 2) using the Tango enabled mobile phone. 3D scanned models are exported using OBJ format and can be visualized by using external applications. Also provides support to uploading models to Sketchfab.

Fig. 2. 3D model reconstructed using Open Constructor for Tango [23]

2.3 RTAB-Map

RTAB-Map (Real-Time Appearance-Based Mapping) [17] allows online 3D scanning/mapping of the environment (Fig. 3) based on multi-session incremental appearance-based loop closure detector [12]. RTAB-Map allows to export the 3D reconstructed model in PLY or OBJ (with textures up to 720p) format.

Fig. 3. 3D model reconstructed using RTAB-Map [18]

2.4 Matterport Scenes

Matterport Scenes [24] is another free 3D scanning application for Tango-enabled devices that has some useful features, like: the ability to trim a 3D scan and to crop object of interest, the ability to make real time measurements, to take photos while scanning and to share 3D scans (Fig. 4).

Fig. 4. 3D model reconstructed using Matterport Scenes [25]

2.5 Scandy Pro

Scandy Pro [26] capture 3D meshes with Tango device, having high resolution and accurate scans of objects by combining Tango scanning technology with its own 3D scanning algorithms. It is able to provide a maximum resolution of 1 mm and render a 3D mesh on-device within seconds [27] (Fig. 5).

Fig. 5. 3D model reconstructed using Scandy Pro [28]

3 Materials and Data Collection

With the advent of the 3D data capture image-based methodologies, new scenarios are opening up for the construction of true 3D models of artifacts, statues, buildings or other object belonging to cultural heritage. The input images are acquired in different experimental configuration, with different cameras and the proposed procedure has the purpose to compare 3D models starting from the two input data (Tango and Photogrammetry).

Project Tango is a platform developed by the Advanced Technology and Projects (ATAP) that uses computer vision to give devices like smartphones and tablets the ability to understand their position relative to the environment. The software works by integrating three types of functionality: motion-tracking, area learning, and depth perception [29]. In Fig. 6 is presented the diagram of Tango 3D reconstruction offline process, with used techniques for each stage.

For depth perception, Tango devices use three technologies: structured light, time-of-flight and stereo. The first two require the use of an infrared sensor to estimate the distance to the surrounding objects from the time difference between the emission of the infrared wave and its return to the sensor as a result of the reflection. Stereo technique uses two cameras for taking pictures and calculates the distance between

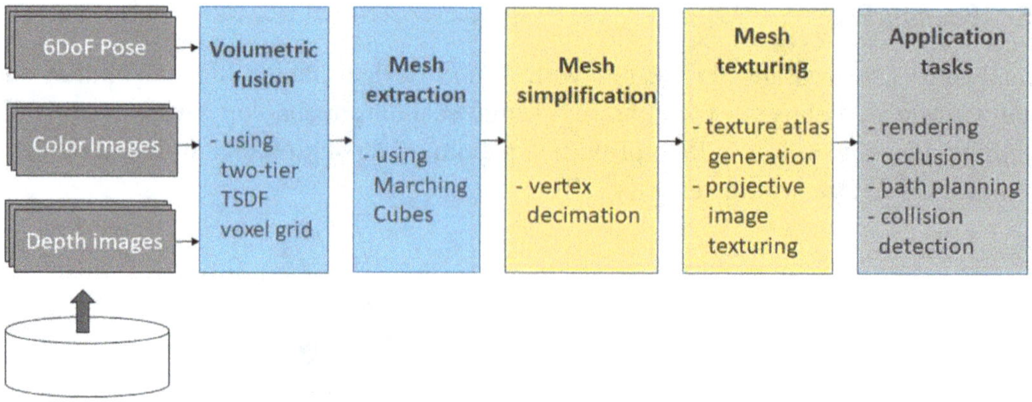

Fig. 6. Tango 3D reconstruction process [29]

them, like to the human eyes do. Project Tango's developers provides APIs that return point clouds from the depth sensor in the form of xyz coordinates.

A statue of Horea from the statuary group representing Horea, Cloşca and Crişan, located on Griviţei Boulevard, in front of the Building V of Transylvania University of Braşov was selected as subject for analysis (Fig. 7). The statuary group representing three personalities of the Romanian national history was subjected this year to a process of cleaning and restoration of mosaic tiles. These personalities were the leaders of the 1784 Romanian Peasants' Revolt of Transylvania. They were executed by the Hungarian authorities by breaking on the wheel in 1785.

Fig. 7. The statuary group "Horia, Cloşca şi Crişan" (a) and the bust of Horia (b)

For photogrammetry method, the images were collected using a Samsung Galaxy S7 smartphone, that employs a ISOCELL S5K2L1 sensor (1.4 μm pixel size), with a maximum resolution of 12 effective Megapixels (4032 × 3024). In order to reduce the errors of 3D model, the smartphone camera was placed at close distance from the object (about 1.5 m). The images were captured at different angles with respect to the statue surface. The smartphone camera was rotated horizontally and vertically with 10 degrees, maintaining a 70–80% overlap between consecutive photos. Having this overlapping percentage, the acquisition of 173 images was enough for obtaining a good 3D model of the statue.

The images sets were imported into Agisoft PhotoScan [30], a commercial tool used for processing digital images and to generate 3D spatial data, to realize the 3D modeling process: from the sparse point cloud to the final 3D textured model (Fig. 8a).

Fig. 8. Point cloud obtained by photogrammetry (a) and using Tango Constructor (b)

The Tango model (Fig. 8b) was obtained using Lenovo Phab2, a large Android smartphone with numerous cameras and infrared sensors that could make use of the Google's Tango software. It has a 16 MP rear camera, depth sensor, motion tracking camera and a 6.4" QHD display. The phablet not only tracks motion, but also has depth perception thanks to an IR emitter and other sensors, remembering the space around it. Another features are accelerometer, gyroscope, ambient light sensor, compass, a powerful Qualcomm Snapdragon, 652 processor optimized for Tango, and an 8 MP front camera. With this device, you are able even to measure distances in the environment.

The image sets were acquired in different sessions, keeping the same procedural steps in order to obtain comparable results for the two methods. The models are imported first in MeshLab [31], an advanced 3D mesh processing software system, free and open source, to improve the quality of the meshes.

4 Results

The 3D point clouds generated from the two different recording techniques were analyzed for variations in their quality, to determine which method is most appropriate for generating 3D models in an easy and fast way.

In a first stage, the .obj files obtained from Tango Constructor and from PhotoScan were imported in CloudCompare and they are converted in .pts files. When comparing two models obtained with different methods, the first problem that arises is the difference of resolution of the two corresponding point clouds. The RGB model acquired with the Samsung camera has about 400 times more points in the dense cloud than the one obtained with Tango camera, 5530620 and 13855 points, respectively. Before doing the comparison, the points on the mesh were sampled at 3000000 points.

Before comparing the 3D models, the meshes must be carefully aligned (Fig. 9a). For this purpose, we used the open source CloudCompare software [32]. CloudCompare is an advanced 3D data processing software for quickly detecting changes and comparing 3D point clouds data. Point pair based alignment tool was firstly used for rough alignment, then we used the registration automatic method to finely register the two datasets by the Iterative Closest Point (ICP) algorithm. The quality of the obtained alignment depends on choosing good pairs of corresponding points in the two datasets. The alignment parameters were previously optimized by minimizing the ICP alignment error for two identical point clouds.

Fig. 9. Aligned point cloud (a) Photogrammetry/Tango models absolute distances (b)

After registering the two 3D clouds, a quantitatively and qualitatively evaluation of their difference was performed by calculating the Hausdorff distance and the Cloud to Cloud (C2C) distance between the two models. C2C distance computation calculates the nearest neighbor distance, i.e. for each point of the compared cloud, the software looks for the nearest point in the reference cloud and then computes their distance.

In Fig. 10 are presented the histogram of absolute distances between vertices of the two point clouds. We compared Tango/Photogrammetry clouds, keeping the Photogrammetry cloud as reference. The average differences between the models are around 0.07 cm (Fig. 9b), with standard deviation of 0.07. It can be observed that the scalar field shows the distances between points ranging from 0 to 4.5 mm. The number of points for each model was 2999976, of which more than 85% show a difference smaller than 1.5 mm.

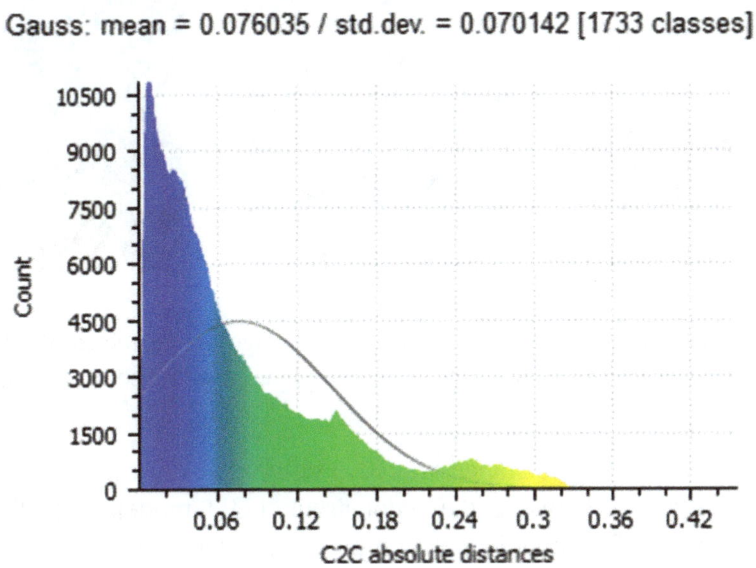

Fig. 10. Histogram of the absolute distance

The models are very similar, showing the larger deviations on the edges of the model where no perfect match was achieved. The model produced by photogrammetry is of higher quality than the Tango-based one and this can be easily seen even when looking at them (e.g. visual comparison of the two models in terms of geometrical details and lack of noise). But this thing is due to the surface properties of the statue: there are no big changes in terms of color – the surface is almost white, there are reflections occurring in some areas or shaded surfaces. Moreover, as there are many powerful features, the accuracy would be better.

On the other hand, comparing the two models, it is clear that the one obtained with depth sensor device does not show the outline of statue details as well as the photogrammetry-based one. Details are more prominent in the case of the second technique, while the Tango mesh have a smoother texture that makes some parts of the model more difficult to distinguish (like, for instance, the ornament carved on the statue's base – Fig. 11 a, b). So, the Tango-based model does not highlight depths as detailed as photogrammetry-based one. The details can be distinguished, but they are not so well shaped. But this is due to considerably lower number of points captured with Tango device. As the manufacturers mentioned, the device could construct a "rough" 3D model in real time, but, in addition, post-processing tools can be applied in order to result a realistic 3D model of an object or a space.

Fig. 11. Photogrammetry reconstructed 3D model (a) Tango reconstructed 3D (b) Photogrammetry/Tango models Hausdorff distance computed for the Tango based model (c)

The one-sided Hausdorff distance was also computed in order to analyze the differences and similarities between the reconstructed 3D models [3]. The geometric difference between the 3D models was achieved by calculating the distance between each point of the models and then measuring the actual dimension in millimeters. The models surfaces at a point are similar if the distance between two points is smaller. To compute the Hausdorff distance was used the feature integrated into MeshLab in the filter Sampling -> Hausdorff Distance.

In order to better visualize the error, the results of the calculated Hausdorff distance were displayed by using red-green-blue colormap. For this representation, the red color is maximum error and the blue color is minimum error. Results of the geometric differences applying Hausdorff distance are presented in Fig. 11c. The maximum error between the 3D models is 0.96% and the average error is 0.16%. Thus, the models generated using Tango technology and photogrammetry are geometrically approximately similar.

However, a critical part of Tango scanning is the influence of lighting conditions and object material. We have chosen an object whose surface is very little reflective and the captures where made in proper conditions, with enough light and with clouds. As is shown in [16, 33], there is an obvious difference in the performance of a Tango device in low light and high light conditions. When there are insufficient lighting conditions, the obtained models have certainly a reduced geometric quality. Moreover, Tango-based device is not able to detect surfaces that are directly illuminated by sunlight or transparent surfaces. Even with these limitations, using this method the restorers have a quick way to record vast amount of data, combined with sufficient accuracy and ease-of-use.

The result shows that it is possible to obtain 3D models that are morphometrically comparable using both image-based techniques. The photogrammetry technique has created clearer details in relief of the artifact and their depth seems much higher than the model captured with depth sensor. However, the conducted analysis shows that the differences between the two models are very small and can be considered as acceptable.

As mentioned above, the transparent, shiny, reflective, but also dark surfaces are problematic for image-based 3D reconstruction. They influence the quality of the resulting model, but there are expectations both on the part of the hardware and the improved algorithms that next devices will be able to overcome the different unfavorable conditions and can provide solutions for the realization of 3D models of artifacts in CH field. In this way, the scientists or the conservators can easily compare different information given by different techniques.

Moreover, even if the native models produce by Tango are not rich in information enough, there are various approaches in the literature that can enrich them with semantic and topological information [5]. The method is very suitable when the time is a critical aspect.

5 Conclusions

The 3D reconstruction is very important to analyze, document and to preserve Cultural Heritage. The aim of this paper was to investigate the application of an image-based reconstruction methodology based on Google Tango for 3D reconstruction of historical artifacts. We have attempted to evaluate the quality of the data generated by Google's Tango Constructor Android application compared to photogrammetry-based 3D reconstruction using commercial software for a relatively large artifact with low features of the surface.

The 3D data evaluation comparison indicates that Tango-based method is an efficient way for 3D reconstruction of historical artifacts and is able to provide morphometric data comparable with photogrammetry-based data. The analysis was performed by comparing the point clouds obtained using the two mentioned methods and the variation of them in terms of distances between point is relatively small and thus quite accurate.

The performance of Tango Constructor free standalone application was evaluated for an outdoor artifact that was considered suitable for 3D reconstruction due to the bright color and low reflectivity of the surface. Tango Constructor allows users to capture and view 3D models of objects or of their surroundings, and the models can be shared as mesh files. This is a quick way of creating 3D models, which can be used in other applications or software environments.

The presented method has a series of advantages, like saving time required for data collection, fast generation of the 3D model, cost saving, less maintenance, and ease of use. However, there are certain limitations of this method: the accuracy of the 3D reconstructed model is influenced by object materials and lighting conditions. Another limitation is related to the size of the object. If the object to be scanned is small or very small, it is reconstructed with very few details, distorted or even it cannot be identifiable in the scanned scene.

It is certain fact that mobile devices equipped with sensors and appropriate software for depth sensing can find their application in CH field. Since laser scanners have already proven their usefulness and potential on acquiring high quality 3D data, and photogrammetry or image-based techniques have their advantages, but a combination of them lead to better results [34].

Concluding, due to the versatility in terms of cost, time and ease of use, Google Tango represent a viable solution for conservators and restorers, enlarging their choice in the range of 3D reconstruction instruments. However, as a preliminary test, this study need to be extended in order to asses if Tango devices are adequate for specific applications and to determine whether this low cost solution has the potential to make the difference in 3D reconstruction.

As future work, we plan to continue the investigation by using different scenarios (e.g. indoor, outdoor), more objects with different shapes and different lightning conditions. We also intend to conduct a study to evaluate the performance of various reconstruction applications that use Google Tango technology and which were presented (some of them) in Sect. 2 of this article.

Acknowledgments. This paper is supported by European Union's Horizon 2020 research and innovation programme under grant agreement No. 692103, project eHERITAGE (Expanding the Research and Innovation Capacity in Cultural Heritage Virtual Reality Applications).

References

1. Aicardi, I., Chiabrando, F., Lingua, A.M., Noardo, F.: Recent trends in cultural heritage 3D survey: the photogrammetric computer vision approach. J. Cult. Herit. **32**, 257–266 (2018)
2. Alsadik, B.: Practicing the geometric designation of sensor networks using the Crowdsource 3D models of cultural heritage objects. J. Cult. Herit. **31**, 202–207 (2018)
3. Cignoni, P., Rocchini, C., Scopigno, R.: Metro: measuring error on simplified surfaces. Comput. Graph. Forum **17**(2), 167–174 (1998)
4. Chung, M., Callin, J.: Point Cloud Framework for Rendering 3D Models Using Google Tango. Thesis, Santa Clara University (2017)
5. Diakite, A., Zlatanova, S.: First experiments with the Tango tanglet for indoor mapping. ISPRS Ann. Photogramm. Remote Sens. Spat. Inf. Sci. **3**(4), 67–72 (2016)
6. Donlic, M., Petkovic, T., Pribanic, T.: On tablet 3D structured light reconstruction and registration. In: Proceedings of the IEEE Conference on Computer Vision and Pattern Recognition, pp. 2462–2471 (2017)
7. Erica, N., et al.: 3D reconstruction with a collaborative approach based on smartphones and a cloud-based server. In: 5th International Workshop LowCost 3D-Sensors, Algorithms, Applications, vol. 42, pp. 187–194 (2017)
8. Froehlich, M., Azhar, S., Vanture, M.: An investigation of Google Tango® tablet for low cost 3D scanning. In: Proceedings of the International Symposium on Automation and Robotics in Construction, ISARC, vol. 34. Vilnius Gediminas Technical University, Department of Construction Economics & Property (2017)
9. Golodetz, S., Cavallari, T., Lord, N., Prisacariu, V., Murray, D., Torr, P.: Collaborative Large-Scale Dense 3D Reconstruction with Online Inter-Agent Pose Optimisation (2018). arXiv preprint: arXiv:1801.08361

10. Grifoni, E., et al.: Construction and comparison of 3D multi-source multi-band models for cultural heritage applications. J. Cult. Herit. **34**, 261–267 (2018)
11. Kwon, S., Park, J.-W., Moon, D., Jung, S., Park, H.: Smart merging method for hybrid point cloud data using UAV and LIDAR in earthwork construction. Procedia Eng. **196**, 21–28 (2017)
12. Labbé, M., Michaud, F.: Long-term online multi-session graph-based SPLAM with memory management. Auton. Robots **42**(6), 1133–1150 (2018)
13. Lachat, E., Landes, T., Grussenmeyer, P.: Investigation of a combined surveying and scanning device: the trimble SX10 scanning total station. Sensors **17**(4), 730 (2017)
14. Nocerino, E., et al.: 3d reconstruction with a collaborative approach based on smartphones and a cloud-based server. In: International Archives of Photogrammetry, Remote Sensing and Spatial Information Sciences, vol. XLII-2/W8, pp. 187–194 (2017)
15. Schöps, T., Sattler, T., Häne, C., Pollefeys, M.: Large-scale outdoor 3D reconstruction on a mobile device. Comput. Vis. Image Underst. **157**, 151–166 (2017)
16. Senthilvel, M., Soman, R.K., Varghese, K.: Comparison of handheld devices for 3D reconstruction in construction. In: Proceedings of the International Symposium on Automation and Robotics in Construction, ISARC, vol. 34. Vilnius Gediminas Technical University, Department of Construction Economics & Property (2017)
17. RTB-Map. https://play.google.com/store/apps/details?id=com.introlab.rtabmap&hl=en. Accessed 21 Nov 2017
18. RTB-Map 3D model example. https://sketchfab.com/models/b782694a0e93428ebbe8df688634f7a3?ref=related. Accessed 21 Nov 2017
19. Tango Constructor App. https://play.google.com/store/apps/details?id=com.projecttango.constructor&hl=en. Accessed 21 Nov 2017
20. Tango Constructor. https://sketchfab.com/models/cd5fe7388c16419caf4945837a40cbec. Accessed 21 Nov 2017
21. Open-Constructor. https://github.com/lvonasek/tango/wiki/Open-Constructor. Accessed 21 Nov 2017
22. Open-Constructor App. https://play.google.com/store/apps/details?id=com.lvonasek.openconstructor&hl=en. Accessed 21 Nov 2017
23. Open-Constructor example. https://sketchfab.com/models/4e9804f548454c30b06ad31f37a8638c?ref=related. Accessed 21 Nov 2017
24. Matterport Scenes. https://play.google.com/store/apps/details?id=com.matterport.capture&hl=en. Accessed 24 Nov 2017
25. Matterport Scenes example. https://sketchfab.com/models/a5e3dd2e31194a1e982e75cacb747fb8?ref=related. Accessed 24 Nov 2017
26. Scandy Pro. https://play.google.com/store/apps/details?id=co.scandy.scandypro.production&hl=en. Accessed 16 Jan 2018
27. Scandy Pro. https://www.scandy.co/blog/four-reasons-for-scandy-pro/. Accessed 16 Jan 2018
28. Scandy Pro example. https://sketchfab.com/models/bfd1841b23174ab09e82086bccecdd36. Accessed 16 Jan 2018
29. Dryanovski, I.: 3D reconstruction with tango. In: 2016 IEEE Hot Chips 28 Symposium (HCS) (2016)
30. Agisoft PhotoScan. http://www.agisoft.com/. Accessed 21 Apr 2018
31. MeshLab. http://www.meshlab.net/. Accessed 21 Apr 2018

32. CloudCompare. http://www.danielgm.net/cc/. Accessed 8 May 2018
33. Gülch, E.: Investigations on Google Tango development kit for personal indoor mapping. In: Proceedings of the 19th AGILE International Conference on Geographic Information Science, Helsinki, 14–17 June 2016
34. Koutsoudis, A., Vidmar, B., Ioannakis, G., Arnaoutoglou, F., Pavlidis, G., Chamzas, C.: Multi-image 3D reconstruction data evaluation. J. Cult. Herit. **15**, 73–79 (2014)

Towards a Novel User Satisfaction Modelling for Museum Visit Recommender Systems

George Pavlidis(✉)

Athena Research Centre, University Campus at Kimmeria, PO BOX 159, 67100 Xanthi, Greece
gpavlid@ceti.athena-innovation.gr

Abstract. Modern recommender systems technology appeared in Cultural Heritage application relatively recently, particularly during the dawn of the 21st century. There is already a significant amount of relevant works in the bibliography, which has been primarily empowered by large-scale research and development projects. Various approaches have been adopted from the recommender systems technology, including collaborative filtering, content-based, knowledge-based and hybrid systems. In most of these approaches that focused on museum guidance, which is the focus of this paper, the museum has been assumed to be a form of a gallery and the visitor was treated primarily as a user in seek on engagement and enjoyment. The free museum roaming was the main form of visit that has been considered and targeted, while the educational factors and storytelling aspects have been markedly overlooked. In this paper a new framework for the user satisfaction modelling is being presented that quantifies user satisfaction based on a weighted combination of various probabilistic factors that are being estimated during a museum visit. The goal is to provide a model of user satisfaction that can be used for museum recommenders that could guide either free-roaming visits or guided-tour scenarios for visitors of various motivations and backgrounds.

Keywords: User satisfaction · User modelling
Museum guide · Recommender system · Recommendation
Cultural heritage · Machine learning · Artificial intelligence

1 Introduction

Recommender technologies have been widely adopted in various fields of applications since the late-20th century. Recommender systems are, typically, systems that exploit some form of knowledge for a group of users and user preferences on a list of items, in order to provide recommendations to the known or new users about unseen items that might be of possible interest. This recommendation can take any form of suggestion for any kind of interaction and engagement, that might depend on the context, including, for example, buying options,

M. Duguleană et al. (Eds.): VRTCH 2018, CCIS 904, pp. 60–75, 2019.
https://doi.org/10.1007/978-3-030-05819-7_6

music selections, movie suggestions, or even path following. Generally, recommender systems can be considered to be a form of narrow artificial intelligence applications, adapted to perform efficiently for particular cases. The goal of recommender systems is to create meaningful and personalised recommendations, which is an effective solution to the pervasive and persistent problem of information overload. This personalisation takes any form that complies with a particular user group and a contexts (such as educational, recreational, location-based, time-dependent) [1,2,7,35].

Recommender systems draw on theoretical background from cognitive science, approximation theory, information retrieval, forecasting, management, consumer modelling and more [1]. As computational systems that are able to provide contextually valid recommendations they are studied as machine learning application in information technology, and they are already being massively applied in online advertising and general items recommendation [20]. Based on that specific goal of creating valid recommendations, these systems focus on creating associations among users and items for a pre-defined motive. If all potential users are modelled as a gaussian sample the most obvious strategy of a naive recommender system would be to create recommendations based purely on popularity; this includes ranking the items in a decreasing order of popularity (statistically estimated) and suggesting the top ranked items to the active user (this is the terminology for the current system user). Although this user model is simple, the results by such a recommender are usually valid and thus any new recommender technology has to be compared against a popularity-based recommender that serves as the baseline.

Recommender technology is heavily based on existing data that might include user demographics and user assumptions, item features, ratings of items by the users and contextual information. Apparently the situation is far from being ideal, and the data are largely 'incomplete'; the user data and model assumptions are incomplete and inaccurate, the item ratings are significantly scarce and contextual data are not usually considered as having temporal dynamics and biases. Ratings are of particular interest for a specific type of recommender systems, those that employ *collaborative filtering*, which is a method of predicting item ratings for users that have not rated these items yet. The item ratings are mathematically formulated as a *ratings matrix*, which is expected to be significantly sparse. Another challenge for the recommender systems is what is called the *cold-start problem*, which relates to the difficulty in creating valid recommendations for new users (or users that do not rate the items or they do not express any preferences). Typically this problem is tackled by exploiting user model assumptions by following the activity of the user and any user (demographic) data available. Of course, recommenders need also to deal with *fraud* and *attacks*, which are forms of manipulation of the system to generate biased recommendations [3,13,29,34,35,46,47].

There is a vast bibliography regarding recommender systems in various domains and settings, that has appeared since the 1990s [1,2,5,12,18,19,24–26,28,30,40,41]. Equally massive is the bibliography of recommender systems in cultural heritage and particularly museum recommenders, although there have been recommender systems focusing primarily on wider applications of cultural tourism. In the following section a brief account of those works is presented, focusing on the user modelling aspects and assumptions, and in the subsequent sections of the paper a new framework for user satisfaction modelling is presented that is able to provide quantitative measures for effective museum recommenders. Throughout the paper the terms 'user' and 'visitor and also 'item' and 'exhibit' are used interchangeably, but fundamentally correspond to analogies between a generalised setting and the domain of museum visits and exhibition tours. The terms 'user' and 'item' with the wider sense are used to denote a more general notion or application.

2 User Satisfaction in Museum Recommenders

In 1999 the *nomadic guide Hippie* [38] was developed within project HIPS, as an electronic guide capable for adaptive guided exhibition presentation, which exploited visitor location data by tracking visitors with IR sensing devices. User modelling was a mixture of the explicit visitor preferences, user interactions with items and localisation. An interesting feature of Hippie was the support for communication among visitors that enhanced the social dimension of a visit.

In 2002 the *Sotto Voce* was developed [6]. Sotto Voce was an audio guide for PDA devices that focused largely on the social aspects of a visit. The users where supposed to be socially active entities that draw satisfaction by the social interactions among them, so this work resulted a guide that supported a mediated sharing of audio content. The approach was named *eavesdropping*, since it was a form of overhearing what other visitors were listening to at any given close distance. In this work the recommender was based on the localisation and social interaction.

Some years later, project PEACH presented another approach and a mobile system for an engaging experience in a museum visit [42]. Cinematic techniques were primarily employed as means for young visitor engagement, and user localisation was also implemented for better user modelling and context building. A technique for dynamic image sequence generation and sound synchronisation was the engine for the content personalisation. Interestingly, temporal dynamics were considered in the user modelling in this case, as the content personalisation was based on a user profile that evolved during the visit.

In 2005, semantics and context-awareness were used in a set of museum guide applications for PDA devices presented in [16]. Their aim was to adapt to visitor models that included visitor behaviours, which were initialised using typical demographics and preferences. Sensing technologies were employed to provide localisation context, based on [36]. This was a case of a content-based recommender that assumed a semantics-based and proximity-based visitor satisfaction model.

In 2006 the *ARCHIE mobile guide system* [32] proposed a mobile guide that focused largely on social awareness. Social interaction was of paramount importance in the assumption for the user modelling in this work, drawing on studies like [17]. ARCHIE supported the building of an evolving visitor profile, and relied on mechanisms similar to those in PEACH to personalise the content, along with visitor localisation.

In 2007 a system was proposed that extracted semantic similarities from textual descriptions for accurate user modelling and item matching [21]. In this work the proximity, text-based metadata, and popularity were combined to support the recommendation process. Interestingly, in this work any exhibit was symbolised as a word and any path (or tour) was symbolised as a sentence. The system was able to combine the visitor activity, collaborative data, proximity and textual semantics and similarities into a naive Bayes approach to predict the most probable next exhibit that might by of the active visitors interest. Nevertheless, and despite the insightful design and formulation of this purely machine learning approach the reported results did not outperform a naive popularity-based recommender, and special heuristics were employed to improve the performance of the new system. In this work, the user is a dynamically evolving entity which is influenced by the semantics and proximities in each point of interest.

In 2007 a first version of museum recommender approaches within the framework of project CHIP appeared, the *CHIP interactive tour guide*, which was a content-based personalisation framework [39] that focused on effective user model learning and the recommendation of web content. The next year another approach within the same project resulted in recommendations based on semantics [50], in which a concrete ontology was created to support the new content-based recommender, which was also coupled with localisation data. In 2009 an updated version was presented in an annual student research competition, focussing on the mobile implementation for museum visits [43]. Finally, in 2010 the most advanced version of the system was presented that included routing functionalities based on connectivity graphs [49].

In 2008, and within project CHAT, a content-based recommender system was developed that was able to learn user profiles from static and user-generated content [8]. The system was based on a folksonomy based on integrating static and user-generated content in the form of tags. The visitor profile learning was based on probabilistic models, and the recommender was based on naive Bayes text categorisation. The same year, another interesting work focused on an newly studied aspect, that of recommending based on *visitor lifestyles* [31]. Although technically the method was based on typical collaborative filtering, the novel contribution was the introduction of interesting *lifestyle factors* for a different user modelling approach.

In 2012 a personalised guide was presented that focused on the educational aspect of museums and the tackling of the information overload [23]. The activity of visitors is monitored to create and update personalisation rules online, formulating a rule-based recommender. A case-based approach was used to switch between collaborative and content-based filtering for either collective or individual patterns that were augmented with localisation. In this work user satisfaction factors, as defined in [37] and upgraded by the authors were used to assess the system performance. During the same year, a recommender that relied on a semantic network on museum exhibits was presented [33], which generated recommendations based on item relations, user preferences, and the limited timeframe of a visit. The item relations captured influences of any exhibit by other exhibits and the recommender resulted in an estimate of the probability that the active user would appreciate the exhibit in question

In 2015, personalised museums tours on smart mobile devices have been presented in a system that combined content-based and collaborative filtering [9]. The system exploited relevance and contextual information, to provide accurate context-aware recommendations, and adopted an ontology-based approach using CIDOC-CRM. In this system users are grouped by their demographics and the recommender is a complex hybrid system. The same year, within the AMMICO project a museum recommender was presented that focused on enhanced audio guidance in museum tours [27]. Once more, the user satisfaction modelling was based on the assumption that linear predefined narratives with no interactions are uninteresting. Like in any content-based recommenders, the method creates neighbourhoods for users and items based on a modified similarity measure, adopting definitions of local communities from [15], and of communities from [11], taking also into account a disjointed active visitor [10].

In 2016, another system motivated by a pre-supposed uninteresting linear narratives approach in museums appeared, in which a collaborative filtering-based system was developed, focusing on increasing both individual and group visitor satisfaction [44]. Technically, matrix factorisation was adopted for the collaborative filtering implementation and the localisation context was integrated by describing the museum with a directed acyclic graph. Influenced by the work in [45] the method quantified the individual or group satisfaction by estimating the accumulated user satisfaction by viewed items. The same year a hybrid recommender was presented in the framework of the eHERITAGE project adopting a mash-up approach, that integrated intelligent virtual assistant, Google Street View and recommender technology for virtual museum tours [48].

In 2017, within project meSch, another hybrid recommender appeared that focused on free-roaming museum visits and localisation [22]. What is interesting in this work is the integration of online and on-site user activity in the user modelling approach. Users are described in an eighteen-dimensional feature space. Logistic regression and a deep neural network were used to learn the recommendation model, the former targeting the understanding of the contribution of each feature in the recommendation, and the latter targeting the cold-start problem. The same year, an association rule-based approach was proposed within project M5SAR [14]. This was a hybrid method for museum visit recommendation, capable of supporting multiple visitors and multiple museums and sites, based on the Apriori algorithm [4] for rules learning.

3 A Novel User Satisfaction Modelling Framework

Clearly, in most of the reviewed works on museum recommenders, the conceptualisation of a museum as a gallery that provides linear narratives seems to prevail. This view draws a frame on what users expect to gain by museum visits and how their engagement should be quantified or predicted and their satisfaction could be modelled. The free-roaming visitor model also seems to prevail, completing the gallery-like picture. Social engagement and participatory factors have been exploited by some of the works, but the museum role has been somehow diminished to an academic repository.

On the technical side, collaborative filtering approaches model user satisfaction in terms of items ratings and latent factors that, unfortunately, lack explainability. This approach relies on existing ratings to create predictions on missing ratings, and, consequently to predict a user's satisfaction in interactions with unvisited items. On the other hand, content-based approaches rely on grouping users and items by similarities and trying to match a user to a user group and to items so as to predict the user satisfaction by the interaction with unvisited items. Hybrid approaches try to combine the best of both worlds by employing domain knowledge, context awareness, assumptions and ratings to improve the prediction of items that would potentially enhance a user's satisfaction by their interaction. In the most complex cases, all those aspects are complemented with temporal dynamics to capture time-based changes in user behaviour, and possible biases in how users rate the items or in how specific items enhance user satisfaction.

This paper presents a novel approach in modelling user satisfaction based on the modelling of user dissatisfaction, or better, the probability that a user will be dissatisfied by an item during the interaction with a sequence of items. The formulated framework takes into account four basic factors, that is

- temporal dynamics in user behaviour;
- biases in an item's proximity neighbourhood;
- biases in an item's content-based neighbourhood;
- influences by obstacles, obtrusions and access difficulties.

Quantification of these factors in the novel framework is based on

- the usage of the available visit time by a user and the patterns in the way time is spent on each item, in relation to a 'required' (or desired) time for an effective appreciation of an item;
- items 'reputation' expressed by both the involved parties, the users and the stakeholder, which means that a museum exhibit can have ratings by users (which express the popularity of this item) and also ratings by the museum itself, the latter denoting a degree of significance of an exhibit by the stakeholder (how featured the item is considered by the museum);
- proximity based attractions, corresponding to highly rated or featured items in the close neighbourhood of an item;
- content based attractions, corresponding to highly rated or featured items that are thematically or semantically related to an item;
- proximity based obtrusions due to crowded locations, possible scheduled or un-scheduled stakeholder interventions and any other possible access difficulty.

These user satisfaction modelling assumptions and factors that are taken into account are, in essence, an attempt towards a mathematical formulation of the most influential stimuli for divergence during a visit, which is abstractly presented in Fig. 1. In this conceptualisation of a typical museum visit that can be either in a free-roaming visit or a guided tour, the visit is depicted as a set of points of interest, physical and semantic distances and groupings and local obtrusions. Each item is depicted by a circle with a size proportional to the item's average popularity; the shading of each circle depicts how significant (featured) the item is considered by the stakeholder; thus dark large circles correspond to highly popular and featured items, whereas light small circles correspond to less popular and featured items. The straight arrowhead lines show the tour path depicted with a length that corresponds to a physical distance. In addition, closely grouped circles (items) correspond to physical neighbourhoods of items and obtrusions, the latter represented by shaded squares (with a size proportional to the level of local obtrusion). A physical neighbourhoods is depicted as an area enclosed by a dotted grey ellipse. Finally, content-based similar items in various locations are semantically grouped into content-based neighbourhoods, as the one depicted with the dashed grey line.

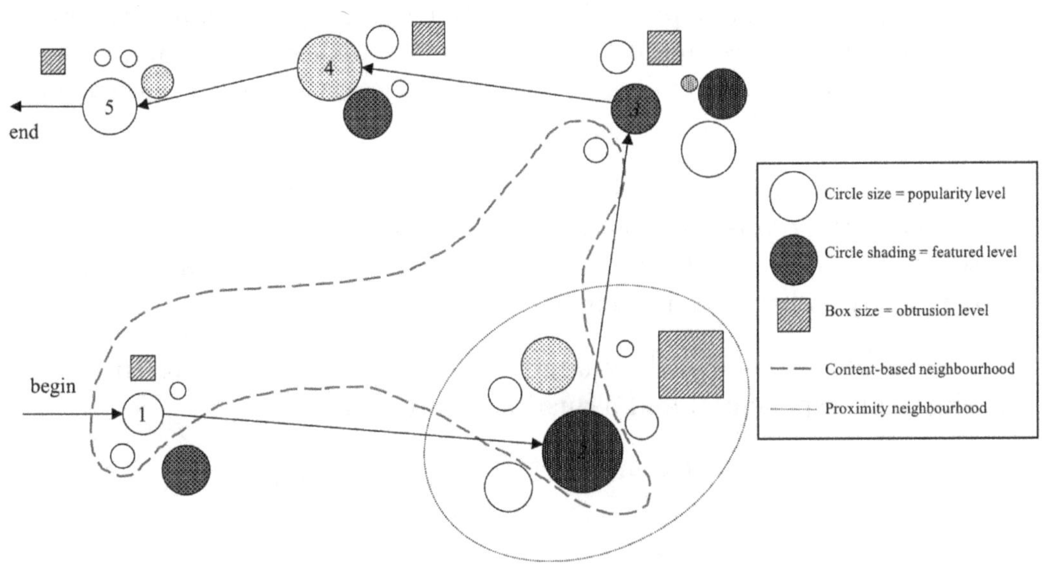

Fig. 1. The conceptualisation of a museum visit adopted in the proposed framework.

The way those entities are quantified is pretty straightforward; (a) there are the average user ratings and also (b) the featured item scores provided by the stakeholder, (c) there are Internet of Everything (IoE) and localised notification approaches to assess obtrusions (or scheduled interventions), (d) the physical distances can naturally form proximity neighbourhoods and (e) content-based similarities among items can form similarity neighbourhoods by exploiting the items dataset and features.

This conceptualisation of a museum visit or tour is the basis for the development of probabilistic features that aim to capture the probability of a user being attracted by items not in the user's initial schedule or not in the list of items suggested by a recommender system. Experimental study in simulated settings of the aforementioned visit conceptualisation, the influencing factors and the notion of focusing on dissatisfaction estimation (rather than satisfaction) resulted in the design of four features which are being presented in the following subsections. The feature that relates to obtrusions (denoted as $p_o \in [0, 1]$) is not further analysed as it is a pure normalised estimate of any available information relating to obstacles or access issues in the vicinity of an item.

3.1 Temporal Dynamics in User Behaviour

Time is a very important factor in human activities and even more important in time-constrained settings like a typical museum visit. In museum visits there is a clock ticking for the user, based on the interactions with items that gradually consume the initially (in many cases predetermined) available time, but with some inherent fuzziness, as this available time can be easily shortened or prolonged according to various factors. On the other hand there is another clock that is ticking according to a prescribed duration of interactions among users and items, stemming from the amount of information attached to each item and the item to item distances. By exploiting those two clocks the temporal behaviour of a user can be modelled based on the pretty apparent assumptions by which

- a user that skips a provided item description is highly likely to have been dissatisfied by the presentation of an item or by the item itself
- a user that spends more time than the minimum required in front of an item is more likely to have been fascinated by the item

The situation can be modelled by adopting a piecewise continuous function, a composite of an exponential and a quadratic function,

$$p_t = 1 - \begin{cases} e^{-\alpha(t_f-1)^2} & t_f > 1, \quad \alpha \in [5, 10] \\ \frac{1}{t_f^2} & t_f \leq 1 \end{cases} \tag{1}$$

where p_t is the estimate of the probability of user dissatisfaction due to temporal dynamics, α is the exponential function steepness factor accepting values $\in [5, 10]$ and t_f is a time factor computed as the ratio of the user available time and the total 'required' tour time up to the current (or next) point of interest. This function is depicted in Fig. 2, in which the horizontal axis is the time factor t_f. The exponential (left side) function quantifies the dissatisfaction probability in cases in which the user skips item presentations. The inverse quadratic (right side) function quantifies the dissatisfaction probability in cases in which the user seems to spend too much time with items, thus need to be more 'conservative' than the exponential part. Apparently, this function estimates a probability, since the mapping values are bounded in the $[0, 1]$ interval, and its inverting influence leads to high values near 1 in cases in which there is significant disagreement between the estimated required times and the times actually spent by the user. Values close to 0 (around the 1 in the horizontal axis) correspond to a user that should be more or less considered 'satisfied', since the two running clocks seem to be in synchronisation. Obviously, a beta or a gamma distribution function could be used to approximate the temporal dynamics behaviour instead of this piecewise continuous function, which, nevertheless, provides better control over the modelled situation.

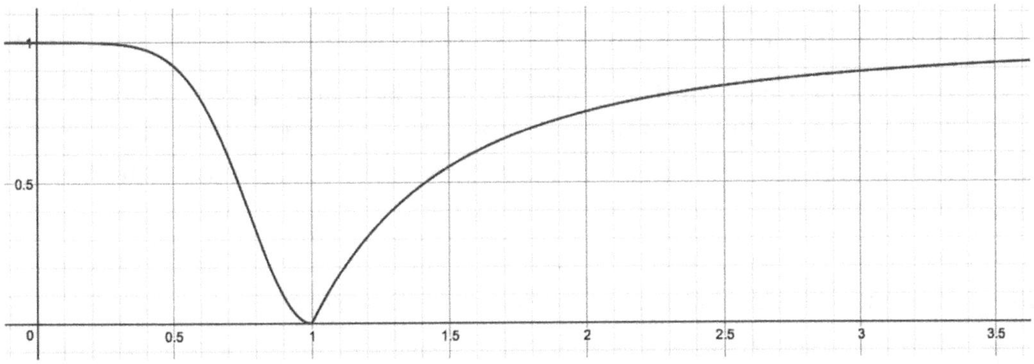

Fig. 2. The temporal user behaviour modelling function.

3.2 Proximity Dynamics in User Behaviour

As popular or significant items in the physical proximity of a viewed item are likely to become attractions for the active user, they have a potential to divert the user from a predefined (in any way or concept) course. Thus their influence in their neighbourhood need to be modelled and quantified as a probability of producing a dissatisfaction by the initially intended item interaction. Simply, the satisfaction by an item may be reduced by a popular or significant item in its immediate neighbourhood. This can be modelled as a function of the distances, the popularities and featured item scores,

$$p_p = 1 - \sum_{j=1}^{3} \beta^{(j)} \cdot p_f^{(j)} \tag{2}$$

where p_p is the estimate of the probability of user dissatisfaction by item i due to proximity dynamics computed as a weighted summation of three features p_f, β are heuristic weights for the three features (scaling in the range $[0, 1]$), and the features p_f are defined as[1]

[1] The $^{(j)}$ superscripts in parentheses correspond to indices and not powers.

$$p_f^{(j)} = \begin{cases} \omega^{(1)} \cdot \overline{R}^{(i)} + \omega^{(2)} \cdot F^{(i)} & j = 1 \\ \frac{p_f^{(1)}}{\sum_{k \in \text{proximity}} \omega^{(1)} \cdot \overline{R}^{(k)} + \omega^{(2)} \cdot F^{(k)}} & j = 2 \\ \frac{p_f^{(1)}}{\max_{k \in \text{proximity}} \omega^{(1)} \cdot \overline{R}^{(k)} + \omega^{(2)} \cdot F^{(k)}} & j = 3 \end{cases} \tag{3}$$

where, essentially, $p_f^{(1)}$ is the weighted summation of the average popularity and featured score of the examined item i, $p_f^{(2)}$ is the same quantity normalised by the summation of all the corresponding weighted summations in the proximity, and $p_f^{(3)}$ is the normalisation with respect to the maximum influence in the proximity, $\overline{R}^{(k)}$ is the average rating of item k and $F^{(k)}$ is the featured item score for item k. Apparently the weights in β and in ω are either predefined based on domain knowledge and experimental result, or can be learned within a machine learning framework (which is not the focus of this paper).

3.3 Content-Based Dynamics in User Behaviour

Content-based and semantic similarities among items have already been highlighted and studied in the relevant research and many works try to take into account that users might be biased towards (or against) specific families or groups of items that are possibly linked in multiple ways. This item linkage can be based on ontological connections, hierarchical relations, or even description similarities. When a recommender is hinted by the repetitive preference of the active user towards similar items (and possibly not nearby or popular items) then it is reasonable to assume that the user draws satisfaction by the specific type or group of items and should focus in recommending items based on some learned item clustering. Nevertheless, even under this line of reasoning that promotes similar items, the impact of proximity cannot be totally neglected. Apparently, a fairly relevant item in the vicinity of the user might be a more probable target than a more relevant item in a distance. Thus the quantification of content-based dynamics in the modelling of user satisfaction has to combine both content similarity and distance. In addition, there is still a strong influence by those items that are considered to be popular and this influence has to also be accounted for. In the presented framework the content-based user satisfaction model by the current (or next) item i is defined as

$$p_c = \max_{j \in \{\text{content neighb.}\}} \left\{ \gamma^{(1)} \cdot \left(\text{sim}^{(j)} \cdot \text{prox}^{(j)} \right) + \gamma^{(2)} \cdot \text{pop}^{(j)} \right\} \tag{4}$$

where p_c is the estimate of the probability of user dissatisfaction due to content-based dynamics (influenced by proximities and popularities), $\text{sim}^{(j)}$ is the content-based similarity of the active item i with item j that is in the high similarity (content-based) neighbourhood of i, $\text{prox}^{(j)}$ is the normalised inverse distance of item i with item j, and $\text{pop}^{(j)}$ is the average popularity of item j. The estimate takes into account the strongest influence in the neighbourhood of similar items and results a value for $p_c \in [0, 1]$. Again, heuristically predefined or learned weights are being used (γ) in order to emphasise the influence of similarity, proximity or popularity in this composite feature computation.

3.4 The Composite Feature for User Satisfaction Modelling

The four probabilistic factors (or features) defined in this framework can be used to either create a composite (vectorised) four-dimensional feature or a final one-dimensional feature that models user dissatisfaction at any point during a museum visit. The estimation of all four features at each new item creates an estimate of the dissatisfaction of the next probable items, either in a list of items created by collaborative filtering, either in a list of items generated by content-based approaches, or knowledge based item lists, and thus it can be used to propose adjustments to the predictions for the minimisation of the dissatisfaction. As the proposed framework focuses on the dissatisfaction rather than the user satisfaction modelling, it assumes a *minimax* approach, since it can be used for minimising the possible worst-case loss, that is for minimising the maximum possible estimated dissatisfaction, and is inherently a 'defensive' or conservative approach. Formally, the final dissatisfaction model can be expressed as a four-dimensional vector

$$p_d = \begin{bmatrix} p_t \\ p_p \\ p_c \\ p_o \end{bmatrix} \tag{5}$$

or a composite one-dimensional factor

$$p_d = \delta^{(1)} \cdot p_t + \delta^{(2)} \cdot p_p + \delta^{(3)} \cdot p_c + \delta^{(4)} \cdot p_o \tag{6}$$

in which the $\delta^{(k)}$ values are weights imposed on the features that can either be heuristic or learned based on an iterative machine learning technique.

In order to visualise how this user satisfaction modelling framework performs, a large-scale simulation has been conducted, including 1,000 items, 10,000 users with about 1% ratings of items. Indicatively Fig. 3 presents a typical representation of all estimated featured during a realistic museum tour along with all proximities, similarities and obstacles in each point of interest in three dimensions (real world relative locations). In this figure, the green circles are the target items, blue circles represent proximity related items, red circles represent content-based similar items, magenta squares depict the localised obtrusions and grey squares with numbers represent the composite overall dissatisfaction factor estimated at each item. The strong dotted line segments connect the target (green) items and represent the distances from point to point. In addition, light red dashed lines stemming from the target items connect with the similar items in various locations, and the number on each such line corresponds to the strength of the attraction ("1" being the strongest). Finally, as defined in the introduction of the framework, the size of the circles corresponds to the popularity of each item

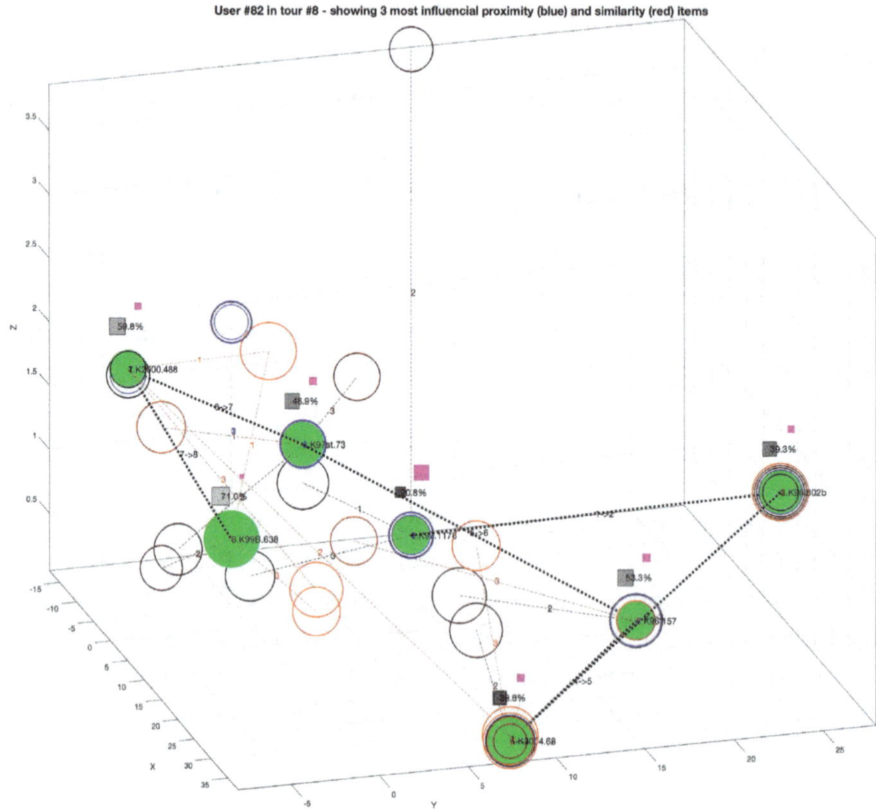

Fig. 3. Visualisation of a tour by a random user and the estimates of all features at each point of interest.

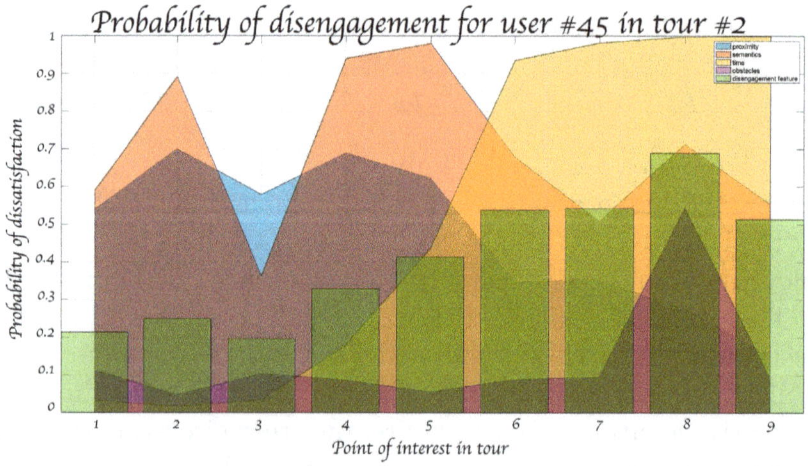

Fig. 4. Visualisation the estimates of all features at each point of interest during a tour by a random user.

and the saturation of the colours of the circles corresponds to the featured score. For tracking the visit direction, all strong dotted line segments denote the connection they correspond to, ie. the label "6 → 7" denotes the pathway from the sixth to the seventh item in the tour. Another visualisation of the evolution of the dynamics estimated by the four features and the final composite feature are shown in the graph of Fig. 4. Here the horizontal axis represents the items visited in the sequence, from left to right, and each feature's evolution is shown with a different area plot for comparison. The foremost bar graph is the composite dissatisfaction estimate.

4 Conclusion

Intelligent recommenders have appeared in Cultural Heritage applications during the recent decade, with promising results. Specifically cultural tourism and museums have been at the centre of development of technologies and techniques to tackle the information overload and increase user satisfaction for whatever the user motivation in the interaction with cultural heritage. This paper reviewed the recent history of recommender systems in museums from a point of view relating to how user satisfaction has been modelled, and presented a novel user satisfaction modelling framework that is able to capture temporal, proximity, content-based and obtrusion dynamics in the user behaviour during a museum visit, either in the form of an organised predefined narrative or a typical free-roaming visit.

The modelling framework was designed primarily having in mind what was missed by the previous works, the support of scenario based (storytelling) guided tours and a needed augmentation of the main notions of satisfaction applicable to any case of individual museum visit. The modelling framework has already been tested with a large amount of simulated data within an overall hybrid museum recommender and interesting preliminary results have been reported in terms of how it can be used as a means to support minimax-based strategies (user dissatisfaction minimisation). It has also been tested for another class of applications, that of the museum curators and visit program designers, where it can provide aid to identify the weak and strong points in each tour or individual item interactions so that decisions may be supported for changes and rearrangements.

Acknowledgement. This work was supported by the project "Computational Sciences and Technologies for Data, Content and Interaction" (MIS 5002437), which is implemented under the Action "Reinforcement of the Research and Innovation Infrastructure", funded by the Operational Programme "Competitiveness, Entrepreneurship and Innovation" (NSRF 2014-2020) and co-financed by Greece and the European Union (European Regional Development Fund).

References

1. Adomavicius, G., Tuzhilin, A.: Toward the next generation of recommender systems: a survey of the state-of-the-art and possible extensions. IEEE Trans. Knowl. Data Eng. **17**(6), 734–749 (2005)
2. Aggarwal, C.C.: An introduction to recommender systems. Recommender Systems, pp. 1–28. Springer, Cham (2016). https://doi.org/10.1007/978-3-319-29659-3_1

3. Aggarwal, C.C.: Recommender Systems: The Textbook. Springer, Cham (2016). https://doi.org/10.1007/978-3-319-29659-3
4. Agrawal, R., Srikant, R., et al.: Fast algorithms for mining association rules. In: Proceedings of 20th International Conference on Very Large Data Bases, VLDB, vol. 1215, pp. 487–499 (1994)
5. Anand, S.S., Mobasher, B.: Intelligent techniques for web personalization. In: Mobasher, B., Anand, S.S. (eds.) ITWP 2003. LNCS (LNAI), vol. 3169, pp. 1–36. Springer, Heidelberg (2005). https://doi.org/10.1007/11577935_1
6. Aoki, P.M., Grinter, R.E., Hurst, A., Szymanski, M.H., Thornton, J.D., Woodru, A.: Sotto voce: exploring the interplay of conversation and mobile audio spaces. In: Proceedings of the SIGCHI Conference on Human Factors in Computing Systems, pp. 431–438. ACM (2002)
7. Asanov, D., et al.: Algorithms and methods in recommender systems. Berlin Institute of Technology, Berlin, Germany (2011)
8. Basile, P., et al.: Augmenting a content-based recommender system with tags for cultural heritage personalization. Personalized Access to Cultural Heritage PATCH 2008, p. 25 (2008)
9. Benouaret, I., Lenne, D.: Combining Semantic and collaborative recommendations to generate personalized museum tours. In: Morzy, T., Valduriez, P., Bellatreche, L. (eds.) ADBIS 2015. CCIS, vol. 539, pp. 477–487. Springer, Cham (2015). https://doi.org/10.1007/978-3-319-23201-0_48
10. Bernardes, D., Diaby, M., Fournier, R., FogelmanSoulié, F., Viennet, E.: A social formalism and survey for recommender systems. ACM SIGKDD Explor. Newsl. **16**(2), 20–37 (2015)
11. Blondel, V.D., Guillaume, J.L., Lambiotte, R., Lefebvre, E.: Fast unfolding of communities in large networks. J. Stat. Mech. Theory Exp. **2008**(10), P10008 (2008)
12. Bobadilla, J., Ortega, F., Hernando, A., Gutiérrez, A.: Recommender systems survey. Knowl. Based Syst. **46**, 109–132 (2013)
13. Burke, R., Mobasher, B., Bhaumik, R., Williams, C.: Segment-based injection attacks against collaborative filtering recommender systems. In: Fifth IEEE International Conference on Data Mining, pp. 4-pp. IEEE (2005)
14. Cardoso, P.J.S., Rodrigues, J.M.F., Pereira, J.A.R., Sardo, J.D.P.: An object visit recommender supported in multiple visitors and museums. In: Antona, M., Stephanidis, C. (eds.) UAHCI 2017. LNCS, vol. 10277, pp. 301–312. Springer, Cham (2017). https://doi.org/10.1007/978-3-319-58706-6_24
15. Chen, J., Zaïane, O., Goebel, R.: Local community identification in social networks. In: International Conference on Advances in Social Network Analysis and Mining, ASONAM 2009, pp. 237–242. IEEE (2009)
16. Chou, S.C., Hsieh, W.T., Gandon, F.L., Sadeh, N.M.: Semantic web technologies for context-aware museum tour guide applications. In: 19th International Conference on Advanced Information Networking and Applications, AINA 2005, vol. 2, pp. 709–714. IEEE (2005)
17. Falk, J.H., Dierking, L.D.: Learning from Museums: Visitor Experiences and the Making of Meaning. Altamira Press, Walnut Creek (2000)
18. Goldberg, D., Nichols, D., Oki, B.M., Terry, D.: Using collaborative filtering to weave an information tapestry. Commun. ACM **35**(12), 61–70 (1992)
19. Good, N., et al.: Combining collaborative filtering with personal agents for better recommendations. In: AAAI/IAAI, pp. 439–446 (1999)
20. Goodfellow, I., Bengio, Y., Courville, A., Bengio, Y.: Deep Learning, vol. 1, pp. 465–469. MIT press, Cambridge (2016)

21. Grieser, K., Baldwin, T., Bird, S.: Dynamic path prediction and recommendation in a museum environment. In: Proceedings of the Workshop on Language Technology for Cultural Heritage Data (LaTeCH 2007), pp. 49–56 (2007)
22. Hashemi, S.H., Kamps, J.: Where to go next?: Exploiting behavioral user models in smart environments. In: Proceedings of the 25th Conference on User Modeling, Adaptation and Personalization, pp. 50–58. ACM (2017)
23. Huang, Y.M., Liu, C.H., Lee, C.Y., Huang, Y.M.: Designing a personalized guide recommendation system to mitigate information overload in museum learning. J. Educ. Technol. Soc. **15**(4) (2012)
24. Iaquinta, L., de Gemmis, M., Lops, P., Semeraro, G., Molino, P.: Can a recommender system induce serendipitous encounters? In: E-commerce. InTech (2010)
25. Jannach, D., Zanker, M., Felfernig, A., Friedrich, G.: An Introduction to Recommender Systems. Cambridge University Press, New York (2011)
26. Kaminskas, M., Ricci, F.: Contextual music information retrieval and recommendation: state of the art and challenges. Comput. Sci. Rev. **6**(2–3), 89–119 (2012)
27. Keller, I., Viennet, E.: Recommender systems for museums: evaluation on a real dataset. In: Fifth International Conference on Advances in Information Mining and Management (2015)
28. Konstan, J.A.: Introduction to recommender systems: algorithms and evaluation. ACM Trans. Inf. Syst. (TOIS) **22**(1), 1–4 (2004)
29. Lam, S.K., Riedl, J.: Shilling recommender systems for fun and profit. In: Proceedings of the 13th International Conference on World Wide Web, pp. 393–402. ACM (2004)
30. Lü, L., Medo, M., Yeung, C.H., Zhang, Y.C., Zhang, Z.K., Zhou, T.: Recommender systems. Phys. Rep. **519**(1), 1–49 (2012)
31. Luh, D., Yang, T.: Museum recommendation system based on lifestyles. In: 9th International Conference on Computer-Aided Industrial Design and Conceptual Design, CAID/CD 2008, pp. 884–889. IEEE (2008)
32. Luyten, K., Van Loon, H., Teunkens, D., Gabriëls, K., Coninx, K., Manshoven, E.: Archie: disclosing a museum by a socially-aware mobile guide. In: 7th International Symposium on Virtual Reality, Archaeology and Cultural Heritage (2006)
33. Maehara, C., Yatsugi, K., Kim, D., Ushiama, T.: An exhibit recommendation system based on semantic networks for museum. In: Watanabe, T., Jain, L.C. (eds.) Innovations in Intelligent Machines - 2. SCI, vol. 376, pp. 131–141. Springer, Heidelberg (2012). https://doi.org/10.1007/978-3-642-23190-2_10
34. Melville, P., Mooney, R.J., Nagarajan, R.: Content-boosted collaborative filtering for improved recommendations. In: AAAI/IAAI, vol. 23, pp. 187–192 (2002)
35. Melville, P., Sindhwani, V.: Recommender Systems. In: Sammut, C., Webb, G.I. (eds.) Encyclopedia of Machine Learning, pp. 829–838. Springer, Boston (2011). https://doi.org/10.1007/978-0-387-30164-8
36. Miller, N., et al.: Context-aware computing using a shared contextual information service. In: Advances in Pervasive Computing. A Collection of Contributions Presented at the 2nd International Conference on Pervasive Computing (Pervasive 2004) (2004)
37. Ong, C.S., Day, M.Y., Hsu, W.L.: The measurement of user satisfaction with question answering systems. Inf. Manag. **46**(7), 397–403 (2009)
38. Oppermann, R., Specht, M.: A nomadic information system for adaptive exhibition guidance. Arch. Mus. Inform. **13**(2), 127–138 (1999)
39. Pechenizkiy, M., Calders, T.: A framework for guiding the museum tours personalization. In: Proceedings of the Workshop on Personalised Access to Cultural Heritage (PATCH07), pp. 11–28. Citeseer (2007)

40. Resnick, P., Iacovou, N., Suchak, M., Bergstrom, P., Riedl, J.: Grouplens: an open architecture for collaborative filtering of netnews. In: Proceedings of the 1994 ACM Conference on Computer Supported Cooperative Work, pp. 175–186. ACM (1994)
41. Ricci, F., Rokach, L., Shapira, B., Kantor, P.B. (eds.): Recommender Systems Handbook. Springer, Boston (2011). https://doi.org/10.1007/978-0-387-85820-3
42. Rocchi, C., Stock, O., Zancanaro, M., Kruppa, M., Krüger, A.: The museum visit: generating seamless personalized presentations on multiple devices. In: Proceedings of the 9th International Conference on Intelligent User Interfaces, pp. 316–318. ACM (2004)
43. Roes, I., Stash, N., Wang, Y., Aroyo, L.: A personalized walk through the museum: The Chip Interactive Tour Guide. In: CHI 2009 Extended Abstracts on Human Factors in Computing Systems, pp. 3317–3322. ACM (2009)
44. Rossi, S., Barile, F., Improta, D., Russo, L.: Towards a collaborative filtering framework for recommendation in museums: from preference elicitation to group's visits. Procedia Comput. Sci. **98**, 431–436 (2016)
45. Rossi, S., Cervone, F.: Social utilities and personality traits for group recommendation: a pilot user study. In: Proceedings of the 8th International Conference on Agents and Artificial Intelligence, pp. 38–46. SCITEPRESS-Science and Technology Publications, Lda (2016)
46. Schein, A.I., Popescul, A., Ungar, L.H., Pennock, D.M.: Methods and metrics for cold-start recommendations. In: Proceedings of the 25th Annual International ACM SIGIR Conference on Research and Development in Information Retrieval, pp. 253–260. ACM (2002)
47. Su, X., Khoshgoftaar, T.M.: A survey of collaborative filtering techniques. Adv. Artif. Intell. **2009**, 4 (2009)
48. Tavcar, A., Antonya, C., Butila, E.V.: Recommender system for virtual assistant supported museum tours. Informatica **40**(3), 279 (2016)
49. van Hage, W.R., Stash, N., Wang, Y., Aroyo, L.: Finding your way through the Rijksmuseum with an adaptive mobile museum guide. In: Aroyo, L., Antoniou, G., Hyvönen, E., ten Teije, A., Stuckenschmidt, H., Cabral, L., Tudorache, T. (eds.) ESWC 2010. LNCS, vol. 6088, pp. 46–59. Springer, Heidelberg (2010). https://doi.org/10.1007/978-3-642-13486-9_4
50. Wang, Y., Stash, N., Aroyo, L., Gorgels, P., Rutledge, L., Schreiber, G.: Recommendations based on semantically enriched museum collections. Web Semant. Sci., Serv. Agents World Wide Web **6**(4), 283–290 (2008)

Visualization Methods/Audio

DinofelisAR: Users' Perspective About a Mobile AR Application in Cultural Heritage

Anabela Marto[1(✉)], Alexandrino Gonçalves[1], and A. Augusto de Sousa[2]

[1] Department of Informatics Engineering, ESTG, CIIC, Polytechnic Institute of Leiria, Leiria, Portugal
anabela.marto@ipleiria.pt
[2] Department of Informatics Engineering, INESC TEC, Faculty of Engineering of the University of Porto, Porto, Portugal

Abstract. Augmented reality has seen an increased popularity among the last decades due to technological advances and, a consequent growth of the amount of augmented reality systems, became available. However, in order to diffuse this technology successfully, understand users' feelings when using augmented reality applications is considered a major issue. This study implemented this technology in a cultural heritage outdoor context and tested it *in-situ* to evaluate user's perspective regarding to personal satisfaction – including cultural enrichment acquired –, ease of use and their intention to use it. The results obtained, through questionnaires, presented the visitors acceptance regarding the usage of this type of solutions among a cultural heritage context, since it may become future visits more pleasant and desirable. The user's majority expressed the request to use this technology more often in cultural heritage spaces.

Keywords: Mobile augmented reality · Cultural heritage · User tests

1 Introduction

Museums are striving for having their spaces full of visitors whom, by their side, want to learn, enrich themselves and have fun. It is known, through an internal survey made in the Conimbriga Monographic Museum-National Museum in 2014, that the main reason that motivates visitors to come to Conimbriga is cultural enrichment (50,6%). Other motivations are related to leisure time (20,2%), to improve their knowledge about history and archaeology (17,7%), to Ruins' mosaics, architecture and urbanism (6,5%), and to the object collection in the museum (5,0%).

To fulfil the expectations of both – museums and visitors – museums are attempting to provide information by means of different and innovative methods. Aside from their historic artefacts and infrastructures (or what remain of them), they usually provide images added to specific places (digital and real), mock-ups reconstructions, multimedia content (audio-visual information), etc. Therefore, new technologic approaches, such as augmented reality, has been exploited in the last few years among different museums. The Monographic Museum of Conimbriga-National Museum, an archaeological space with the ruins of an important ancient Roman City, presented a report in

M. Duguleană et al. (Eds.): VRTCH 2018, CCIS 904, pp. 79–92, 2019.
https://doi.org/10.1007/978-3-030-05819-7_7

2016 [1], where visitors stated that this museum is interesting from the historic point of view (9,4/10) and worthwhile a visit to the ruins (9,2/10). However, less satisfactory results were obtained when visitors were questioned if Conimbriga knows how to use technology in the space in a way to provide a more interesting visit (6,9/10) and when questioned about the enjoyability for children while visiting Conimbriga (6,7/10). Hence, a proper and user-oriented use of technology should be prospected to cultural heritage contexts, profiting visitors and institutions. Notwithstanding, the way that visitors from archaeological spaces look and feel about technology applications in cultural heritage spaces, may differ in a way that technology could be considered as intrusive and unexploited instead of being profitable.

AR has been recognized as a good solution to use in distinct areas and its usage has a positive impact in users' perspective (Liu, Zhang and Bao 2016).

The main purpose of this study is to better comprehend the users' opinion about the use of AR technology when visiting a cultural heritage space regarding to its satisfaction, the ease of use, and their desire to use this technology.

This research presents a case study whereby the visitors of a space – an archaeological space – the Roman Ruins of the Conimbriga Monographic Museum-National Museum – were invited to test an AR application for mobile devices. The usage of a smartphone for the experiment brings this technology closer to people since there is no need to resort to further gadgets as head-mounted devices, being less intrusive to visitors whilst saves money for cultural institutions. The visitors who accepted this challenge, used a smartphone themselves to test the AR app with no time limit and without restrictions. The outcome obtained across this experiment are the results acquired from questionnaires on a Likert-type five-level scale.

2 State of the Art

This chapter intends to introduce the concept of augmented reality and to present relevant conclusions from studies related to AR and users. A summary of recent studies where this technology was tested with users is made.

2.1 Virtual and Augmented Reality

To allude the concept of augmented reality, it is suitable to mention virtual reality as well, since augmented reality is a correlation between real environment and virtual reality. In 1994, Milgram and Kishino [2] presented the concept of *Virtuality Continuum*: a term used to describe the concept through a continuous scale, ranging the totally virtual and the totally real environment. Thus, according to their concept, while in virtual reality the user is totally immersed in a virtual environment, the experience with augmented reality allows the user to be aware of both environments: virtual and real.

Augmented Reality (AR), despite its early appearance during the 60's [3], it was among the last decades that has become more popular, acquiring preponderance and prominence. Due to technological advances, today it is possible to access to AR experiences using handy and ubiquitous devices, like smartphones or tablets, bringing this technology closer to general public. AR has been known as a good solution to use in distinct areas and its usage has a positive impact in users' perspective [5]. Although this technology has seen popularity grow and being present among a vast variety of areas, such as publicity [6], entertainment [7], education [8], [9], medicine [10], architecture [11], manufacturing [12] and, the particular case for this study, in cultural heritage [13–15], it is not very common to find AR experiences available for visitors in archaeological spaces whereby they can experience it among their visits. This lack is even more noticeable for engaging AR experiences in outdoor spaces, a fact that sparked interest to unleash this research.

2.2 Previous Studies with Users Using AR

In the first years of the new millennium, a mobile augmented reality implementation in cultural heritage sites, arose as one of the pioneers projects named *Archeoguide* [16]. That same year, Vlahakis *et al.* [17] published the first results of the *Archeoguide* project. This study, where younger users appeared as the most enthusiastic, some problems using the system were detected. As examples of these problems, they found the fact that users felt uncomfortable while using the technological devices and the difficulty of visualizing the digital information outdoors due to the sunlight.

Meanwhile, mobile AR became lighter to carry, since today is implemented in single handheld devices, various approaches were developed, and several cultural institutions have made their own mobile augmented reality applications. Some examples are found in Philadelphia Department of Records, the city of Christchurch, the Museum of London, the Netherlands Architecture Institute and the Powerhouse Museum in Sydney.

Recently, several studies tested the usage of AR in cultural heritage contexts using different approaches to understand the acceptance and the intention to use the technology. Hence, the necessity to understand how other researches evaluated their systems arose.

All in all, a collection of recent studies – from 2014 up to now – related to AR applications developed in order to, somehow, preserve or disseminate cultural heritage spaces, was made and is summarised in Table 1.

Table 1. Collection of studies published since 2014 using AR in cultural heritage environment.

Context	Methodology		Sample	Reference
	Method	Instrument		
Mobile AR app in urban heritage	Three examples of AR including three modalities, text/image; video; an example of GPS-based AR (before and during the interview)	In-depth interviews (40 min)	26 international and domestic tourists in Dublin, Ireland	[15]
AR Travel Guide	Participants used the system as a guiding tool	Questionnaire	105, Corfu island visitors, Greece	[18]

(*continued*)

Table 1. *(continued)*

Context	Methodology		Sample	Reference
	Method	Instrument		
AR for tourism: destinations and attractions	Used the app	(not specified)	145, Deoksugung Palace, South Korea	[19]
AR and VR in a museum – Geevor Tin Mine Museum	Participants tried the apps (AR and VR)	Questionnaire	163 in Cornwall, UK	[20]
Mobile AR for tourist guide	Tested the app	Questionnaire	30 non-experts in Brno, Czech Republic	[21]
Mobile AR to learn in cultural heritage	Tested the app	Questionnaire	200 in Melaka, Malaysia	[22]
Outdoors mobile AR guide for archaeology	Tested the prototype (4 groups of 4 elements)	Questionnaire	16 students – educational visit to Knossos	[23]
AR for historic factors	A between-subjects experiment. (1) used AR in space; (2) – watched on computer	Questionnaire	45 students, Warsaw, Poland Experimental group = 22 Control group = 23	[24]
AR – wearable devices in tourism	Used the system on a tour to the museum – Museum Zoom Google Glass	Questionnaire	126 + 211. art gallery in the UK for 30 min	[25]

Observing the previous studies where AR was implemented and tested with users within diverse cultural heritage purposes, it is noticeable that the most common instrument used to evaluate the systems implemented – for those that present results related to users – is the questionnaire and the number of participants vary amid 16 and 200 volunteers.

3 Methodology

A mobile AR prototype was developed to allow the visitors of the archaeological space in study – the Roman Ruins of Conimbriga – to experience mobile AR technology. This prototype, named DinofelisAR, was developed for Android devices and an image was used as mark to detect the position and orientation of the user in order to place the virtual information in the right position when overlapped to the real scenario perceived trough the smartphone's camera. Using this prototype *in-situ*, the user could see a virtual reconstruction of the *Forum* superimposed over its existing ruins.

3.1 Prototype Development

Due to a large quantity and diversity of frameworks available to support the development of AR systems, a research study was made in order to identify which were the frameworks that would fulfil the requirements needed for this project [26]. Considering this prototype requirements, three frameworks seemed comply the requisites: Vuforia SDK[1], Kudan SDK[2] and, Wikitude SDK[3]. The referred study revealed that, for the specific tests made, Vuforia SDK was the one which best fulfilled the needs for this prototype. In addition to the good performance tests achieved by Vuforia SDK, this framework was the only one that, in the free version for developers, allowed to track the camera with natural features when the marker gets out of the field of view with a feature named by Vuforia as *Extended Tracking*. Although this technique appeared to be less stable when compared to the marker-based tracking, especially with restricted light conditions, this feature enhanced the application flexibility and freedom to navigate in space.

DinofelisAR, the prototype created to be tested *in-situ*, was developed in Unity 3D[4] and using a Vuforia package for Unity. An image was used as mark (Fig. 1) and the functionality *Extended Tracking* was activated in order to allow users to explore the surroundings even if the image used as mark, got out of the field of view.

Fig. 1. Image used as mark for the experiment using the AR app DinofelisAR *in-situ*.

[1] More information about Vuforia SDK on https://developer.vuforia.com/.

[2] More information about Kudan SDK on https://www.kudan.eu/overview/.

[3] More information about Wikitude SDK on https://www.wikitude.com/.

[4] More information about Unity 3D on https://unity3d.com/pt.

Since the museum requested for infographics in place to inform visitors about the place of the AR experiment, the image presented in Fig. 1 was created for two purposes: as an informative image about the existence of an AR experience in the space; and as a mark for the AR app.

3.2 Local of the Experiment

The intention to evaluate DinofelisAR app by users when used in cultural heritage contexts, took us to test the prototype in Conimbriga.

Conimbriga is a Roman provincial city which was abandoned during the medieval age and it was inhabited between centuries IX B.C. and A.D. VII–VIII [27]

DinofelisAR app was tested in the location where used to be edified the *Forum* – a public monument with large dimensions which was virtually reconstructed – and its position corresponds to the centre of the ancient city (Fig. 2). Its dimensions were approximately 48 × 96 m and it would be around 9 m high.

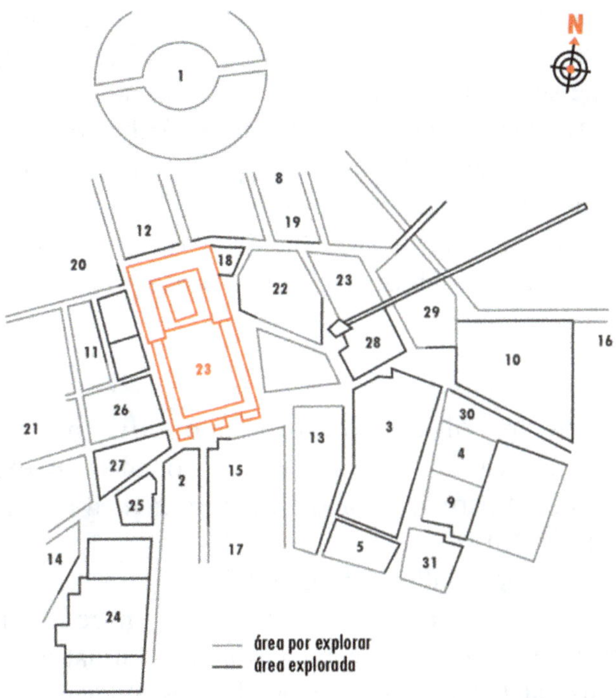

Fig. 2. Identified by number 23, highlighted in red, the *Forum*'s location is stressed (image created based on the information available at www.conimbriga.pt). (Color figure online)

Within the *Forum's* ruins, an ample and open space, the experience occurred in square's centre, as illustrated on Fig. 3.

Fig. 3. Identification of the central position where the experience took place. (Color figure online)

A green circle in Fig. 3 identifies the place where the experience with the DinofelisAR app took place. The volunteers who agreed to participate in this study, could visualize, in the smartphone and around their surroundings, the virtual building corresponding to the Roman *Forum* that used to be edified there during the Roman Era. In the beginning of the experience, *Forum*'s Temple would be right in front of the users and the surroundings would be composed by the peristyle, with columns and walls. The *Forum* was edified all around the square which means that all its structure, composed by columns, roofs and walls, established a closed space.

3.3 Tests Procedure

The tests occurred between 17th and 19th of May of 2017 in the Ruins of the Conimbriga Monographic Museum-National Museum. For this AR experience, a smartphone[5] was handed to each participant and they were invited to perform several steps that are hereinafter described.

1. First, to launch the application DinofelisAR.
2. Second, to point the smartphone's camera to the image provided (this image is the mark used as target for the AR experience) until a virtual cube appears over the referred image as illustrated in Fig. 4. Technically, this moment was where the user's position and orientation were identified.
3. To explore the surroundings with the smartphone to visualize the virtual model over its ruins (Fig. 5 [A] and [B]). Users were able to navigate in a 360° angle.
4. For the last step, participants were invited to fill a questionnaire (English or Portuguese version) on a five-point scale.

[5] The smartphone used for this experiment was a Motorola 3rd Generation 5.0" (*Quad-core* 1.4 GHz *Cortex*-A53, 1 GB RAM, camera 13 MP, f/2.0).

Fig. 4. The virtual cube over the real image grantees that the app detected the image mark and is able to show the virtual information around the user.

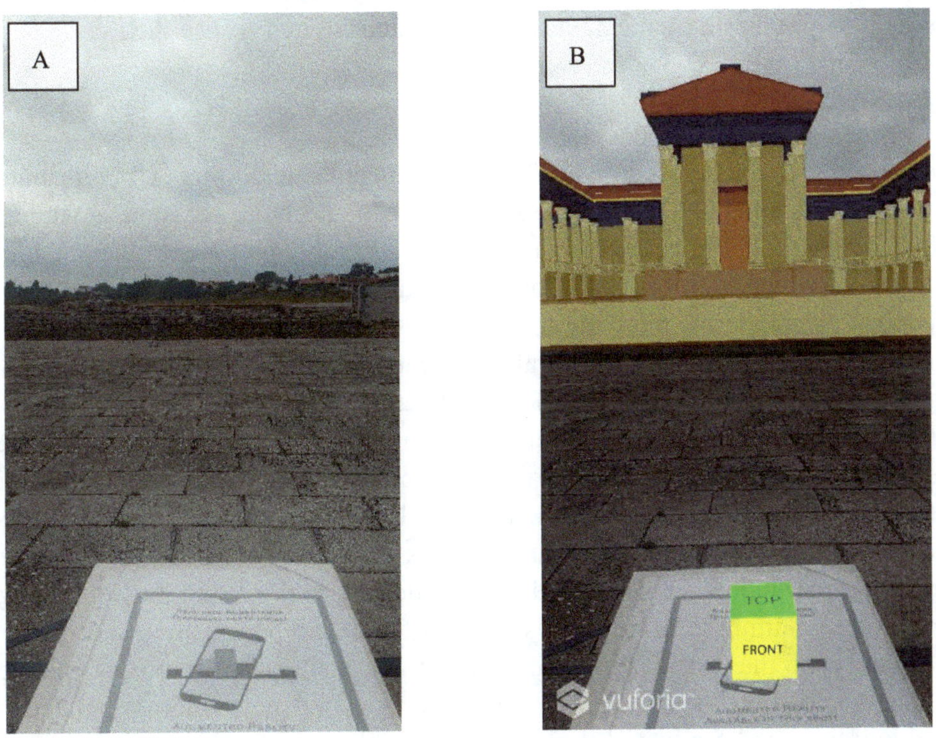

Fig. 5. View of the place before the AR experience [A] occurs and, during the AR experience with DinofelisAR, with the virtual model visible over *Forum*'s ruins [B].

Looking at Fig. 5, it is possible to observe that the ground is part of the real content around user. The virtual model is overlapped over the ruins to give the user a glimpse of the building's appearance back in the Roman Era.

4 Presentation and Discussion of Results

The visitors of Conimbriga's Roman Ruins which accepted the invitation to be part of this study, after testing AR experience by their hands, filled in a questionnaire whose questions intended to ascertain the users' opinion related to (1) satisfaction, which includes the pleasure, dynamism and activity among the visit to the *Forum*, as well as the level of engagement in the visit and achievements obtained; (2) the ease of use of AR technology; and (3) the desire to use this technology in cultural heritage spaces.

A total of 90 participants accepted to be part of this study (51% female and 49% male). Among this heterogeneous group of participants, 44% of them were more than 55 years old, 19% between 40 and 55 years old, 21% between 25 and 39 years old, 9% between 18 and 24 years old and, 7% were less than 18 years old. Considering their level of education, while 1% preferred not to answer this question, 73% of the respondents were higher educated, contrasting to 26% that were not.

The participants were also questioned about why they decided to be part of this experiment and, the majority (72%), stated the interest of augmented reality applied to archaeological context. Even the participants that affirmed not to know the technology in study, they got curious to try it (18%) while 10% asserted other reasons. These results help to predict the tendency of people when invited to use AR.

4.1 User's Satisfaction

The results collected disclosed that the participants considered that AR contributed for a more dynamic and active visit to the *Forum* (94%) and more pleasant as well (94%).

Moreover, 92% of the participants agreed or strongly agreed with the allegation of being more involved with this tour zone when using the AR app.

Keeping in mind the motivation of visitors about people's motivation to visit Conimbriga – the majority, for cultural enrichment –, it was asked about the cultural enrichment provided by using the AR app when they were visiting the *Forum*. The results presented a majority agreement: 97% of the participants agreed or strongly agreed that AR applications can contribute to cultural enrichment during their visits.

Considering the *Forum* features acquired, 91% of participants stated that became able to describe better the *Forum* characteristics – *e.g.* size, colours, architecture.

In short, participants emphasized a significant level of satisfaction using AR technology in Conimbriga's Ruins. Using DinofelisAR when visiting the *Forum*, the clear majority of the participants stated that their visit became more dynamic and active, more pleasant, they felt more involved, acquired new findings related to the referred building, and facilitated their cultural enrichment.

4.2 Ease of Use

An interesting fact about the use of AR technology, is that even people who never used this technology before this experiment (61%), considered it easy to use, as well as those who already had tried it before (Fig. 6).

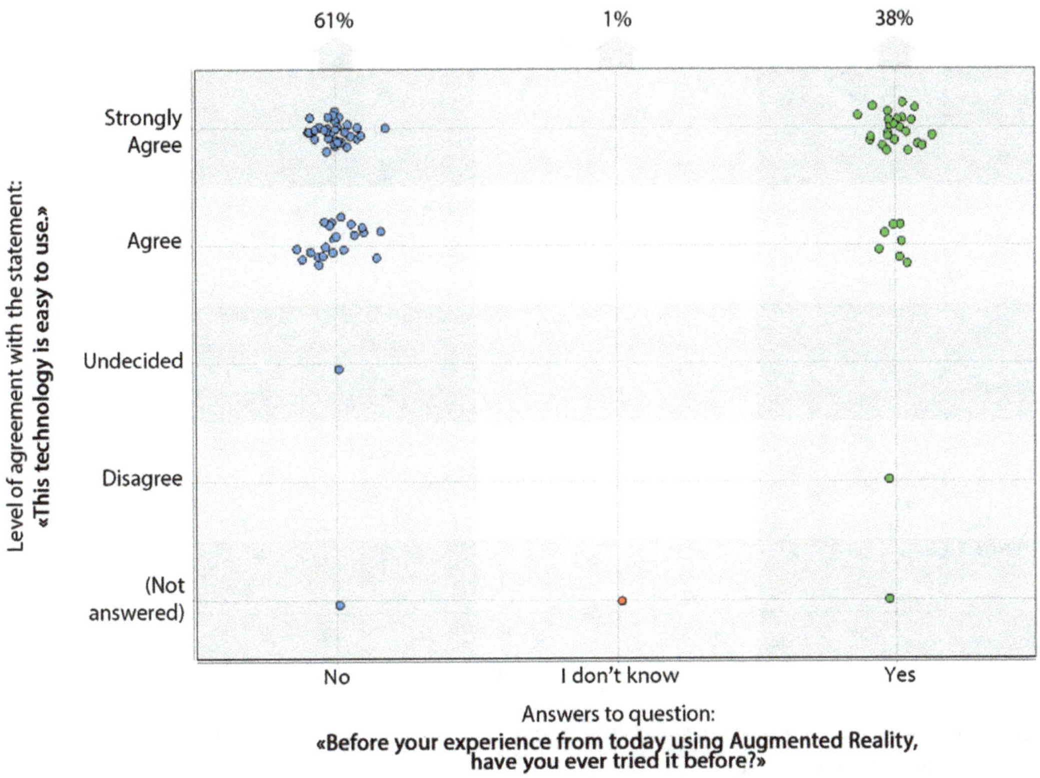

Fig. 6. Representation of participants' opinion related to the ease of use (vertical axes) compared to their experience using AR (horizontal axes).

Figure 6 displays that, regardless the previous experience using AR, the majority affirmed that this technology is easy to use. In fact, 96% of the participants agreed or strongly agreed that this technology is easy to use.

The majority (84%) didn't feel lost during the experience, not knowing very well where to point the smartphone in order to see the virtual model.

Furthermore, most of the participants (88%) assumed that after some short moments using AR technology, they already were comfortable using it and understanding how to use it correctly.

In brief, the usage of AR technology was revealed as a very easy and rapid learning tool to handle, independently of the individual participant's characteristic – age, gender or level of expertise.

4.3 Desire to Use

And because the participants' intention to use this technology is also a point of interest for this study, the visitors were asked about their interest in installing an app similar to the one provided in the experiment in their own smartphones. The results were also positive, and the majority stated that they would be interested (Fig. 7).

In Fig. 7 is shown that, regardless of the average age of this study sample, participants confirmed their desire to install an AR mobile app in their phones with the intension to use it among cultural heritage spaces.

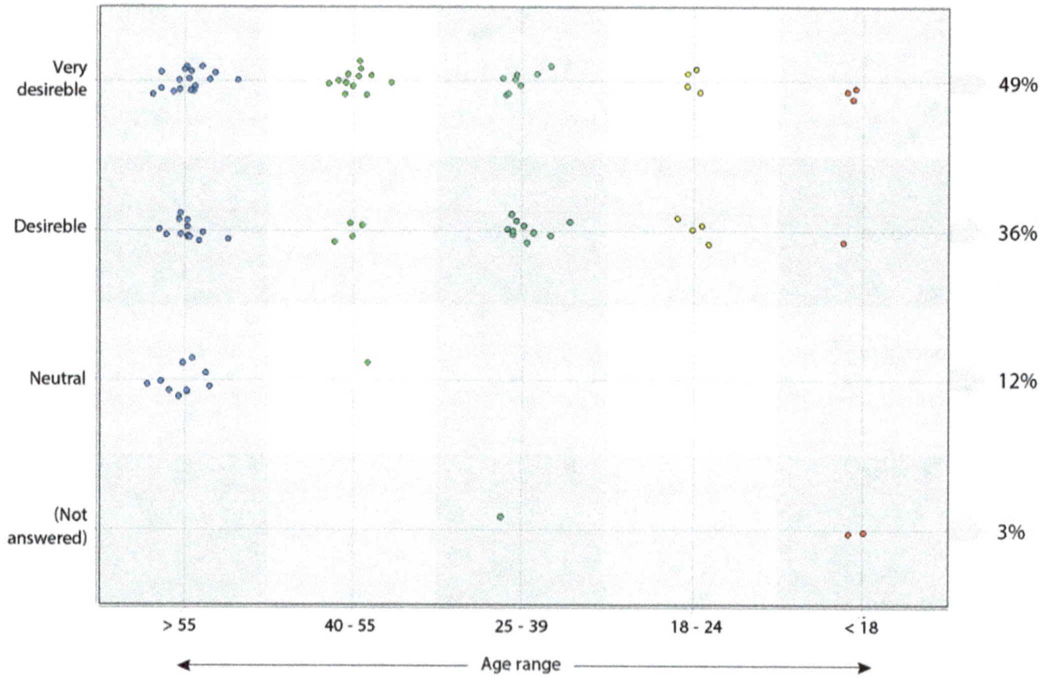

Fig. 7. Graphic representation related to the level of desire of the users in installing an AR app on their personal smartphones.

As visitors of Conimbriga, it was asked if the use of this technology could contribute to an increase number of visitors to this archaeological space where 90% of the participants agreed or strongly agreed.

Additionally, through open-ended questions related to suggestions and issues found during their experience, the participants specifically requested to extend AR technology to other places – inside Conimbriga's Roman Ruins and other archaeological spaces as well – (33%); to freely explore the space without the need of being close to the mark (28%); to look through a bigger screen (13%) – this suggestion was made mainly (83%) from people with more than 55 years old –; to provide a more detailed virtual model; and to add people/avatars to the virtual scene. Other requests made by the participants included the use of sounds and the ability to zoom the virtual model in order to observe it with more detail.

In sum even though the future installation of these AR applications implies the usage of their personal mobile devices, these results reveal that most participants confirm their interest using AR technology when visiting cultural heritage spaces. Their intent is also noticeable among their suggestions presented in the open-ended questions.

5 Conclusion

This study intended to implement and test a mobile AR application with visitors of a cultural heritage space, which in our case is the Roman Ruins of Conimbriga, and to evaluate its use with visitors. This rollout was specifically guided to evaluate an application of mobile AR used in outdoor spaces, among an archaeological space, where a virtual building was superimposed in its correspondent ruins.

A total of 90 visitors participated in this study which was accomplished in the centre of the ancient city *Forum*'s square. These volunteers used a smartphone (an Android device was provided) to run the mobile AR app named DinofelisAR. They were able to perceive and explore the virtual reconstruction of the *Forum* overlapped on its real ruins. Each user could observe, in real-time and in a 360-degree view, the virtual model while perceiving real images trough the camera. After this experience, the participants filled a questionnaire and the results had exposed that this technology may be an excellent opportunity to improve and spotlight cultural heritage spaces. Analysing participants' opinions related to their satisfaction, including the achievements acquired, their opinion related to the ease of use, and their intention to use AR technology in this context, had highlighted an unequivocal benefit from users' perspective.

Looking ahead, the importance of deeply understand users' perspective when using a new technology such as mobile AR, is well known to accomplish better approaches that would fit the visitors' expectations and needs when visiting cultural heritage spaces. Hence, arises also the necessity of comprehend the acceptance and the intention to use technology among other cultural heritage spaces beyond the Ruins of Conimbriga.

Analysing the results presented among this paper, it is our opinion that AR technology has great potential to engage people and seemed to be easy to use amid everyone who tested it. Therefore, dwell on AR technology is appropriate and stimulates opportune and useful new fields of research for scientific community and for society.

Acknowledgments. This work was supported by national funds through the Portuguese Foundation for Science and Technology (FCT) under the project UID/CEC/04524/2016.

References

1. Santander Chair- Universidad Complutense de Madrid. Conimbriga's Visitor Satisfaction (2016)
2. Milgram, P., Takemura, H., Utsumi, A., Kishino, F.: Augmented reality : a class of displays on the reality-virtuality continuum. In: SPIE - The International Society for Optical Engineering, pp. 282–292 (1994)
3. Sutherland, I.E.: The ultimate display. In: Proceedings of the IFIP Congress, pp. 506–508 (1965)
4. Bae, H., Walker, M., White, J., Sun, Y., Golparvar-Fard, M.: Fast and scalable structure-from-motion based localization for high-precision mobile augmented reality systems fast and scalable structure-from-motion based localization for high-precision mobile augmented reality systems. mUX J. Mob. User Exp. **5**(1), 4 (2016)
5. Liu, H., Zhang, G., Bao, H.: Robust keyframe-based monocular SLAM for augmented reality. In: 2016 IEEE International Symposium on Mixed and Augmented Reality (ISMAR) (2016)
6. Kim, Y., Kim, W.: Implementation of augmented reality system for smartphone advertisements. Int. J. Multimed. Ubiquit. Eng. **9**(2), 385–392 (2014)

7. Hamasaki, M., Takeda, H., Nishimura, T.: Network analysis of massively collaborative creation of multimedia contents. In: Proceedings of the 1st International Conference on Designing Interactive User Experiences for TV and Video, UXTV 2008, pp. 165–168 (2008)
8. Yuen, S.C., Yaoyuneyong, G., Johnson, E.: Augmented reality: an overview and five directions for AR in education. J. Educ. Technol. Dev. Exch. **4**(1), 119–140 (2011)
9. Bower, M., Howe, C., McCredie, N., Robinson, A., Grover, D.: Augmented reality in education – cases, places and potentials. EMI. Educ. Media Int. **51**(1), 1–15 (2014)
10. Paolis, L.T.: augmented visualization as surgical support in the treatment of tumors. In: Rojas, I., Ortuño, F. (eds.) IWBBIO 2017, Part I. LNCS, vol. 10208, pp. 432–443. Springer, Cham (2017). https://doi.org/10.1007/978-3-319-56148-6_38
11. Meža, S., Turk, Ž., Dolenc, M.: Measuring the potential of augmented reality in civil engineering. Adv. Eng. Softw. **90**, 1–10 (2015)
12. Regenbrecht, H., Baratoff, G., Wilke, W.: Augmented reality projects in automotive and aerospace industry. IEEE Comput. Graph. Appl. **25**(6), 48–56 (2005)
13. Canciani, M., Conigliaro, E., Del Grasso, M., Papalini, P., Saccone, M.: 3D Survey and augmented reality for cultural heritage. The case study of Aurelian wall at Castra Praetoria in Rome. Int. Arch. Photogramm. Remote Sens. Spat. Inf. Sci. **41**, 931–937 (2016)
14. Fidas, C., Sintoris, C., Yiannoutsou, N., Avouris, N.: A survey on tools for end user authoring of mobile applications for cultural heritage. In: Proceedings of the 6th International Conference on Information, Intelligence, Systems and Applications (IISA), pp. 1–5 (2015)
15. Han, D.-I., Jung, T., Gibson, A.: Dublin AR: implementing augmented reality in tourism. In: Xiang, Z., Tussyadiah, I. (eds.) Information and Communication Technologies in Tourism 2014, pp. 511–523. Springer, Cham (2013). https://doi.org/10.1007/978-3-319-03973-2_37
16. Gleue, T., Dähne, P.: Design and Implementation of a mobile device for outdoor augmented reality in the archeoguide project. In: Proceedings of the 2001 Conference on Virtual Reality, Archeology, and Cultural Heritage, VAST 2001, pp. 161–168 (2001)
17. Vlahakis, V., et al: Archeoguide: first results of an augmented reality, mobile computing system in cultural heritage sites. In: Proceedings of the 2001 Conference on Virtual Reality, Archeology, and Cultural Heritage (VAST 2001), pp. 131–140 (2001)
18. Kourouthanassis, P., Boletsis, C., Bardaki, C., Chasanidou, D.: Tourists responses to mobile augmented reality travel guides: the role of emotions on adoption behavior. Pervasive Mob. Comput. **18**, 71–87 (2015)
19. Chung, N., Han, H., Joun, Y.: Tourists' intention to visit a destination: The role of augmented reality (AR) application for a heritage site. Comput. Hum. Behav. **50**, 588–599 (2015)
20. Jung, T., tom Dieck, M.C., Lee, H., Chung, N.: Effects of virtual reality and augmented reality on visitor experiences in museum. In: Inversini, A., Schegg, R. (eds.) Information and Communication Technologies in Tourism 2016, pp. 621–635. Springer, Cham (2016). https://doi.org/10.1007/978-3-319-28231-2_45
21. Střelák, D., Škola, F., Liarokapis, F.: Examining user experiences in a mobile augmented reality tourist guide. In: Proceedings of the 9th ACM International Conference on Pervasive Technologies Related to Assistive Environments (PETRA 2016) (2016)
22. Pendit, U.C., Zaibon, S.B., Bakar, J.A.A.: Measuring enjoyable informal learning using augmented reality at cultural heritage site. J. Telecommun. Electron. Comput. Eng. **8**(10), 13–21 (2016)
23. Kasapakis, V., Gavalas, D., Galatis, P.: Augmented reality in cultural heritage: field of view awareness in an archaeological site mobile guide. J. Ambient Intell. Smart Environ. **8**(5), 501–514 (2016)

24. Oleksy, T., Wnuk, A.: Augmented places: an impact of embodied historical experience on attitudes towards places. Comput. Hum. Behav. **57**, 11–16 (2016)
25. Tussyadiah, I.P., Jung, T.: Embodiment of wearable augmented reality technology in tourism experiences. J. Travel Res. **57**, 597–611 (2017)
26. Marto, A.G.R.: Realidade Aumentada Móvel num Contexto de Herança Cultural. Faculty of Engineering, University of Porto (2017)
27. Correia, V.H.: A Arquitectura Doméstica de Conimbriga e as Estruturas Económicas e sociais da Cidade Romana. Simões & Linhares Lda (2013)

Exploring Cultural Heritage Using Augmented Reality Through Google's Project Tango and ARCore

Gheorghe-Daniel Voinea[1(✉)], Florin Girbacia[1], Cristian Cezar Postelnicu[1], and Anabela Marto[2]

[1] Transilvania University of Brasov, Brasov, Romania
daniel.voinea@unitbv.ro

[2] Department of Informatics Engineering – ESTG, CIIC, Polytechnic Institute of Leiria, Leiria, Portugal

Abstract. This research is focused on the importance of using modern technologies in preserving and exploring Cultural Heritage (CH). Specifically, Augmented Reality (AR) has the potential to enhance the user experience related to cultural heritage. We briefly present the main technological approaches in CH and a state of the art in mobile augmented reality. The latest Software Development Kit (SDK) for building AR applications are reviewed and compared. The 3D object that participants could place in the real environment was obtained using photogrammetry, a popular and relatively easy to use digitization technique. The virtual object represents a fortified church and is part of a group of UNESCO monuments from the historical and ethnographical region called "Țara Bârsei", located in Brasov, Romania. We also provided some guidelines to ensure an accurate 3D reconstruction of any object. We assess users' perception regarding two mobile AR applications, one based on Project Tango while the other was developed using ARCore. Results confirm that AR improves user experience and increases the enjoyment of learning about cultural heritage.

Keywords: Cultural heritage · Augmented reality · Project Tango

1 Introduction

Cultural Heritage (CH) represents an expression of the ways of living that were developed by people inside a community and passed on to the new generations. CH encompasses several components, such as customs, places, practices, artistic expressions and values. UNESCO (United Nations Educational, Scientific and Cultural Organization) classifies heritage in three main categories: cultural heritage (tangible or intangible), natural heritage and heritage in the event of armed conflict [1]. Tangible cultural heritage is further defined as having three components: movable cultural heritage, such as manuscripts, paintings, coins, sculptures; immovable cultural heritage, for example archaeological sites and monuments; underwater cultural heritage, which is represented by underwater ruins and cities, shipwrecks [2].

M. Duguleană et al. (Eds.): VRTCH 2018, CCIS 904, pp. 93–106, 2019.
https://doi.org/10.1007/978-3-030-05819-7_8

Computer applications applied to cultural heritage are mainly focused at improving the processes of digitization and documentation of artifacts and sites, digital preservation and exploration [3]. In the past modern technologies were used only by CH professionals, such as archaeologists, architects and civil engineers. Recently, more and more museums, archaeological places and exhibitions have begun to explore the use of new technologies to create new types of interaction with the aim to enhance the user experience (UX). There are several interactive solutions that are used in CH, such as location-aware audio guides, online and mobile applications, games, interactive multi-touch displays, virtual/augmented reality systems, 3D virtual worlds and other types of installations which include even kinesthetic control [4].

The term "augmented reality" has been used since the 60's [5] and represents a bridge between the real environment and virtual reality. The best way to understand AR is with the help of the "Virtuality Continuum" concept introduced in 1995 by [6]. The term refers to a scale that starts from a real environment and shows the "road" to a totally virtual environment, passing through augmented reality and augmented virtuality. Therefore, augmented reality is the first stage in which virtual objects are superimposed on a real scene. The advances of technology are allowing developers to create user friendly AR applications that work on mobile devices, thus bringing AR closer to the general public.

Project Tango is a platform for augmented reality that offers a simple API for non-experts in computer vision. Its primary use case is to create interactive applications that have the capability to recognize the environment. The devices that support this technology need to be equipped with a complex package of cameras consisting of an RGB camera, a depth camera and a fisheye camera for motion tracking. A capable processor is required to analyze and fuse the data from the cameras and from inertial sensors of the device. The depth camera can be used to detect distances to surfaces in the environment. Another interesting use case is to create 3D models very fast and convenient. However, the 3D objects obtained using a Project Tango device are of poor quality and with limited functionality. The ability to recognize the environment allows developers to create applications that will no longer require the use of visual markers, thus enabling a more natural interaction with cultural heritage. As the name suggest, this technology was only a project and was shut down since the 1st of March in 2018. Developers can still create AR applications based on Tango, but there is no support provided and no future releases.

ARCore is based on Project Tango with fewer features that are not dependent on specialized cameras, thus allowing a larger number of devices to be compatible with its technology. The main drawbacks of ARCore is the lack of Area Learning and occlusion detection. There is a wide variety of Android phones running Android 7.0 (Nougat) and later that support this technology, as opposed to the two commercial devices that are compatible with Project Tango.

The main purpose of this study is to evaluate the users' perception regarding two mobile augmented reality applications that allow the exploration of a 3D representation of a fortified church. The questionnaire includes empirical items to determine if participants noticed any significant differences between the two AR apps and to find out which they prefer. A secondary focus is to highlight the importance of preserving cultural heritage and to show how the use of advanced technology can bring tangible and intangible CH back to life.

The remainder of the paper is structured as follows. Section 2 provides theoretical background on technological approaches in cultural heritage, presents a comparison of frameworks for mobile AR development and also shortly approaches the digitization techniques that are commonly used in CH. Section 3 presents the methodology of the study, including the questionnaire that was used. Results are presented and discussed in Sect. 4, while the conclusions are organized in Sect. 5.

2 Theoretical Background

2.1 Technological Approaches in Cultural Heritage

Preservation, education, and entertainment are essential points regarding to cultural heritage sites, and technology integration is viewed as an essential element of service delivery in a museum environment [7]. Thus, new ways have been exploited to enhance the communication between users and heritage sites. The aim of technological approaches can vary from preservation and valorization of cultural heritage, support for artistic creation, facilitating access to and involvement in culture, protecting pluralism, freedom of expression, and cultural diversity [8].

A variety of different technological solutions are found in previous studies in order to improve the relationship between cultural heritage content and users. Among the several solutions proposed, it is found different kinds of games like: educational games, e.g. the role-play digital game named "Taiwan Epic Game" where it was intended to create the historical context of Southern Taiwan in the late nineteenth century [9]; or location-based games, e.g. "Gossip at Palace," a location-based mobile game developed for an Italian historical residence to communicate its 18th-century history to teenagers [10]. Another technological solution frequently found are virtual reality explorations, e.g. a 3D model of the lost township of Caen [11]; or a virtual exploration on mobile devices based on a natural interaction approach of cultural heritage sites which are not accessible [12]; or a proposal for better access and communication of the Cultural Heritage information through to the visualization and disclosure of 3D digital contents [13]. A set of the main interactive technologies and interaction styles are presented in a study published by Koutsabasis, namely, 3D game engine, mobile, kinesthetic interaction, mobile AR, virtual reality, web, multi-touch display, physical computing, multimedia, virtual world, location-based audio, wearable, and AR [4].

Notwithstanding the riches facilitated by the use of the various technological solutions, regarding to AR in cultural heritage sites, it has economic, experiential, social, epistemic, cultural and historical, and educational value from both internal and external stakeholders' perspectives [14].

2.2 Mobile AR in Cultural Heritage

The adoption of AR in cultural heritage began as early as 1999 with the MARS project [15] and the ARCHEOGUIDE Project [16], which were considered as mobile AR although the large amount of heavy devices needed to carry in these experiments. In the last few years, mobile AR refers to mobile devices easily portable such as smartphones or tablets [17]. These pioneer projects were followed by other research projects related to mobile AR applied to cultural heritage sites aiming at exhibition enhancement, being followed by reconstruction and exploration [18].

Looking at some of the several studies that tested the use of AR in cultural heritage with the aim of improving the visitors' experience among these spaces, it is common to find acceptance studies to understand the users' acceptance and intention to use a technology like the study of acceptance and use of AR in cultural heritage outdoors through the exhibition of photographs [19], or a study made to test users' satisfaction and intention to recommend marker-based augmented reality applications in Jeju Island, South Korea [20].

Regarding to some recent AR technology approaches, a virtual restoration of the religious heritage objects through 3D AR technology content was proposed [21]. The CHESS project introduced an overview of handheld AR in museums, aiming to design and evaluate personalized interactive stories for visitors of cultural sites [22]. The potential of AR for supporting mobile tourism applications is emphasised with CorfuAR, a mobile augmented reality tour guide presented by Kourouthanassis et al. [23]. An adaptive mixed reality system was proposed aiming to achieve the visualization of in-situ virtual ancient building reconstructions with the MixAR project [24]. A mobile augmented reality guide for cultural heritage to examine user experiences was evaluated in the historic city centre of Brno in Czech Republic [25]. KnossosAR is an outdoors mobile AR guide implemented for the archaeological site of Knossos which intended to improve the user's perception about its surrounding space hiding or utilizing appropriate visual metaphors for occluded objects/locations [26].

2.3 Comparison of Frameworks for Mobile AR Development

A research related to the frameworks available to implement AR mobile apps on mobile devices was made and an overview of this research is described below. According to this study concern, all frameworks presented provide the development of its AR application for Android or iOS devices. Among this research, the frameworks which provided their latest versions before 2016 were dropped. The following description is made considering the characteristics that each framework points out the most. Considering specific features, the results of the comparative study is presented in Table 1.

In the following, we will summarize the most popular AR platforms available on the market, presenting them in a concise manner, in alphabetical order as they appear in the table.

ARKit [27] is an Apple's platform that combines different techniques and algorithms, like motion tracking, camera scene capture or advanced scene processing in order to allow users to easily build AR experiences. ARCore [28] is Google's version of AR platform that uses different APIs, enabling the device to sense its environment, understand the world and interact with information.

ARToolKit [29] is an open-source AR software library providing support for three categories of tracker: natural feature tracking (NFT), traditional template square maker,

Table 1. Comparative study of the SDKs available to implement AR mobile systems.

Framework	Last version found	Markers		Sensors		SLAM	Dynamic occlusion	Implementation
		2D tracking	3D object tracking	GPS	IMU			SDK package
Apple ARKit		✓	✓	✓	✓	Not found	✗	iOS
AR Core	8 May 2018	✓	✗	✓	✓	✓	✗	Unity Unreal
ArUco	17 May 2018	✓	✗	✗	✗	✗	✓	✗
Augmented Pixels	26 Apr 2017 (protype)	✗	✗	✓	✓	✓	✗	✗
Catchoom CraftAR	28 Mar 2017	✓	✗	✗	✗	✗	✗	Unity
EasyAR SDK Basic	6 Mar 2018	✓	✗	✗	✗	✗	✗	Unity
EasyAR SDK Pro			✓			✓		
Kudan	23 Mar 2018	✓	✓	✓	✓	✓	✗	Unity
MAXST AR	19 Mar 2018	✓	✓	✗	✗	✓	✗	Unity
NyARToolkit	24 May 2016	✓	✗	✗	✗	✗	✗	Unity
Tango	1 Mar 2018	✓	✗	✓	✓	✓	✓	Unity
Vuforia	1 Mar 2018	✓	✓	✗	✓	✓	✗	Unity
Wikitude	21 Feb 2018	✓	✓	✓	✓	✓	✗	Unity

and 2D Barcode Markers. ARToolKit was acquired by DAQRI since 2015 and, for this reason, this framework will not be considered in the comparative study. Another AR open-source minimal library for detecting squared fiducial markers in images is ArUco [30]. It is written in C++, is extremely fast and can calibrate cameras to make camera pose estimation (static or moving).

Augmented Pixels [31] has proprietary simultaneous localization and mapping technology (SLAM SDK) optimized for low CPU usage (Raspberry Pi 3 with standard Raspberry Pi camera sensor for SLAM real time processing). Also, it gets autonomous navigation by connecting to a drone or a robot through a Vision Processing Unit. Catchoom's toolbox, from the Catchoom CraftAR Pixels [32] offers Image Recognition and AR tools in their branded apps targeted to transform the way consumers discover and shop for products in the real world using visual search.

EasyAR SDK [33] is a free AR engine developed by VisionStar Information Technology (Shanghai) which provides a number of cutting-edge features (such as SLAM, 3D tracking, and screen recording). Kudan AR SDK [34] can support marker or markerless tracking and location requirements, having a very robust single-camera SLAM tracking technology.

MAXST AR SDK [35], a cross-platform AR engine, also provides features and environments needed to develop AR apps. The main focus of this platform is on Natural Feature Tracking. Based on ARToolKit, NyARToolkit [36] is a free open-source project developing a vision-based AR written in Java.

Tango [37] was a phone and tablet-based mobile AR solution that relied on advanced camera hardware to build 3D meshes of spaces developed by a division of Google. Google shut down Tango in order to focus on the more mass market ARCore product. Vuforia [38] allows to develop AR apps with advanced vision and recognition of a range of everyday images, objects and environments.

The last but not least, Wikitude's all-in-one AR SDK [39] combines instant tracking technology (SLAM[1]), object recognition and tracking, top-notch image recognition and tracking, as well as geo-location AR for mobile, tablets and smart glasses.

In order to get to know all of the cited frameworks in this study, a comparative study was made and it is resumed in Table 1.

Observing Table 1 it is possible to realize that the great majority of the frameworks listed allows the image 2D tracking and the majority provides a package to implement the technology using Unity software. The usage of a 3D object to accomplish the tracking process is limited to few frameworks, where, in the case of the EasyAR it's confined to the Pro version. The usage of sensors to find the localization of the device, typically, the frameworks which appeal to GPS also provide IMU sensors usage. In the case of Vuforia, that does not provide geo-localization with GPS sensors, it still uses IMU sensors to undertake the AR experience. The SLAM is assured by a large part of the frameworks presented, whereas the occlusion is covered by a small part of them, namely, ArUco and Tango. Albeit this two, ArUco does not provide an SDK to implement the technology which is important to help its implementation to reach a larger number of developers.

2.4 Digitization Techniques in Cultural Heritage

The digital preservation of CH is more important than ever due to several factors: the deterioration of the materials, natural phenomena like earthquakes, hurricanes, tsunami or other, armed conflicts and other human related problems. The main motivations for preserving CH are: (1) to create a digital replica; (2) to create a database with information related to the shape and appearance of an object; (3) to create new types of applications that are based on digital media collections to enhance the users' experience

[1] SLAM – Simultaneous Localization and Mapping. This technique allows AR applications to perform instant tracking.

[40]. A brief state of the art regarding the 3D digitization process related to cultural heritage is presented in Table 2.

Table 2. State of the art solutions for the 3D digitization process applied to cultural heritage

Stage no.	Stage name	Methods/Components	Remarks
1	Data acquisition	Triangulation laser scanning	Choosing the appropriate method has to take into consideration the nature of the object that will be digitized, the necessary equipment and the purpose of its digitization [41]
		Time-of-flight laser scanning	
		Shape from structured light	
		Contact digitization methods	
		Topographic methods	
		Shape from focus	
		Shape from photometry	
		Shape from stereo	
		Shape from motion	
		Shape from silhouette	
		Shape from shading	
		Pre-processing	
2	Registration	Initial registration	In order to obtain accurate 3D models, the best alignment between overlapped images or point clouds has to be found
		Fine registration	
		Global registration	
		Simultaneous all view alignment	
3	Integration	Delaunay-based methods	The aim of this stage is to integrate all the raw data into a single mesh without losing information and without unwanted holes. The volumetric approaches yield good results when combined with equipment that has appropriate processing power
		Surface-based methods	
		Parametric or deformable methods	
		Volumetric methods	
		Hole filling	
4	Texture	Calibration	The visual aspect of the 3D model is greatly improved by precise color data and adds more details to the geometry of the mesh
		Texture generation	

Structure from Motion or multi-image photogrammetry is a practical and versatile technique that is being adopted widely for accurate digital capture of 3D objects and surfaces related to cultural heritage [42–45]. Photogrammetry is a method that analyzes and matches features detected in overlapping photos, and is fundamentally based on trigonometry. There are a few guidelines that need to be taken into consideration when any object is photographed for 3D reconstruction that ensure accurate and reliable results:

- The most important rule is to keep an overlapping percentage of 60% to 80% between successive photos;
- The light and white balance should be the same or with few changes. In the case of large scale objects, such as buildings or other monuments, a cloudy sky offers the best lighting conditions due to a uniform spread of light, thus avoiding the appearance of hard shadows;
- Use a professional digital camera with at least 24 megapixels (relatively good results can be obtained also with a smartphone camera), at a small aperture to have a "large" depth of field.

3 Methodology

The aim of the experiment is to obtain a subjective evaluation of two mobile augmented reality applications that use different technologies. The virtual object was obtained using photogrammetry and it represents the Prejmer fortified church from Brasov, a UNESCO monument.

3.1 Participants

For this study 38 participants (average age = 24.08, SD = 5.43) have used the AR applications. There were no requirements necessary in order to participate. Participants have confirmed that they use a smartphone very frequently, however only 18 have experienced augmented reality prior to the experiment.

3.2 Procedure

The experiment took place at a public event organized by the Transilvania University of Brasov. Participants were first presented the aim of the study after which they received instructions on how to use the applications. The AR application based on Project Tango was installed on a Lenovo Phab 2 Pro (see Fig. 2), while the one based on ARCore was tested using the Huawei P20 Pro (see Fig. 1). Half of the participants started with the Phab 2 Pro, while the other half started with the P20 Pro. Their task was to explore the 3D model of the fortified church without having a time limit. After using one technology participants were asked to complete an evaluation questionnaire and then move on to the second technology.

For the Project Tango application we used the Ikariotikos package, while for the ARCore we used package version 1.2. The only difference in the usage of the two applications is that for the ARCore version, users first have to scan the surroundings in order to detect a surface on which they can then place the virtual object.

Fig. 1. Screenshot from the Huawei device

Fig. 2. Screenshot from the Lenovo device

3.3 Questionnaire Design

The questionnaire is adapted from the Handheld Augmented Reality Usability Scale (HARUS) [46] and contains 21 items based on a 7-point Likert scale, ranging from 1 – "strongly disagree", to 7 – "strongly agree" (see Table 3). There are two questions (Q1–Q2) that are meant to reveal the familiarity of the participants with AR applications and their normal usage of a mobile device. In order to evaluate the comprehensibility parameter we used eight items (Q3–Q10) and seven items (Q11–Q17) to assess how difficult or physical demanding it was to interact with the two applications. Four items (Q18–Q21) reflect if the participants found the applications pleasant or boring. Using the last three questions (Q19–Q21) we wanted to find out their general perception of the experiment, if they believe that an AR application can help them learn more about cultural heritage and if they notice any significant differences between the two devices.

4 Results

Results showed that the application is easy to use, intuitive and with relevant information. Related to comprehensibility, the scores computed for the Project Tango device were slightly better due to the bigger size of the display. A large display offers a better user experience, however in the case of handheld devices this can cause discomfort in a long term usage. Regarding manipulability, the ARCore device was rated a bit better, mostly because of its size and weight.

There was no significant difference when it comes to enjoyment. Using augmented reality allowed users to explore cultural heritage in a new and exciting way (Figs. 3 and 4).

Table 3. Evaluation questionnaire

Personal skills	Q1: Have you experienced Augmented Reality (AR) applications before this test? Q2: How often do you use mobile devices?
Comprehensibility	Q3: I think that interacting with this application requires a lot of mental effort Q4: I thought the amount of information displayed on screen was appropriate Q5: I thought that the information displayed on screen was difficult to read Q6: I felt that the information display was responding fast enough Q7: I thought that the information displayed on screen was confusing Q8: I thought the words and symbols on screen were easy to read Q9: I felt that the display was flickering too much Q10: I thought that the information displayed on screen was consistent
Manipulability	Q11: I think that interacting with this AR application requires a lot of body muscle effort Q12: I felt that using the AR application was comfortable for my arms and hands Q13: I found the device difficult to hold while operating the AR application Q14: I felt that my arm or hand became tired after using the AR application Q15: I think the AR application is easy to control Q16: I felt that I was losing grip and dropping the device at some point Q17: I think the operation of this AR application is simple and uncomplicated
Enjoyment	Q18: I enjoyed using the AR application Q19: I found the AR application unpleasant Q20: I found the AR application exciting Q21: I found the AR application boring
Empirical	Q19: By using the AR application, I learn more about heritage Q20: Rate the overall experience you had during the experiment? Q21: After using the AR application on two different devices, did you notice any significant differences?

Other observations regarding the empirical questions:

- Participants declared that the AR application increased their interest in learning about cultural heritage
- The experience using the AR application was very positive
- Some participants declared that the Tango enabled device was more stable, however most of the users did not notice any significant differences between the two technologies.

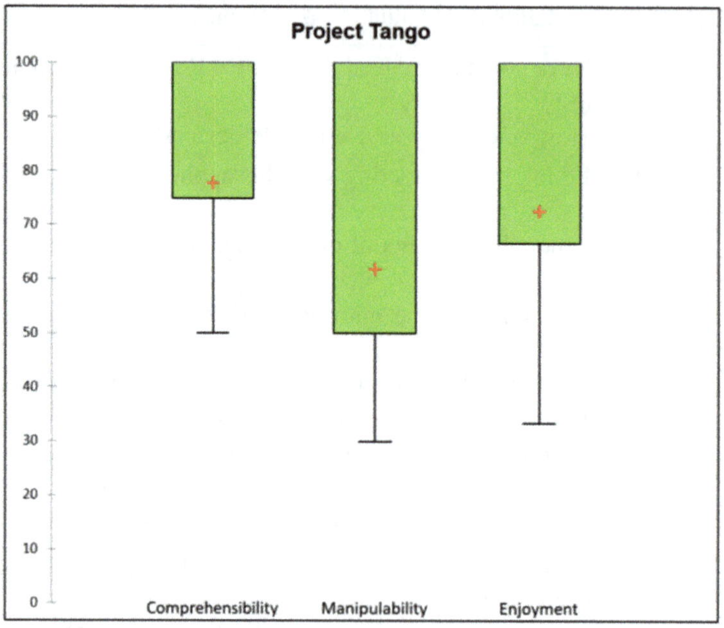

Fig. 3. Box plots showing the results from Project Tango

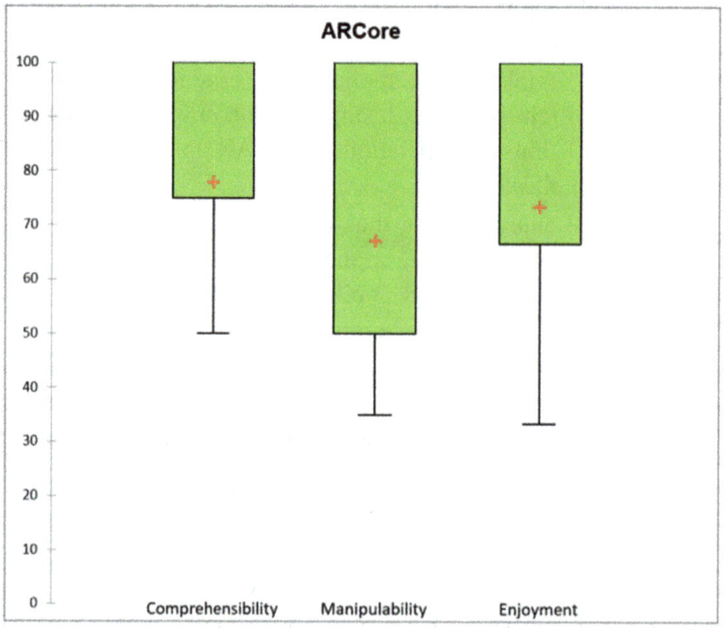

Fig. 4. Box plots showing the results from ARCore

5 Conclusions

Cultural heritage stands for more than just an object, it represents the way we used to live and could even be considered a national treasure. Finding new methods to preserve, document and explore CH using modern technologies is of great interest and many breakthroughs have been made by archaeologists, researchers or museum curators.

In this paper we developed an augmented reality application that gives users the chance to visualize and explore a 3D model of a fortified church. The virtual model was obtained by our project team using photogrammetry with the aim to obtain a digital replica of a recognized UNESCO monument.

Project Tango has gained the attention of many entities during its development as it offered a practical and easy to use technology to implement augmented reality. With the help of specialized sensors and powerful hardware it yielded great results. However, it was more of a niche solution with relatively small potential to be adopted widely by regular consumers. Nonetheless, several museums and other commercial companies have developed attractive and interesting applications using this technology. Project Tango had a lot of potential, however it was replaced by ARCore in a move to boost the number of mobile AR applications.

The present study shows that there is no significant difference between the two technologies in simply exploring a virtual object. Things would be different in the case of a marker-less application or trying to use the device for 3D reconstruction, where only Project Tango is feasible.

Acknowledgements. This paper is supported by European Union's Horizon 2020 research and innovation programme under grant agreement No 692103, project eHERITAGE (Expanding the Research and Innovation Capacity in Cultural Heritage Virtual Reality Applications).

References

1. ICOMOS, International Cultural Tourism Charter. Principles And Guidelines For Managing Tourism At Places Of Cultural And Heritage Significance. ICOMOS International Cultural Tourism Committee (2002)
2. Definition of cultural heritage. http://www.unesco.org. Accessed 21 Apr 2018
3. Pavlidis, G., Koutsoudis, A., Arnaoutoglou, F., Tsioukas, V., Chamzas, C.: Methods for 3D digitization of cultural heritage. J. Cult. Herit. **8**(1), 93–98 (2007)
4. Koutsabasis, P.: Empirical evaluations of interactive systems in cultural heritage: a review. Int. J. Comput. Methods Herit. Sci. **1**(1), 1–23 (2017)
5. Sutherland, I.E.: The ultimate display. In: Proceedings of the IFIP Congress, pp. 506–508 (1965)
6. Milgram, P., Takemura, H., Utsumi, A., Kishino, F.: Augmented reality: a class of displays on the reality-virtuality continuum. In: Telemanipulator and Telepresence Technologies, vol. 2351, pp. 282–293. International Society for Optics and Photonics (1995)
7. Hume, M.: To technovate or not to technovate? Examining the inter-relationship of consumer technology, museum service quality, museum value, and repurchase intent. J. Nonprofit Public Sect. Mark. **27**(2), 155–182 (2015)

8. Vicente, E., Camarero, C., Garrido, M.J.: Insights into innovation in European museums. Public Manag. Rev. **14**(5), 649–680 (2012)
9. Shih, J.-L., Jheng, S.-C., Tseng, J.-J.: A simulated learning environment of history games for enhancing players' cultural awareness. Interact. Learn. Environ. **23**(2), 191–211 (2015)
10. Rubino, I., Barberis, C., Xhembulla, J., Malnati, G.: Integrating a location-based mobile game in the museum visit: evaluating visitors' behaviour and learning. J. Comput. Cult. Herit. **8**(3), 1–18 (2015). Article No. 15
11. McCaffery, J., Miller, A., Vermehren, A., Fabola, A.: The virtual museums of Caen: a case study on modes of representation of digital historical content. In: Digital Heritage, pp. 541–548 (2015)
12. Malomo, L., Banterle, F., Pingi, P., Gabellone, F., Scopigno, R.: VirtualTour: a system for exploring cultural heritage sites in an immersive way. In: 2015 Digital Heritage, pp. 309–312 (2015)
13. Fernández-Palacios, B.J., Morabito, D., Remondino, F.: Access to complex reality-based 3D models using virtual reality solutions. J. Cult. Herit. **23**, 40–48 (2017)
14. tom Dieck, M.C., Jung, T.H.: Value of augmented reality at cultural heritage sites: a stakeholder approach. J. Destin. Mark. Manag. **6**(2), 110–117 (2017)
15. Höllerer, T., Feiner, S., Terauchi, T., Rashid, G., Hallaway, D.: Exploring MARS: developing indoor and outdoor user interfaces to a mobile augmented reality system. Comput. Graph. **23**(6), 779–785 (1999)
16. Vlahakis, V., Ioannidis, N., John, K., Tsotros, M., Gounaris, M.: Archeoguide: an augmented reality guide for archaeological sites. Comput. Graph. Art Hist. Archaeol. **22**(5), 52–60 (2002)
17. Höllerer, T.H., Feiner, S.K.: Mobile Augmented Reality. CRC Press, Boca Raton (2004)
18. Bekele, M.K., Pierdicca, E., Frontoni, E., Malinverni, S., Gain, J.: A survey of augmented, virtual, and mixed reality for cultural heritage. J. Comput. Cult. Herit. **11**(2), 1–36 (2018). Article No. 7
19. Haugstvedt, A.-C., Krogstie, J.: Mobile augmented reality for cultural heritage: a technology acceptance study. In: Proceedings of the IEEE International Symposium on Mixed and Augmented Reality (ISMAR), pp. 247–255 (2012)
20. Jung, T., Chung, N., Leue, M.C.: The determinants of recommendations to use augmented reality technologies: the case of a Korean Theme Park. Tour. Manag. **49**, 75–86 (2015)
21. Gîrbacia, F., Butnariu, S., Orman, A.P., Postelnicu, C.C.: Virtual restoration of deteriorated religious heritage objects using augmented reality technologies. Eur. J. Sci. Theol. **9**(2), 223–231 (2013)
22. Keil, J., et al.: A digital look at physical museum exhibits. In: Proceedings of the Digital Heritage International Congress (DigitalHeritage), vol. 2, pp. 685–688 (2013)
23. Kourouthanassis, P., Boletsis, C., Bardaki, C., Chasanidou, D.: Tourists responses to mobile augmented reality travel guides: the role of emotions on adoption behavior. Pervasive Mob. Comput. **18**, 71–87 (2015)
24. Narciso, D., Pádua, L., Adão, T., Peres, E., Magalhães, L.: MixAR mobile prototype: visualizing virtually reconstructed ancient structures in situ. Procedia Comput. Sci. **64**, 852–861 (2015)
25. Střelák, D., Škola, F., Liarokapis, F.: Examining user experiences in a mobile augmented reality tourist guide. In: Proceedings of the 9th ACM International Conference on Pervasive Technologies Related to Assistive Environments (PETRA 2016) (2016)
26. Kasapakis, V., Gavalas, D., Galatis, P.: Augmented reality in cultural heritage: field of view awareness in an archaeological site mobile guide. J. Ambient Intell. Smart Environ. **8**(5), 501–514 (2016)
27. ARKit. developer.apple.com/arkit. Accessed 20 Mar 2018

28. ARCore. developers.google.com/ar. Accessed 20 Mar 2018
29. ARToolKit. https://www.hitl.washington.edu/artoolkit. Accessed 20 Mar 2018
30. ArUco. www.uco.es/investiga/grupos/ava/node/26. Accessed 20 Mar 2018
31. Augmented Pixels. augmentedpixels.com. Accessed 20 Mar 2018
32. Catchoom CraftAR Pixels. catchoom.com. Accessed 20 Mar 2018
33. EasyAR SDK. www.easyar.com. Accessed 20 Mar 2018
34. Kudan AR SDK. www.kudan.eu. Accessed 20 Mar 2018
35. MAXST AR SDK. maxst.com/#/en/arsdk. Accessed 20 Mar 2018
36. NyARToolkit. nyatla.jp/nyartoolkit/wp. Accessed 20 Mar 2018
37. Tango. https://www.impossible.com/tango. Accessed 20 Mar 2018
38. Vuforia. www.vuforia.com. Accessed 20 Mar 2018
39. Wikitude website. www.wikitude.com. Accessed 20 Mar 2018
40. Gomes, L., Bellon, O.R.P., Silva, L.: 3D reconstruction methods for digital preservation of cultural heritage: a survey. Pattern Recogn. Lett. **50**, 3–14 (2014)
41. Di Angelo, L., Di Stefano, P., Fratocchi, L., Marzola, A.: An AHP-based method for choosing the best 3D scanner for cultural heritage applications. J. Cult. Herit. (2018)
42. McCarthy, J.: Multi-image photogrammetry as a practical tool for cultural heritage survey and community engagement. J. Archaeol. Sci. **43**, 175–185 (2014)
43. Younes, G., et al.: Virtual and augmented reality for rich interaction with cultural heritage sites: a case study from the Roman Theater at Byblos. Digit. Appl. Archaeol. Cult. Herit. **5**, 1–9 (2017)
44. Yastikli, N.: Documentation of cultural heritage using digital photogrammetry and laser scanning. J. Cult. Herit. **8**(4), 423–427 (2007)
45. Yu, D., Jin, J.S., Luo, S., Lai, W., Huang, Q.: A useful visualization technique: a literature review for augmented reality and its application, limitation & future direction. In: Huang, M., Nguyen, Q., Zhang, K. (eds.) Visual Information Communication, pp. 311–337. Springer, Boston (2009). https://doi.org/10.1007/978-1-4419-0312-9_21
46. Santos, M.E.C., Polvi, J., Taketomi, T., Yamamoto, G., Sandor, C., Kato, H.: Toward standard usability questionnaires for handheld augmented reality. IEEE Comput. Graphics Appl. **35**(5), 66–75 (2015)

Sensors and Actuators

From Exploration of Virtual Replica to Cultural Immersion Through Natural Gestures

Catalin Diaconescu(✉), Matei-Ioan Popovici, and Dorin-Mircea Popovici

Ovidius University of Constanta, 124 Mamaia Bd, Constanta, Romania
diaconescucatalin97@gmail.com,
matei_popovici@hotmail.com,
dmpopovici@univ-ovidius.ro

Abstract. We investigate in this work the potential of multimodal rendering for assisting users during culturally-related navigation and manipulation tasks inside virtual environments. We argue that natural gestures play an important role for engaging users in experiencing the cultural dimension of a given environment. To this end, we propose an open system for multi-user visualization and interaction that enables users to employ natural gestures.

We explored different configurations and controls in order to achieve the most accurate and natural user experience. One being switching between the navigation and manipulation mode based on distance and orientation towards different points of interest and the other being based on interacting with a virtual UI used for switching between the two modes.

We also implemented both a single-user and a multi-user version. The single-user version having a normal, computer monitor based, point of view is better for a more accurate and detailed viewing experience. Also, in this version the user would be wearing the Myo armband and also using the Leap Motion for a more immersed experience. The multi-user version is based on a holographic pyramid which has two user perspectives, one of the Myo user and the other being the Leap Motion user's, and two for the spectators' point of view.

Finally, we discuss findings on the users' perceptions of experienced cultural immersion.

Keywords: Cultural immersion · Natural gesture-based interaction
Holographic display · Virtual environment

1 Introduction

Common ways available today to experience cultural heritage are visiting sites (real and on-line), registering to museum tours and actively participating in guided hands-on activities, acquiring memorabilia and taking photos of the historical sites, but also immersing into virtual reality exhibits [1].

M. Duguleană et al. (Eds.): VRTCH 2018, CCIS 904, pp. 109–121, 2019.
https://doi.org/10.1007/978-3-030-05819-7_9

Virtual heritage has been disseminated to the public at large in various forms, starting with multimedia provided on CD's and websites [2] up to dedicated desktop solutions [3, 4], virtual reality, and augmented reality installations [5].

The benefits of the latter consist in the opportunity for their users to visit realistically reconstructed historical sites, which, by means of novel technologies, are being augmented with 3-D content [6]. Among all commonly-used interaction modalities, haptic interaction started to be explored [7] in installations that promote cultural values through interaction with the virtual artifacts.

User experience inside a virtual heritage environment may be enhanced also by supporting natural interactions and, consequently, many researchers have proposed multimodal metaphors to support these types of interaction beyond haptic [8], e.g., mouse pointing, click and drag [9], head, eye, and body tracking [10, 11], and face, gesture, and speech recognition [12].

In this work, we focus on natural gesture interaction as it has no language barriers and can rapidly turn into reflex due to its naturalness. Moreover, dealing with cultural heritage artifacts represents a specific challenge because the intrinsic fragility, inaccessibility, or even the lost meaning of these artifacts. Consequently, when users face technological barriers, they quickly become overwhelmed by technology and may lose the original interest for the artifacts, known as the gulf of execution that amplifies for technologies driving virtual environments [13].

To this end we focused on low-cost and accessible technology as Myo [19] and Leap Motion [20] devices. Both Myo wireless armband and Leap Motion desktop device enables the user to control computer generated content using various hand gestures and motions, but they rely on different technologies in user gesture recognition. Myo uses a set of electromyographic sensor which detect activity in the forearm muscles, together with a gyroscope and accelerometer to help recognize motions and magnetometer for gesture recognition, while Leap Motion uses IR cameras and infrared LEDs that observes a roughly hemispherical working area in which the user hands are detected.

Morgan et al. consider Myo arm-swinging as a way to explore a virtual environment and comparing it to joystick locomotion and physical walking [14]. They concluded that people made fewer errors if they explored the virtual environment physically or with Myo arm–swinging than with the joystick. Participants performed equally well in the walking and Myo arm– swinging conditions in terms of errors.

A similar approach was made by Mulling et al. by considering a 2D map [15]. According to them, navigation on interactive maps through the movement of hands and arms through the Myo showed that improvements need still to be performed both on the device and in the same graphical interface (GUI). The use of hand gestures and arms to control interactive maps can be optimized, first from the design of native applications for Myo, in order to explore the device at its maximum performance.

Another attempt uses mixed-reality based interaction system for digital heritage exploration [16]. Here the advantages of adding a scale 3D-printed replica of the architecture to the user interface was experienced. Based on a user study, Bugalia et al. established the ease of interaction and found that even novices are comfortable with the proposed light-based interface and find it intuitive to use. They think that it would be interesting to explore the effectiveness of adding a gyro-meter to the pointing devices, which is something Myo does have for example, to support more powerful controls during the walk.

Aslan et al. have considered how challenges related with many closely positioned (expanding) targets can be addressed [17]. Prototypes were used as probes to foster the discussions on the results of the driving simulator study. They concluded that by combining mid-air gestures (provided by Leap Motion controller) with touch, it is possible to improve in-car touch-based interaction in situations that rely on visual attention, and therefore to augment the user safety while driving.

Moser explores touch versus mid-air gesture input in physics-based gaming [18]. The study showed that, although the developers adapted the game to suit mid-air gestures, several playability problems occurred that should be considered for future game developments. The observations revealed difficulties with accuracy for small and precise or only partial recognition of very fast swipe mid-air gestures. Another problem was that player lost the orientation and moved towards the monitor when performing mid-air gestures (i.e., the signal was lost). Therefore, the mid-air gestures were rated to be more complex and difficult than touch gestures (i.e., rather easy to use).

2 From Virtual Environment Exploration to Artifact Manipulation

Experiencing a virtual heritage environment usually means letting the user to freely navigate in the 3D replica of the artifact, by bounding its movements to the virtual environment dimensions. To this end, we adopt hand-controlled navigation [9] by using a Leap Motion device or Myo, depending on the system's mode of operation [20].

In our approach, the focal task the users will perform is exploring the environment by interacting with their target artifact, by dividing the task into (a) approaching a target, (b) touching/reaching the target and (c) manipulating the artifact. Touch becomes possible once the user's avatar is close enough to the target. Touch begins when physical contact between the virtual artifact and the user's virtual hand takes place. The Myo device accurately signals this event [19]. Grabbing the object is possible by squeezing the hand, action detected by Leap Motion device [20]. From this point forward, the user can manipulate the object.

2.1 Switching Between Navigation and Manipulation Tasks – First Use-Case

The default task state is navigation. However, when users approach an artifact that may be subject of interaction, navigation switches to manipulation. Interactions may take place locally inside the user's action area (which is denoted "A" in Fig. 1) in the form of observing the artifact (denoted by small "a" in Fig. 1) or manipulating the artifact ("a1"). Should the user decide to manipulate the artifact outside its interaction area then transportation must occur ("a2" in Fig. 1).

Switching between navigation and manipulation becomes relevant as the distance between the user's virtual hand and the artifact is getting smaller. Observation may be achieved if the user is close enough to the artifact, such as for the avatar in the "B"

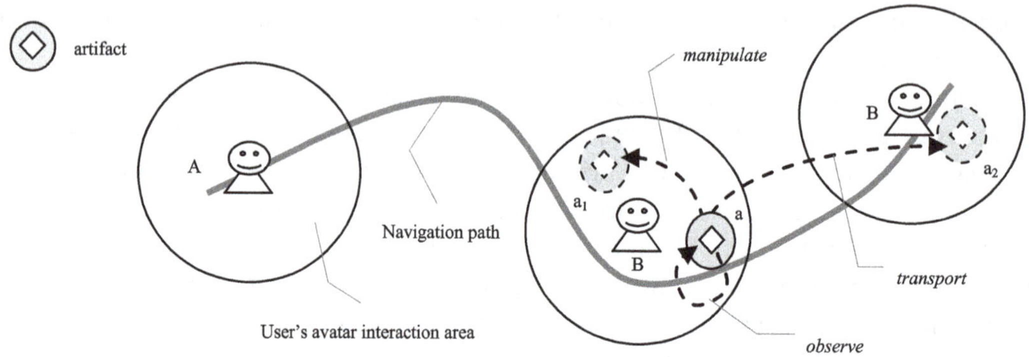

Fig. 1. Manipulation scenarios for different users (A, B) and artifacts (a, b) under various constraints (a_1, a_2).

position with respect to the artifacts located in "a", during user's navigation. But observation may also be considered as special case of manipulation, as for the avatar in location "B" with artifact in "a".

Deciding whether control should be given to the avatar's movement (Fig. 2a) or to the hand (Fig. 2c) depends on the distance to the target and the angle relative to the user's visual focus (*i.e.*, the amount of focus given to a certain target). These conditions must be validated simultaneously and we achieved this behavior by employing a coordinate system composed of the following components: the 3-D distance to target (the X axis), yaw or the horizontal angle (the Y axis), and pitch or the vertical angle (the Z axis). Distances in this coordinate system represent the ratio of interest in manipulating a virtual artifact (Fig. 3).

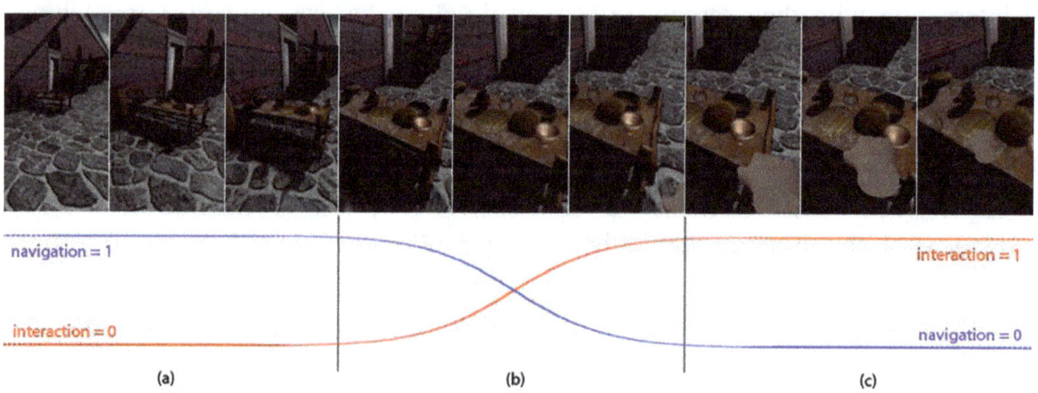

Fig. 2. Transition from navigation to manipulation depending on the position of the user's object of interest.

By constraining that the total sum of interests in manipulation and navigation to be constant, we achieve seamless transition between the two tasks, without requiring users to specifically switch between tasks (Fig. 2b). For the scenario in which multiple targets are present in the environment, the closest one will be selected by default according to the distance measurement described above (Fig. 2).

Fig. 3. The result of a transportation action for several virtual artifacts.

2.2 Switching Between Navigation and Manipulation Tasks – Second Use-Case

Our first solution to switching between navigation and manipulation was tested and deemed hard to use accurately. Therefore, we made a second option that was more reliable.

When the user's character is close enough to an interactable object and he is looking at it the Myo vibrates shortly to notify the user he can interact with that object and also his virtual hand changes color (Fig. 4b). At this point he can grab and move the object at the same pace with his character. This can be achieved by using the distance between the first-person camera and the objects that the user can interact with.

(a) (b)

Fig. 4. The virtual hand changing color when it gets close to an interactable object.

A ray that is casted from the first-person camera towards where the camera is pointed at returns the distance between the camera and the object it hits, if the object is interactable. The returned value is compared with the given average hand length and if the value is the lesser one we consider the user in range to interact with the object.

When the user turns his left palm towards his face, an interface appears near the hand (Fig. 5a) and if the button is pressed he switches to manipulation mode and the button changes color (Fig. 5b). In this mode any object he can interact with loses gravity and navigation is blocked until the same button is pressed again. At which point the navigation and also the object's gravity are switched back on and the button returns to the original color.

(a) (b)

Fig. 5. Using the virtual UI to switch between the navigation and manipulation mode. (Color figure online)

In the manipulation mode the user can grab and rotate object more easily. This is due to the lack of gravity that the object is subjected to. This allows the user to better inspect the heritage until he decides to leave the manipulation mode (Fig. 6).

Fig. 6. User in manipulation mode, interacting with a barrel that is kinematic (has no gravity).

3 Technical Aspects

Our solution is based on three main components: a visualization module responsible with 3D environment real-time rendering – Unity based [21], a hand-oriented interaction module responsible with user navigation inside 3D virtual environment and user manipulation of virtual artifacts – Leap Motion device based [20], and an arm-oriented interaction module responsible with user warning when it approaches to virtual artifacts - Myo device based [19].

In the Leap Motion user-case, moving his hand forwards and backwards makes the user's avatar move at a directly proportional velocity with the difference between the hand and the Leap Motion center. The same thing happens when the hand is moved left/right and up/down for rotation and orientation.

In the Myo user-case (Fig. 7), making a fist would make the character move frontward (Fig. 7a), waving left/right makes the character move left/right (Fig. 7b, c). Grabbing an interactable object can be achieved by making a spread-fingers pose while facing towards it and being at a certain distance from it that makes the Myo vibrate (Fig. 7d). Also, double taping recalibrates the origin of the local coordinates system relative to the user's hand (Fig. 7e).

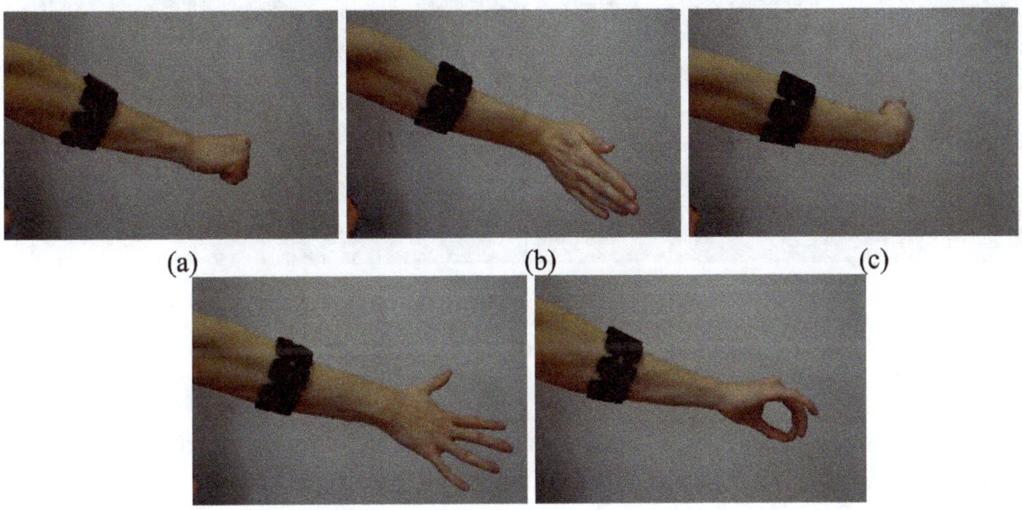

(a) (b) (c) (d) (e)

Fig. 7. Myo poses.

Moreover, for displaying the 3D environment we chose to build a holographic pyramid that opens our system both for single and multi-user real-time cultural heritage exploration (Fig. 8).

In the single-user option, one user would wear the Myo and use the Leap Motion at the same time. Leap Motion is used for movement and orientation of the character and the Myo armband for warnings and feedback in form of vibrations. All though Myo has gesture recognition and gyroscopes, that could be used for interacting with the

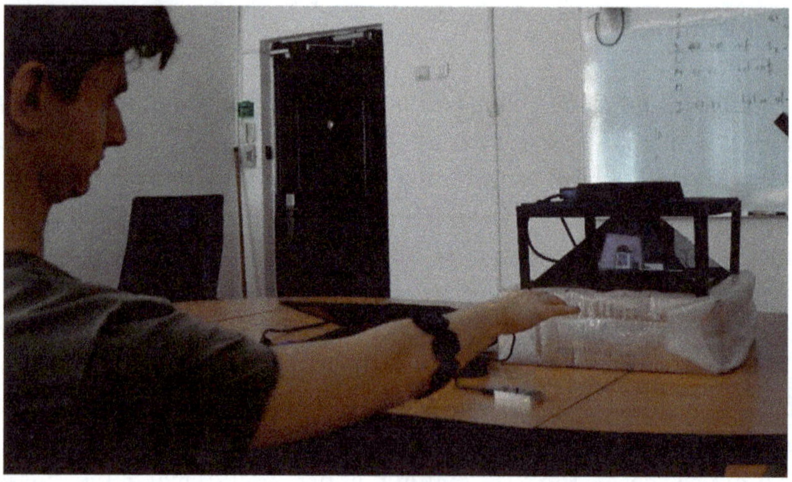

Fig. 8. Multimodal-based experience with a 3D virtual artifact.

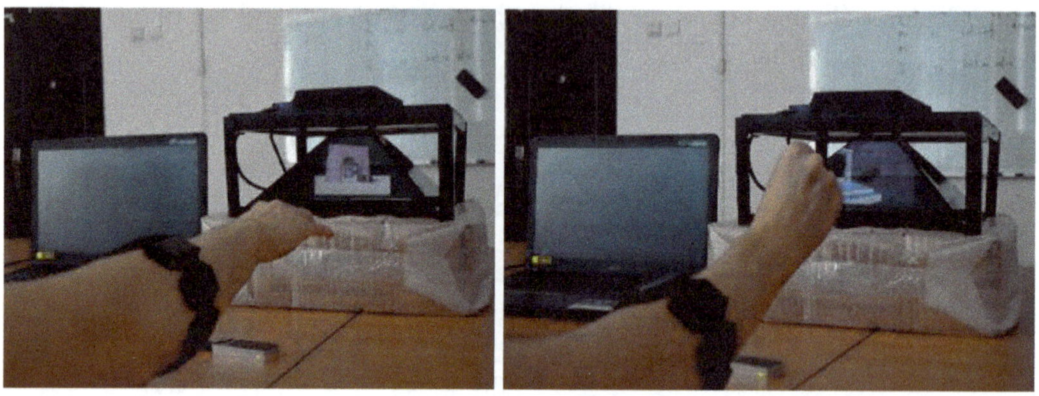

(a) (b)

Fig. 9. Approaching and grabbing virtual artifacts.

environment, we decided to make more use of the Leap Motion because through our testing we concluded that it was more reliable and precise to use.

In the Fig. 9a it is presented the user navigating the environment and, in the Fig. 9b, we can observe him grabbing a heritage object using the grab motion recognized by the Leap Motion.

The multi-user option is based on our holographic pyramid that displays the two users' perspectives. The other two perspectives of the pyramid may be used by spectators to watch as the users interact with the environment. Two users can explore the heritage environment in real time and interact. One of the users uses the Myo armband as a controller to move and interact by making certain gestures and moving the hand he's wearing it on. The other user uses the Leap Motion's interpretation of his hand movements for controlling his character through the environment. He can also naturally grab some objects and also inspect them more thoroughly by entering the manipulation state.

4 Discussion

In order to evaluate the usability of our solution, we start conducting an experiment to verify the following hypothesis on natural gesture-based interaction for cultural environments.

4.1 Hypothesis and Premises

For a user that comes to experiment a cultural heritage virtual reconstruction, natural gesture-based interaction is easier to be accepted rather than using any conventional interaction device.

For our evaluations we adopted the following two premises:

(1) Users know neither the structure nor the topology of the environment beforehand. This premise means that users may become disoriented at the start of their virtual experience and make little sense of the things around them.
(2) Users are not aware a priori neither of the actions that are allowed inside the virtual environment nor of the metaphors to engage into these actions. Simply browsing a new world is not enough to deliver the feeling of being part of that world. Instead, it is the exploration, discovery, and participation to that world's specific cultural activities that are able to deliver the cultural immersive feeling.

4.2 Apparatus

We target about one hundred volunteers to take part in the study, selected from the body of university students and visitors.

We conducted our study using the virtual world platform of the TOMIS project [22] that enables users to engage into the discovery of the reconstructed historical site of the city of Tomis, which was a Greek colony situated on the West coast of the Black Sea.

For the moment, we test our solution only on very few voluntaries in lab setup. Preliminary results showed that natural gesture can provide good guidance for user navigation towards the target implemented as a place in the virtual world or a virtual object to grasp and manipulate, if and only if the system coherently respond to the user gesture.

Although it took a few minutes for the subjects to adjust to the more delicate controls of the system, they learned them quickly because the movements and gestures came naturally.

Given the fact that our previous study was focused on few users we decided to conduct another one. This one's target audience were visitors that came to our faculty for presentations regarding potential registration into our faculty. Considering the time spent on learning the controls and getting used to them and the high-density audience, we were unable to present the full application in order to not disturb the time table of the presentations. With that in mind we made a demo for our holographic display with a few gestures controls using the Leap Motion. We used a questionnaire to gather the opinions of the users that played the demo.

The demo consists of the holographic display from four perspectives of a building from the virtual world platform of the TOMIS project [22]. The building rotates slowly so that it can be seen from all angles. The user could control the rotation of the building by moving his hand above the Leap Motion on the X and Z axis in order to better explore the building.

The demographic of this study is 42 people with the ages between 17 and 24, 26 of them haven't seen a holographic display until testing the application. When asked how often they use gesture-based technology those were the results (Fig. 10).

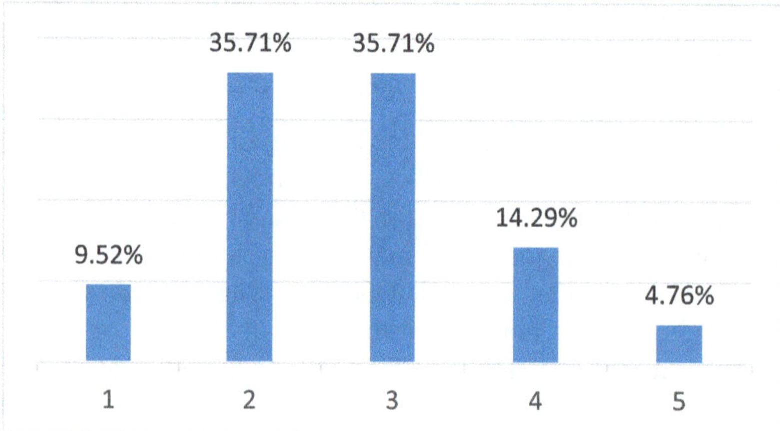

Fig. 10. The frequency our users use of gesture-based technology. (Legend 1-never 2-rarely 3-sometimes 4-often 5-all the time)

In the questionnaire we focused on the following topics: ease of usage, quality of the image, responsiveness and enjoyment of using the application, and final comments. The questionnaire was based on a 1 to 5 rating of the application attributes, based on the previously mentioned topics. For example, responsiveness, it being one of the most important topic, the results are presented in the histogram from (Fig. 11). The other topics had the following highest percentage rating: ease of usage – 4–54%, quality of the image – 4–57%, enjoyment of usage – 5–52%.

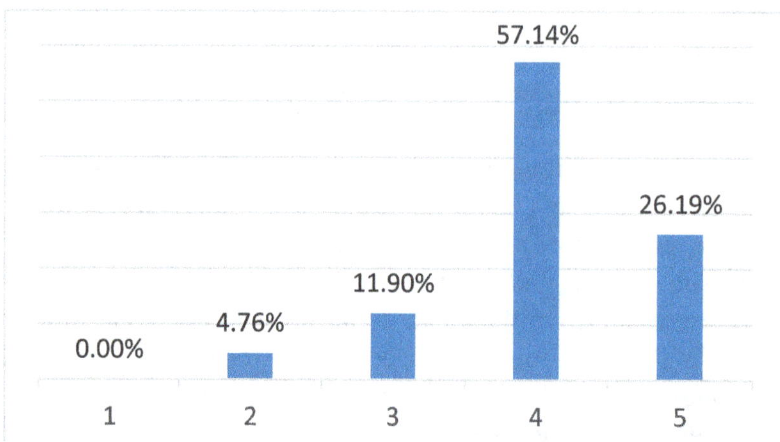

Fig. 11. Rating of our application responsiveness.

We had a few complaints with the image not moving fluently but this was caused by the long time the application was running and heating of our computer.

Under the "what you liked the most?" section of the questionnaire, most common answers were about the holographic display, gesture-based controls and the 3D model.

5 Conclusion and Future Work

In this paper, we have presented different types and approaches on natural, gesture-based interaction with a virtual heritage environment. We have explored the advantages and disadvantages of using two different gesture recognition technologies for VE exploration. The interface setup is also simple and cost effective, consisting of cheap materials used for the holographic setup and a desktop monitor.

Although we were unable to conduct a formal study on a broader user experience in order to determine the best approach with our resources, we believe we came close to an easy to learn and use user interface and configuration. It would be interesting to further explore the effectiveness of adding, say, a virtual-reality headset with an Leap Motion device mounted onto it for a better user experience, or even VR controllers.

We could also add some mini-games that are based on the human interaction that took place in the heritage environment's prime time, for a better heritage understanding and immersion. Further we could add a few Non-Player Characters that you can interact with. For instance, you could help a character make an item or even participate at events. Those characters could be personalities of that time that you could learn more about by interacting with them.

Adding a haptic device for recreating the sense of touch by applying forces, vibrations or motions to the users could make them feel more immersed and make them better understand the texture of the artifacts.

Acknowledgments. This work was supported by a grant of the Romanian Ministry of Research and Innovation, CCCDI - UEFISCDI, project number PN-III-P1-1.2-PCCDI-2017-0917/contract no. 21PCCDI / 2018, within PNCDI III.

Thanks also goes to CeRVA lab from Ovidius University of Constanta for providing 3D models of heritage artifacts obtained during TOMIS project [22].

References

1. Foundation of Helenic World. http://www.fhw.gr/fhw/. Accessed 07 Apr 2018
2. RomeReborn. http://www.romereborn.virginia.edu/. Accessed 07 Apr 2018
3. Abaci, T., et al.: Magic wand and the Enigma of the Sphinx. Comput. Graph. **28**, 477–484 (2004)
4. Fellmann, T., Kavakli, M.: VaiR: system architecture of a generic virtual reality engine. In: International Conference on Computational Intelligence for Modelling, Control and Automation and International Conference on Intelligent Agents, Web Technologies and Internet Commerce, vol. 2, pp. 501–506 (2005)

5. Choudary, O., Charvillat, V., Grigoras, R., Gurdjos, P.: MARCH: mobile augmenting reality for cultural heritage. In: Proceeding of the 17th ACM international conference on Multimedia, pp. 1023–1024 (2009)
6. Noh, Z., Sunar, M.S., Pan, Z.: A review on augmented reality for virtual heritage system. In: Chang, M., Kuo, R., Kinshuk, Chen, G.D., Hirose, M. (eds.) Edutainment 2009. LNCS, vol. 5670, pp. 50–61. Springer, Heidelberg (2009). https://doi.org/10.1007/978-3-642-03364-3_7
7. Carrozzino, M., Bergamasco, M.: Beyond virtual museums: experiencing immersive virtual reality in real museums. J. Cult. Heritage **11**, 452–458 (2010)
8. Čereković, A., Pandžić, I.S.: Multimodal behavior realization for embodied conversational agents. Multimed. Tools Appl. **54**(1), 143–164 (2011)
9. Mine, M.R.: Virtual environment interaction techniques, Technical report TR95-018, Department of Computer Science, University of North California, Chapel Hill, NC 27599-3175 (1995)
10. Bărbuceanu, F., Duguleană, M., Vlad, S., Nedelcu, A.: Evaluation of the average selection speed ratio between an eye tracking and a head tracking interaction interface. In: Camarinha-Matos, L.M. (ed.) DoCEIS 2011. IAICT, vol. 349, pp. 181–186. Springer, Heidelberg (2011). https://doi.org/10.1007/978-3-642-19170-1_20
11. Lee, E.C., Woo, J.C., Kim, J.H., Whang, M., Park, K.R.: A brain–computer interface method combined with eye tracking for 3D interaction. J. Neurosci. Methods **190**, 289–298 (2010)
12. Kehl, R., Van Gool, L.: Real-time pointing gesture recognition for an immersive environment. In: Proceedings of the Sixth IEEE International Conference on Automatic Face and Gesture Recognition, pp. 577–582 (2004). ISBN 0-7695-2122-3
13. Stanney, K.M., Mourant, R.R., Kennedy, R.S.: Human factors issues in virtual environments: a review of the literature. Presence **7**(4), 327–351 (1998)
14. McCullough, M., et al.: Myo arm–swinging to explore a VE. In: Proceedings of the ACM SIGGRAPH Symposium on Applied Perception - SAP 2015, 13–14 September 2015, Tübingen, pp. 107–113. ACM (2015). https://doi.org/10.1145/2804408.2804416. ISBN 978-1-4503-3812-7
15. Mulling, T., Sathiyanarayanan, M.: Characteristics of hand gesture navigation: a case study using a wearable device (MYO). In: Proceedings of the 2015 British HCI Conference (British HCI 2015), pp. 283–284. ACM, New York (2015). https://doi.org/10.1145/2783446.2783612. ISBN 978-1-4503-3643-7
16. Bugalia, N., Kumar, S., Kalra, P., Choudhary, S.: Mixed reality based interaction system for digital heritage. In: Proceedings of the 15th ACM SIGGRAPH Conference on Virtual-Reality Continuum and Its Applications in Industry - Volume 1 (VRCAI 2016), vol. 1, pp. 31–37. ACM, New York (2016). ISBN 978-1-4503-4692-4
17. Aslan, I., Krischkowsky, A., Meschtscherjakov, A., Wuchse, M., Tscheligi, M.: A leap for touch: proximity sensitive touch targets in cars. In: Proceedings of the 7th International Conference on Automotive User Interfaces and Interactive Vehicular Applications (AutomotiveUI 2015), pp. 39–46. ACM, New York (2015). http://dx.doi.org/10.1145/2799250.2799273. ISBN 978-1-4503-3736-6
18. Moser, C., Tscheligi, M.: Physics-based gaming: exploring touch vs. mid-air gesture input. In: Proceedings of the 14th International Conference on Interaction Design and Children (IDC 2015), pp. 291–294. ACM, New York (2015). https://doi.org/10.1145/2771839.2771899. ISBN 978-1-4503-3590-4
19. Myo Gesture Control Armband, Wearable Technology by Thalmic Labs. https://www.myo.com/. Accessed 14 Apr 2018
20. Leap Motion. https://www.leapmotion.com/. Accessed 14 Apr 2018
21. Unity. https://unity3d.com/. Accessed 14 Apr 2018
22. TOMIS Project Homepage. http://tomis.cerva.ro/. Accessed 14 Apr 2018

Natural Interaction in Virtual Reality for Cultural Heritage

Riccardo Galdieri(✉) and Marcello Carrozzino

Institute of Communication, Information and Perception Technologies, Perceptual Robotics Laboratory, Scuola Superiore Sant'Anna, Pisa, Italy
{r.galdieri,m.carrozzino}@santannapisa.it

Abstract. Now that virtual reality has finally become a customer ready product, museums can use this new mean to enhance their exhibitions. The main problem however is that such a tool was not thought for casual users, and to adapt this new technology to short experiences such as the ones museums could provide, it is necessary to reduce the adaptation time to the new mean. In this paper, we discuss how removing physical controllers in favour of visually-tracked virtual hands could significantly reduce the time needed by casual users to adapt to new experiences, underlying the current technological limitations both in terms of technology and design.

Keywords: Human Computer Interaction · Virtual reality · Cultural heritage Interaction metaphors · Natural interaction

1 Introduction

After many decades of incubation, fully immersive virtual reality (VR) has finally become a customer-ready technology. It is not so hard to imagine how such a new way of living surrounding spaces could be used to enhance interaction and fruition of virtual worlds, and many different fields, such as Industrial manufacturing, medicine and entertainment, are adopting these new technologies to improve their products. Despite some initial hesitation, museology and humanities disciplines in general are catching up with this major technological breakthrough, developing dedicated soft-ware to enhance the way in which the public interacts with cultural heritage.

As it often happens with new technologies, in these early stages VR is still far from expressing its full potential. Amongst the remaining problems, the lack of natural interaction within the simulated environments is one of the hardest to solve. Major selling companies ship their head mounted displays (HMDs) with fully tracked controllers, but gameplay interaction is still based on button clicking. This situation is not ideal for casual users such as the ones that museums have, and the time needed by these people to learn new interaction metaphors with controllers could significantly affect their overall enjoyment. Different contexts have different needs, and the inter-action metaphors must be designed in order to produce the best compromise between interaction, presence, enjoyment, learning and fatigue.

Building full hands tracking in VR would be an important breakthrough: natural interaction would speed up the adaptation process for casual users while increasing the

M. Duguleană et al. (Eds.): VRTCH 2018, CCIS 904, pp. 122–131, 2019.
https://doi.org/10.1007/978-3-030-05819-7_10

overall perceived immersion. Unfortunately there is still a conceptual, rather than technological, problem we need to solve. What is keeping real hands out of VR, regardless of the technical implementation, is that virtual and real hands belong to different systems that have different constrains, and an action can be both possible an impossible at the same time when translated from a system to the other. For in-stance, the surrounding space can be perceived as empty in one system but can also be blocked in the other, and when an action performed in the free space is translated to the other world it creates a logical conflict to the scene where the action was not allowed in the first place, resulting in a loss of presence. When the empty space is the simulation, the risk is to hit objects in the real world, and when the empty space is reality, simulated hands can interpenetrate objects in the simulated world, causing non-realistic behaviours.

In this paper we will discuss how to build natural interaction in mono-user immersive controller-free experiences for cultural heritage applications, introducing a test case scenario currently under development. After a summary of the theoretical back-ground in Sect. 2, in Sect. 3 the current state of the art technologies for natural interaction in VR will be explored and current limitations will be exposed. In Sect. 4 an experiment currently under development to test hands free interaction will be presented together with some expected results, before to draw conclusions in Sect. 5.

2 Theoretical Background

2.1 Human Computer Interaction

As human beings, the decisions we take are based on what our senses perceive from the environment. It is therefore important to find a way to feed our sensory apparatus as much as possible in VR, so that our actions can still be based on our perceptions. This is why, when the first home computers came out decades ago, it was important to study users' abilities to interact with these new machines in the smoothest possible way.

The first studies in the so called human-computer interaction (HCI) field, a name that was popularized by Stuart Card in 1983 [1], are dated back to 1976 [2]. During its infancy, HCI research focused on simple interactions such as moving the cursor around the screen: early studies used Fitts' law to measure accuracy with different hardware such as the mouse, trackball, joystick, touchpad, helmet-mounted sight, and eye tracker [3]. With time, HCI evolved from being an engineering problem to an interdisciplinary field [4], benefitting from studies in Psychology [5], cognitive studies [6], and even memory studies [7].

As pointed out by many researches, HCI benefits by a nature-driven approach [8, 9]. Being these interactions always artificial to a certain degree, it was necessary to create some metaphors to mimic a real behaviour in a three-dimensional space [10], the so called interaction metaphors. Through these interactions, it is easier for the public to interact with new environments without any domain specific knowledge or acclimatization programme, by translating their previous knowledge to the new situation.

2.2 Virtual Reality and Hand-Pose Recognition

Historically speaking, in the early stages of virtual reality definitions tended to be strictly related to hardware constrains, categorizing VR based on the different hardware types in use [11]. What those definitions lacked, according to Steuer, was a more human-focussed approach, he therefore proposed a new definition based on the key concepts of presence and telepresence [12], allowing desktop applications to be considered virtual reality even without dedicated hardware. According to Slater, the definition of presence was still too broad and somehow confusing, proposing to categorize VR based on immersion, meant as objective level of sensory fidelity, and presence, which refers to a subjective psychological response [13–15].

With the exponential growth of desktop VR, a wide range of hardware technologies has been released to support and enhance virtual experiences. Among these, head mounted displays (HMD) and non-invasive cameras have attracted a lot of attention, especially in the academic field. In regards of HMD, they have been used for a wide range of topics, including phobias treatment [16], anxiety [17], and education [18], while controller free interaction has been used in scenarios such as Stroke rehab [18], Sign Language recognition [20, 21], surgery [22] and data visualization [23]. Even though these two technologies are widely used in research, only a few experiments have been carried out with active combinations of them [24], and even less seem to address the problem of physically accurate interaction [25]. In one case, given the high efficiency of native controllers shipped with VR, natural interaction has even been defined as "obsolete" [26].

2.3 On Gesture Recognition and Interaction

When discussing hands interaction in virtual worlds, there are two different topics that must be taken into account: pose recognition and interaction. Despite being not mutually exclusive, it is important not to consider them as synonyms, as the first topic studies how to identify the current hands' position in real world and the second topic is interested in understanding how acquired hands can be used to interact with a digital scene [27].

As regards hands position recognition in a three-dimensional space, the two main devices that can perform reliable recognition without haptic interfaces are the Leap Motion and Microsoft Kinect. Leap Motion software return a pre-rigged fully animated mesh of both hands, with advanced API to use the acquired information in custom environments applications. Despite being tested periodically [28, 29], its tracking software is updated almost on monthly basis, and accuracy tests are outperformed most of the times. Also, as proved by Marin [31, 32], Leap Motion results can be further improved by using machine learning algorithms. On the other side, Microsoft Kinect is way more extensible and programmable but it does not provide any hands identification tool. Nevertheless, it has successfully been used to do perform hand gesture recognition [33, 34].

2.4 Museums and Technology

While it is commonly believed that museums are still reticent when it comes to apply technology to exhibitions [30], this tendency has been proven false in recent years [35]. The first milestone in this direction was the creation of the International conference on hypermedia and Interactivity in Museums in 1991 (ICHIM), followed by Museums and the Web established in 1997.

In that period the idea of museums as static exhibitions of art and history was drifting towards the idea of interactive places where people were not passive to their surroundings, but could enhance their experience through new interactive tools [36]. The role of the museum itself was questioned, arguing that museums should not be passive to information, but have an active role in promoting culture and research like other media [37, 38].

As regards user experiences in the so called "Virtual Museums", defined by the International Council of Museums (ICOM) as "A non-profit, permanent institution in the service of society and its development, open to the public, which acquires, conserves, researches, communicates and exhibits the tangible and intangible heritage of humanity and its environment for the purposes of education, study and enjoyment." (ICOM, 2007), it has been proven that the usage of virtual tools to enhance exhibitions does not affect users' enjoyment nor the learning experience in any way [39]. As a matter of fact, it is quite the opposite. Studies have shown that using technology to customize the way guests explore a museum could improve the overall level of satisfaction [40, 41].

3 Background Material

When designing a virtual application for cultural heritage, it is important to keep two elements in mind: the maximum number of simultaneous users and their technological background.

Talking about big audiences, museums want to have as many people as possible to try to enjoy the virtual experience. This leads to an important consequence: unless the application allows many users to control the application simultaneously, all the interaction will be performed by one user at a time with all the other being spectators.

The interaction mean has therefore to be designed to be interactive for one user only, while it has to display data to many. While this is the common case for tools such as CAVE and interactive kiosks, fully immersive VR represents a harder challenge for museums. Given the more immersive nature of the technology, headset users expect a higher degree of interaction with the environment. By default, this interaction is performed through standard controllers in two ways: they can have either have one single action to be performed with a button, which is easy to understand and perform, or a rather complex system of interaction that would require users to learn in advance. For this reason, building a controller free interaction could benefit both immersion and presence, increasing the degree of interactivity while removing the needs of previous knowledge, and speed up the usage time by a significant factor.

While Microsoft Kinect is a valid option for hands tracking acquisition in controlled environments, in a more unsupervised space it could be better to use a shorter-range tool like the Leap Motion. Given the high accuracy that can be reached with it, the consequent step is to blend its data with a fully immersive world. Leap Motion pose data has been used to perform gesture recognition – meant as the interpretation of human gesture – but this data has rarely been used to perform real time interaction with a fully immersive virtual reality system. The main reason for this is realism. Both worlds have physical constraints, but while real world laws cannot be changed, virtual environments' simplified physics interactions are not capable of handling each possible scenario, and when real actions are translated it often happens that the result falls outside the simulated physical model. Something simple like grabbing a glass bottle proves to be a challenge in virtual reality, as physical engines are extremely sensible to mesh interpenetration and are not capable of handling events that, in their own environment would not be allowed, such as having a hand narrow a rigid body.

In June 2017, Leap Motion released an API to tackle this problem. This new software puts himself between the hand poses obtained by the Leap Motion and the 3D engine physics simulation, disabling any collision calculation when the hands are performing a physically inaccurate action. While this approach works from a physical point of view – by preventing the engine from carrying out wrong calculations – it still breaks the perception of reality within the simulation, as it allows the hands to interpenetrate the scene objects without any response. Some applications prefer to limit the degree of visual feedback in the simulation by always showing a physical response to the users, but this creates a mismatch between the perceived hand position and the visual hand. Given the purpose of this project to investigate real hands interaction in VR, the idea of having a mismatch between perception and visualization was discarded, and the compromise offered by Leap Motion accepted and noted.

4 The Experiment

As already discussed, hands free interaction in VR is a rather unexplored field. We designed an experiment to understand how different interactions can be perceived as natural by a variegated audience, hoping to find a preliminary way to categorize single-handed actions. The ideal outcome would be to find common features among gestures that could potentially be used in future natural interaction metaphors design.

To test the previous assertions, we're currently developing a game-like test case scenario application in immersive VR, where users will be required to perform a series of actions on a console in order to unlock a new room with a piece of art in it. The sequence of actions, at the current state of the application, is as follows: in the first instance, users must grab and hold a key, which they must put in a lock. Once inserted, the key must be rotated in order to unlock the case. When unlocked, users will be required to pull it up to access a control panel hidden below. At this point, once a series of switches is activated and the panel powered, a secret box opens and a card is found. The card must be grabbed like the key and slided through a rail. Once the card arrives at the end, the door unlocks and the prize is revealed. Before the simulation starts, the operator will be able to choose whether if he wants to activate a pre-recorded speech that guides the users over the different challenges, or to keep it quiet and leave them to the task (Figs. 1 and 2).

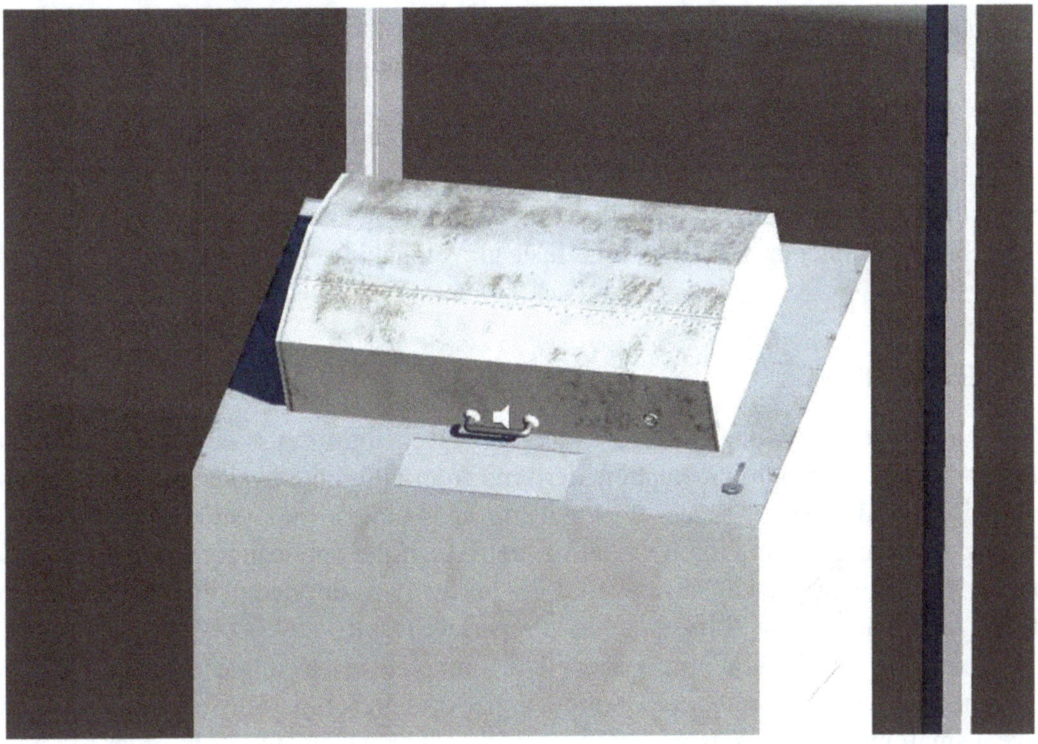

Fig. 1. The closed hatch.

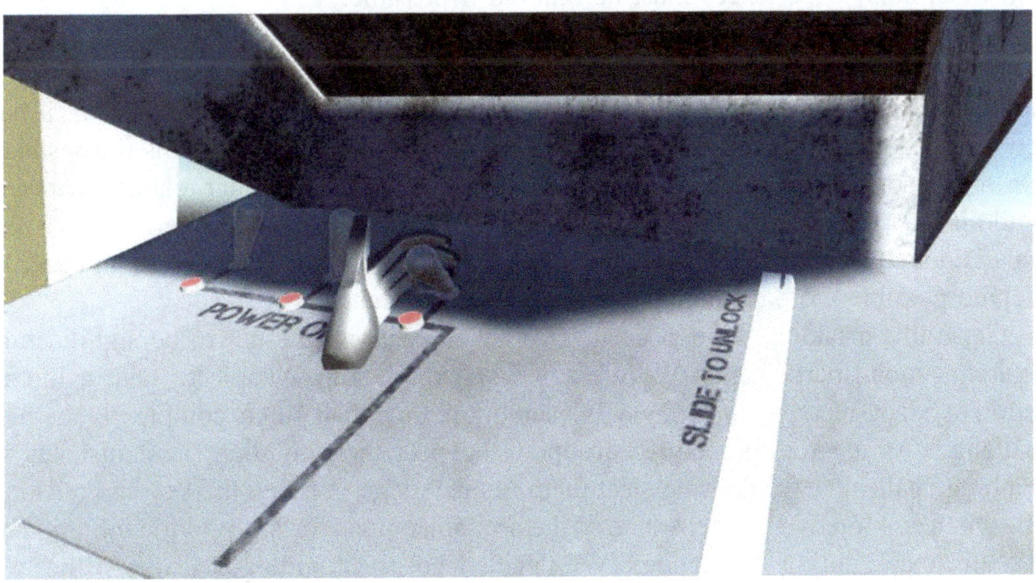

Fig. 2. The virtual hand interacting with the environment. Materials are temporary.

There will be two evaluation metrics for this challenge: time and accuracy. The demo will be monitoring both the overall time needed to access the room and the time needed to complete each single task. If a user takes a significantly longer time but just one attempt to perform a subtask, it means that he was not able to understand what he was required to do in the first place, and the metaphor was not clear. On the other side, if he attempts many times and fail, it could mean that the manipulations were not easy enough to be executed in VR rather than in reality, bringing up further discussion on both technology and design.

A control group has also been created in order to compare how the usage of controllers instead of hands could affect performances. While receiving the same instructions and the same support throughout the tests, the control group will use a single button to interact with the scene instead of touching, grabbing and pulling with his hands.

4.1 Expectations

There are some results that we are expecting, given the discussion above. First and most important, interaction metaphors deriving from different physical interactions will have different degrees of success. In real life, it is almost impossible to insert a key without scratching around the hole, and even though the application gives users some margin, by allowing the key to fit even if not perfectly positioned, they won't be aware of this facilitation and will try to achieve a perfect result.

In addition, the overall time needed to complete each single subtask must be crosschecked with the number of attempts to perform an action. For instance, we might have a small number of users who try to turn the switches on and off in order to repeat the animation. If that is the case, the overall completion time data will be less relevant than in other cases. This behaviour must be noted during the data analysis phase, and data-wise, noisy experiences must be ignored if possible.

Another crucial factor to consider is the size of the objects people will interact with. Every object should have a significant size in order to be physical accurate, and while there is no precise measurement on what the minimum suggested size could b, it has been noticed that small objects such as a key could be subject to problems if too small. For this reason, all graspable objects in the scene are bigger than their real life matches. While it may not seem a significant factor in achieving the desired interaction, as the scale is not so significantly different, further investigations should be made in order to exclude possible score contamination by the scale difference.

Generally speaking, we expect the overall interaction time not to be significantly different among participants. We do however expect some people to take a longer period to adapt, meaning that they will spend more time than others completing the first challenge. As regards the control group, we expect them to score less mistakes in grabbing challenges, while we expect them to take longer rotating the key and clicking the switches. Moreover, current state of the art applications for VR provide vibration as force feedback during interactions. We decided not to provide any, to keep the two interaction means as equal as possible.

5 Conclusions

The experiment we are currently setting up only concerns simple interactions, and purposely avoid complex gestures like throwing, pulling, squeezing or any two hands interaction. While the problem of hands interaction is easy to define, we are far from even scratching the surface of how to handle such complexity.

Now that the quality of virtual reality has reached such a high level of interactivity, it is time to start thinking about immersive virtual experiences as a whole and not as a cluster of problems that can be solved individually. The collision of real and simulated worlds is far too complex, and without an accurate evaluation of colliding aspects, it will be impossible to reach the level of interaction that is expected in a realistic simulation.

Museums could and should be part of this challenge. Given their extremely wide audience, specific interactions must be designed to create immersive controller-free in VR, and general guidelines will not be exhaustive enough to be borrowed and applied to cultural heritage application. Hands interaction among exhibitions could make the difference between being passive to history and actively be part of it.

Acknowledgements. This paper is supported by EU Horizon 2020 research and innovation programme under grant agreement No 692103, project eHERITAGE (Expanding the Research and innovation capacity in Cultural Heritage Virtual Reality Applications).

References

1. Card, S.K., Newell, A., Moran, T.P.: The Psychology of Human-Computer Interaction. L. Erlbaum Associates Inc., Hillsdale (1983)
2. Carlisle, J.H.: Evaluating the impact of office automation on top management communication. In: Proceedings of the June 7–10, 1976, National Computer Conference and Exposition, pp. 611–616. ACM, June 1976
3. MacKenzie, I.S.: Fitts' law as a research and design tool in human-computer interaction. Hum. Comput. Interact. **7**(1), 91–139 (1992)
4. Jaimes, A., Sebe, N.: Multimodal human–computer interaction: a survey. Comput. Vis. Image Underst. **108**(1–2), 116–134 (2007)
5. Newell, A., Card, S.K.: The prospects for psychological science in human-computer interaction. Hum. Comput. Interact. **1**(3), 209–242 (1985)
6. Hollan, J., Hutchins, E., Kirsh, D.: Distributed cognition: toward a new foundation for human-computer interaction research. ACM Trans. Comput. Hum. Interact. (TOCHI) **7**(2), 174–196 (2000)
7. Nass, C., Brave, S.: Emotion in human-computer interaction. In: The Human-Computer Interaction Handbook, pp. 94–109. CRC Press (2007)
8. Villaroman, N., Rowe, D., Swan, B.: Teaching natural user interaction using OpenNI and the Microsoft Kinect sensor. In: Proceedings of the 2011 Conference on Information Technology Education, pp. 227–232. ACM, October 2011
9. Francese, R., Passero, I., Tortora, G.: Wiimote and Kinect: gestural user interfaces add a natural third dimension to HCI. In: Proceedings of the International Working Conference on Advanced Visual Interfaces, pp. 116–123. ACM, May 2012

10. Mackay, W.E., Fayard, A.L.: HCI, natural science and design: a framework for triangulation across disciplines. In: Proceedings of the 2nd Conference on Designing Interactive Systems: Processes, Practices, Methods, and Techniques, pp. 223–234. ACM, August 1997
11. Coates, G.: Program from Invisible Site-a virtual sho, a multimedia performance work presented by George Coates Performance Works. San Francisco, CA (1992)
12. Steuer, J.: Defining virtual reality: dimensions determining telepresence. J. Commun. **42**(4), 73–93 (1992)
13. Slater, M.: Measuring presence: a response to the Witmer and Singer presence questionnaire. Presence **8**(5), 560–565 (1999)
14. Slater, M.: A note on presence terminology. Presence Connect **3**(3), 1–5 (2003)
15. Bowman, D.A., McMahan, R.P.: Virtual reality: how much immersion is enough?. Computer **40**(7) (2007)
16. Carlin, A.S., Hoffman, H.G., Weghorst, S.: Virtual reality and tactile augmentation in the treatment of spider phobia: a case report. Behav. Res. Ther. **35**(2), 153–158 (1997)
17. Wiederhold, B.K., Wiederhold, M.D.: Virtual Reality Therapy for Anxiety Disorders: Advances in Evaluation and Treatment. American Psychological Association, Washington DC (2005)
18. Freina, L., Ott, M.: A literature review on immersive virtual reality in education: state of the art and perspectives. In: The International Scientific Conference eLearning and Software for Education, vol. 1, p. 133. "Carol I" National Defence University, January 2015
19. Bassily, D., Georgoulas, C., Guettler, J., Linner, T., Bock, T.: Intuitive and adaptive robotic arm manipulation using the leap motion controller. In: Proceedings of ISR/robotik 2014; 41st International Symposium on Robotics, pp. 1–7. VDE, June 2014
20. Chuan, C.H., Regina, E., Guardino, C.: American sign language recognition using leap motion sensor. In: 2014 13th International Conference on Machine Learning and Applications (ICMLA), pp. 541–544. IEEE, December 2014
21. Potter, L.E., Araullo, J., Carter, L.: The leap motion controller: a view on sign language. In: Proceedings of the 25th Australian Computer-Human Interaction Conference: Augmentation, Application, Innovation, Collaboration, pp. 175–178. ACM, November 2013
22. Harrison, B., et al.: Through the eye of the master: the use of Virtual Reality in the teaching of surgical hand preparation. In: 2017 IEEE 5th International Conference on Serious Games and Applications for Health (SeGAH), pp. 1–6. IEEE, April 2017
23. Donalek, C., et al.: Immersive and collaborative data visualization using virtual reality platforms. In: 2014 IEEE International Conference on Big Data (Big Data), pp. 609–614. IEEE, October 2014
24. Blaha, J., Gupta, M.: Diplopia: a virtual reality game designed to help amblyopics. In: 2014 iEEE Virtual Reality (VR), pp. 163–164. IEEE, March 2014
25. Lee, P.W., Wang, H.Y., Tung, Y.C., Lin, J.W., Valstar, A.: TranSection: hand-based interaction for playing a game within a virtual reality game. In: Proceedings of the 33rd Annual ACM Conference Extended Abstracts on Human Factors in Computing Systems, pp. 73–76. ACM, April 2015
26. Hilfert, T., König, M.: Low-cost virtual reality environment for engineering and construction. Vis. Eng. **4**(1), 2 (2016)
27. Mitra, S., Acharya, T.: Gesture recognition: a survey. IEEE Trans. Syst. Man Cybern. Part C (Appl. Rev.) **37**(3), 311–324 (2007)
28. Weichert, F., Bachmann, D., Rudak, B., Fisseler, D.: Analysis of the accuracy and robustness of the leap motion controller. Sensors **13**(5), 6380–6393 (2013)
29. Guna, J., Jakus, G., Pogačnik, M., Tomažič, S., Sodnik, J.: An analysis of the precision and reliability of the leap motion sensor and its suitability for static and dynamic tracking. Sensors **14**(2), 3702–3720 (2014)

30. Schweibenz, W.: The" virtual museum": new perspectives for museums to present objects and information using the internet as a knowledge base and communication system. ISI **34**, 185–200 (1998)
31. Marin, G., Dominio, F., Zanuttigh, P.: Hand gesture recognition with leap motion and kinect devices. In: 2014 IEEE International Conference on Image Processing (ICIP), pp. 1565–1569. IEEE, October 2014
32. Marin, G., Dominio, F., Zanuttigh, P.: Hand gesture recognition with jointly calibrated leap motion and depth sensor. Multimedia Tools Appl. **75**(22), 14991–15015 (2016)
33. Tang, M.: Recognizing hand gestures with microsoft's kinect. Department of Electrical Engineering of Stanford University, Palo Alto (2011)
34. Yao, Y., Fu, Y.: Contour model-based hand-gesture recognition using the Kinect sensor. IEEE Trans. Circ. Syst. Video Technol. **24**(11), 1935–1944 (2014)
35. Styliani, S., Fotis, L., Kostas, K., Petros, P.: Virtual museums, a survey and some issues for consideration. J. Cult. Heritage **10**(4), 520–528 (2009)
36. Pearce, S.M.: Thinking about things. In: Pearce, S.M. (ed.) Interpreting Objects and Collections, pp. 125–132. Routledge, London (1994)
37. Silverstone, R.: The medium is the museum: on objects and logics in times and spaces. In: Durant, J. (ed.) Museums and the Public Understanding of Science, pp. 34–42. The Science Museum, London (1992)
38. Macdonald, S.: Theorizing museums: an introduction in Theorizing Museums (Doctoral dissertation, ed. S. Macdonald and G. Fyfe, Oxford: Blackwell Publishers) (1996)
39. Pierdicca, R., Frontoni, E., Zingaretti, P., Sturari, M., Clini, P., Quattrini, R.: Advanced interaction with paintings by augmented reality and high resolution visualization: a real case exhibition. In: De Paolis, L.T., Mongelli, A. (eds.) AVR 2015. LNCS, vol. 9254, pp. 38–50. Springer, Cham (2015). https://doi.org/10.1007/978-3-319-22888-4_4
40. Pagano, A., Armone, G., De Sanctis, E.: Virtual Museums and audience studies: the case of "Keys to Rome" exhibition. In: Digital Heritage 2015, vol. 1, pp. 373–376. IEEE, September 2015
41. Choi, H.S., Kim, S.H.: A content service deployment plan for metaverse museum exhibitions —centering on the combination of beacons and HMDs. Int. J. Inf. Manag. **37**(1), 1519–1527 (2017)

Data Management

Automatic Creation of a Virtual/Augmented Gallery Based on User Defined Queries on Online Public Repositories

Michele Mallia[2], Marcello Carrozzino[1(✉)], Chiara Evangelista[1], and Massimo Bergamasco[1]

[1] Institute of Communication, Information and Perception Technologies, Perceptual Robotics Laboratory, Scuola Superiore Sant'Anna, Pisa, Italy
{m.carrozzino, c.evangelista, m.bergamasco}@santannapisa.it
[2] Department of Filologia, Letteratura e Linguistica, Università di Pisa, Pisa, Italy
mallia.michele@gmail.com

Abstract. Virtual museums are becoming increasingly popular, especially thanks to the recent spread of low-cost immersive technologies enabling a richer technology-based cultural offer. However, creating a virtual museum commonly requires a lot of effort, especially if a certain visual quality is required.

The aim of the project described in this paper is to verify the effectiveness of automatic strategies to create a virtual museum of paintings, whose digital images are retrieved directly from repositories freely available in the network based on specific user queries. The same approach is then applied in order to create an augmented reality application transforming any environment, purposely instrumented with markers, in a virtual museum.

Keywords: Virtual reality · Augmented reality · Cultural heritage
Virtual museums · Procedural generation · Public repository

1 Introduction

Virtual museums are becoming increasingly popular as they allow "to complement, enhance, or augment the museum through personalization, interactivity, user experience and richness of content" [1]. Creating a virtual museum commonly requires a lot of effort in terms of design, content management, and visual rendering, effort unavoidable whenever a given quality of the experience is to be achieved. However, it is possible to think at digital collections which, even if not carefully designed as proper virtual museums, provide an immersive experience richer and, expectantly, more engaging than digital galleries as commonly found in standard web pages.

The aim of the project described in this paper is to verify the effectiveness of automatic strategies to create a virtual museum of paintings, whose digital images are retrieved directly from repositories freely available in the network. The virtual museum is based on a virtual environment, initially empty, that can be populated with various digital elements based on specific user queries. Since the number of artworks can be

M. Duguleană et al. (Eds.): VRTCH 2018, CCIS 904, pp. 135–147, 2019.
https://doi.org/10.1007/978-3-030-05819-7_11

variable, the structure of the museum is modular, i.e. it changes shape based on the number of works selected by the user. The goal of this project is to provide a tool enabling the exploration of a wide variety of artworks taken from public heritage repositories such as Europeana and Google Art Project, or from other generic repositories of multimedia information like Google Images.

Images and the related information are extracted using specific API making use of languages such as Javascript, C++, JSON and XML. The same approach is then applied in order to create an augmented reality application transforming any environment, purposely instrumented with markers, in a virtual museum.

2 Previous Work

Since the advent of VRML, 3D virtual museums have shown their potential as a tool for disseminating culture and knowledge using digital technologies and taking advantage of the advanced features provided by VR such as immersion and presence.

One of the first VR projects applied to cultural heritage was the Nu.M.E, or "New Electronic Museum of the city of Bologna" [2]. Launched in the first half of the 1990s, it can be considered one of the reference points for subsequent works in the field of virtual technologies applied to cultural heritage.

The MUVI [3] (Virtual Museum of Daily Life of the twentieth century) stems from a series of reflections on the memory of people and the events that preceded us above all in relation to the "danger" of losing all the collective heritage that brings together the knowledge related to everyday life and the identity of the various communities. The project, launched in 1999 at the VisIT Lab of CINECA, focuses on the transmission and conservation of past knowledge that can be favored by appropriate technological solutions.

A different approach was proposed in the Museum of Pure Forms [4]: in addition to presenting a VR system including graphic software and sterescopic visualization, it also includes a haptic interface to provide touch feedback. This enables a novel way of presenting historical/artistic artifacts to visitors, allowing them to touch artifacts, albeit in a virtual environment.

The ARCO project [5] aims to develop a series of technologies to "help museums create, manipulate, manage and present digitized cultural objects in virtual exhibitions accessible both inside and outside museums". In the project there is a database storing information regarding digital representations, which can be managed by a system called ACMA (acronym of "ARCO Content Management Application"). ACMA associates each 3D model with a series of metadata outlining four main aspects of the museum's objects: the curatorial aspect, the technical aspect, the exploration of resources and administration.

An investigation on how to go beyond 3D web-based virtual museums and embed virtual technologies in the offer of real physical museums is instead proposed in [6].

An approach similar to the one proposed in this paper was pursued in DynaMus [7]. In this case, also, the virtual content is dynamically downloaded from open data repositories, albeit the generated museum is made available on standard web browsers without any immersive/augmented option.

3 Architecture of the VR Museum

The Virtual Museum architecture (Fig. 1) is organized as follows:

The initial phase is characterized by the selection of the search parameters, i.e. what the user wants to view in the virtual gallery. In this phase, HTML and JavaScript are used for the management of the parameters.

In the second phase the requested information based on the selected search criteria are retrieved. A C++ library is used to this purpose.

The third and last phase consists in the creation of the virtual museum, using the XVR [8] software.

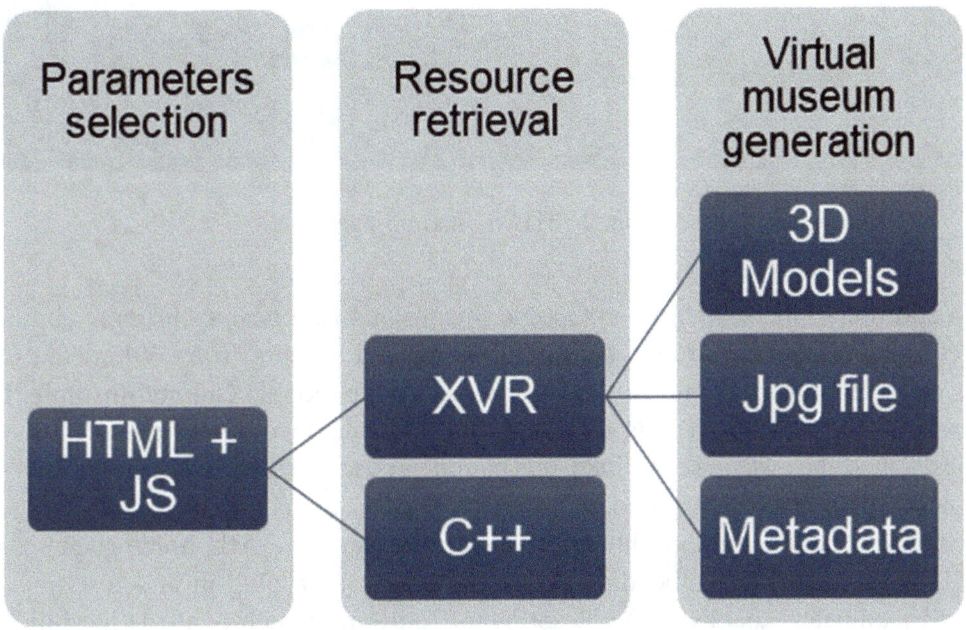

Fig. 1. Data flow of the Virtual Museum generation procedure

3.1 Search Criteria

The selection of the search parameters in order to perform queries to the desired databases is made with a simple HTML page (Fig. 2). From this page, users can select three different repositories: Google Images, Wikimedia Commons and Europeana.

Depending on the repository chosen, the user can perform two types of searches: enter the name of an artist or, in the case of Wikimedia Commons, a collection of works of art. Afterwards the user can choose the number of paintings to be visualize inside the virtual museum (in order to keep the download time within reasonable limits it was decided to set a maximum of 50 artworks, although no investigation has been performed about the optimal value of this parameter).

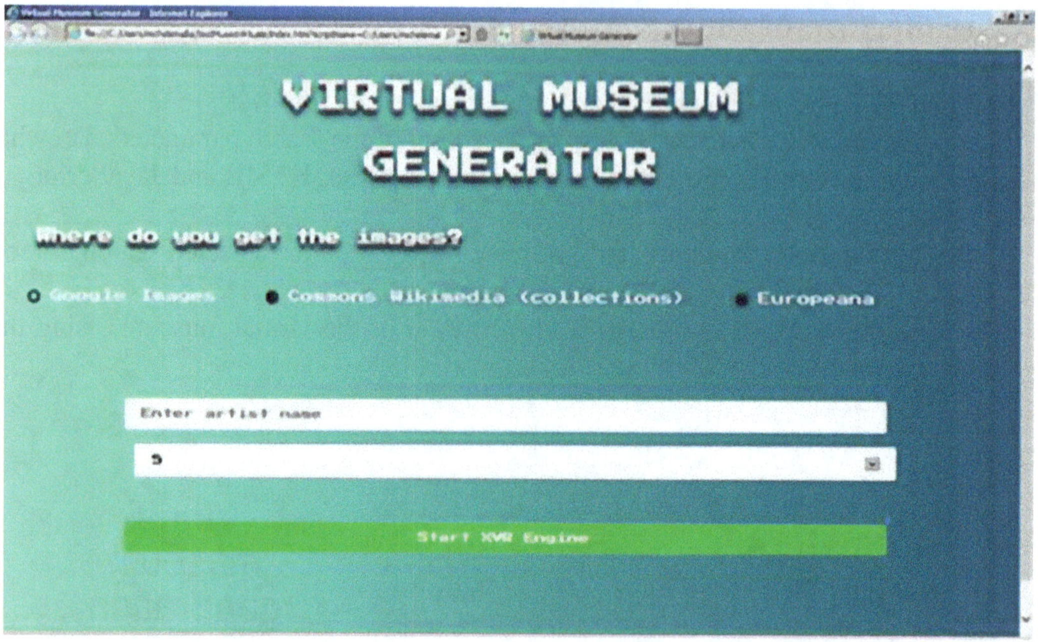

Fig. 2. HTML starting page

In addition to the searching on Google Images and Europeana, currently about 255 collections are indexed through an XML file created starting from Wikimedia Commons collected information regarding the works on the Google Cultural Institute. Each component of the web page is controlled by JS code in order to allow only valid queries. Once the user has outlined the parameters to perform the search, the XVR graphics engine has to be started.

This is obtained through Javascrip inside the same HTML home page: a new HTML page is created embedding the XVR engine as a plug-in and inserting customized parameters thanks to the "UserParam" attribute which contains the following data:

- the first element is an ID corresponding to the chosen repository (Google Images, Wikimedia Commons, Europeana);
- the second element is a string corresponding to the name of the artist or the name of the art gallery;
- the third element is the amount of artworks to be inserted in the virtual museum.

These elements are concatenated into a single text string that is passed to the XVR plugin.

3.2 Resource Retrieval

Once the user XVR application has started, a preliminary phase begins consisting in the retrieval of information that takes place by means of a DLL library written in C++ compiled as a XVR external module, in charge of communicating with the server API of the selected repository.

In the case of Google Images, information retrieval is not a very laborious process, as the only information to be recovered is that relating to the URLs of the images to be downloaded. The solution adopted is to make a simple GET Request to Google's servers to return an HTML page containing high-resolution images links. The HTML page is parsed in order to fill an array containing all the needed links, which are first examined and checked prior to the actual download of the image.

Checks ensure that:

- the resource is actually reachable and returns a response code of 0;
- the image to be downloaded is not be empty;
- the images size is at least 10 K in order to avoid low-resolution resources.

A very different process is used to retrieve resources from Wikimedia Commons. In fact, it is possible to interface with an API in order to request, in addition to links to high-resolution images, also metadata containing information about the works. In addition, instead of receiving an HTML page in response to the GET REQUEST, a JSON object is received that is easily "parsed" through additional library methods.

Initially, a pattern is always used, which must be constructed according to the request that one wants to make. There are two phases for information retrieval:

- the first phase consists in the getting a list of the items present in a given collection;
- the second phase consists in the retrieval of the connection to high resolution images and related metadata.

In Europeana the process is somehow similar to that of Wikimedia Commons. Initially a list of items is obtained accessing the Europeana search engine and, subsequently, the application queries each item in order to retrieve related metadata and multimedia resources. Europeana provides several tools to retrieve information programmatically; dedicated APIs are available to perform searches in databases or to query entities and other open data. The tool used for file retrieval is the Search API.

4 Dynamic Generation of Virtual Museum

After retrieving all the information and resources related to the artworks, the next step is the creation of the virtual museum: a dynamic structure with three-dimensional models and multimedia resources placed in the appropriate spaces.

One of the peculiarities of the gallery is modularity: it does not have a fixed size, but varies according to the number of works requested by the user. 3DS Max software was used for the creation of three-dimensional models.

The virtual museum is divided into blocks: its general shape, corresponding to a box, is initially divided into four parts, with models for the top right, top left, bottom right and bottom left parts. Subsequently, "corridor" blocks are added to create a larger museum, with a shape depending on the side they are placed.

The structure of each block (Fig. 3) is basic: it is composed of a floor of about 7 m2 and three walls, a door and four quads, arranged two by two on two of the walls of the room. The procedural construction starts from the upper left room and then proceeds clockwise (Fig. 4).

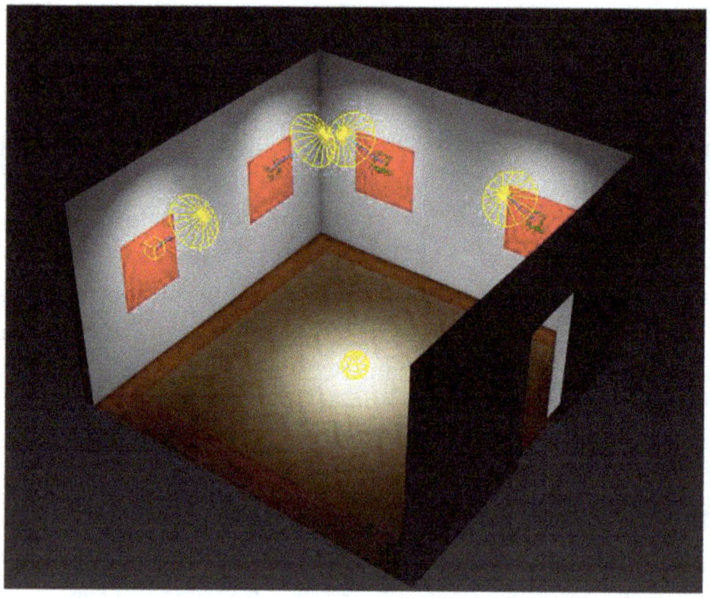

Fig. 3. 3D model of the museum room module

The interactive visit (Fig. 5, top) enables viewing the metadata related to each work (if available) and a simplified navigation of the rooms inside the museum. Metadata (author name, artwork name, period, etc.) are automatically displayed as overlaid text when the user approaches a painting. Information is only displayed when the user is at close range (Fig. 5, bottom).

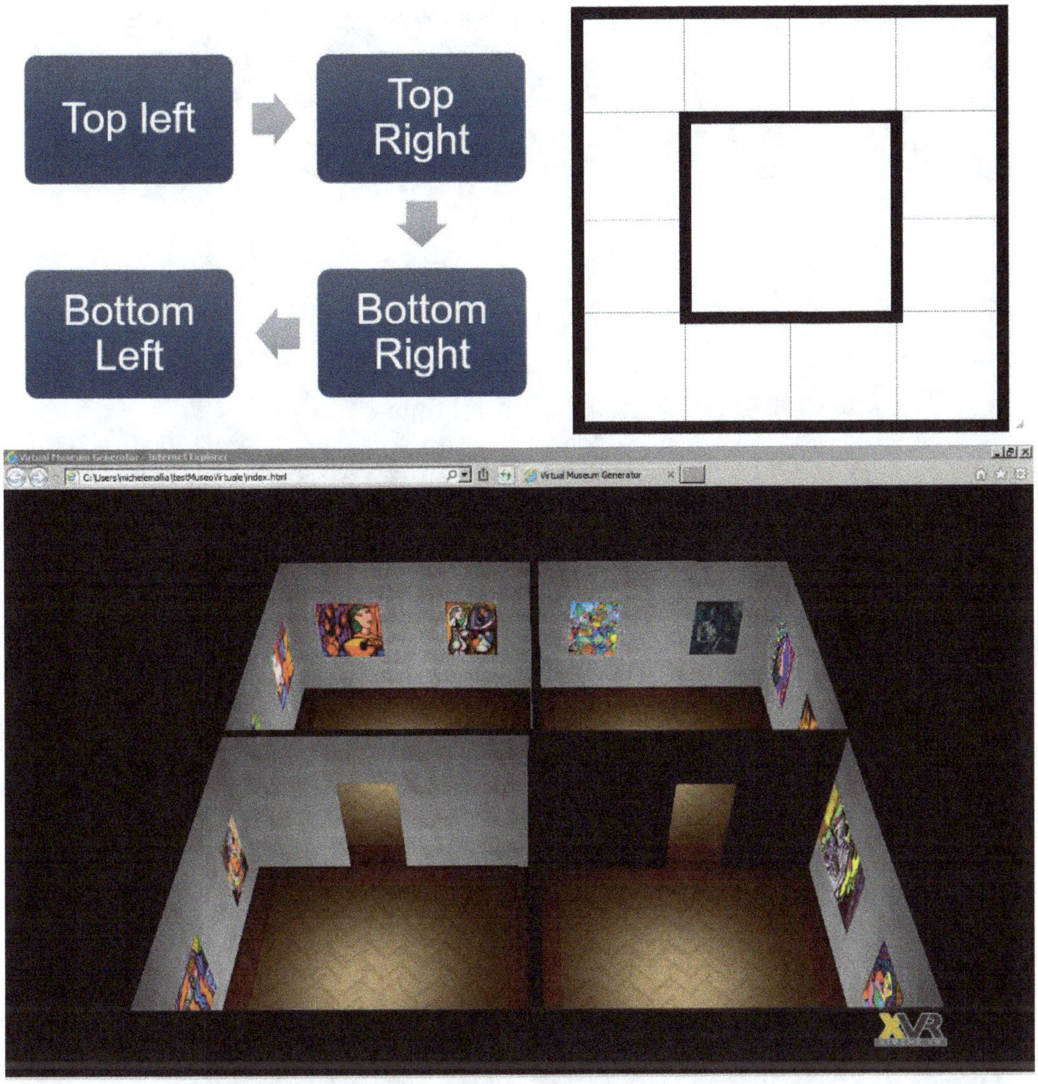

Fig. 4. A possible arrangement of the room modules (top) and the resulting Virtual Museum including paintings mapped as textures onto pre-defined quads

An assisted navigation mode facilitates the exploration of the virtual museum and improves the user experience in visiting the environment. The system consists in labeling the rooms of the museum and providing a list of the artworks present in the different rooms, so that the visitor can move from one room to another to see the desired paintings without having to complete the whole itinerary.

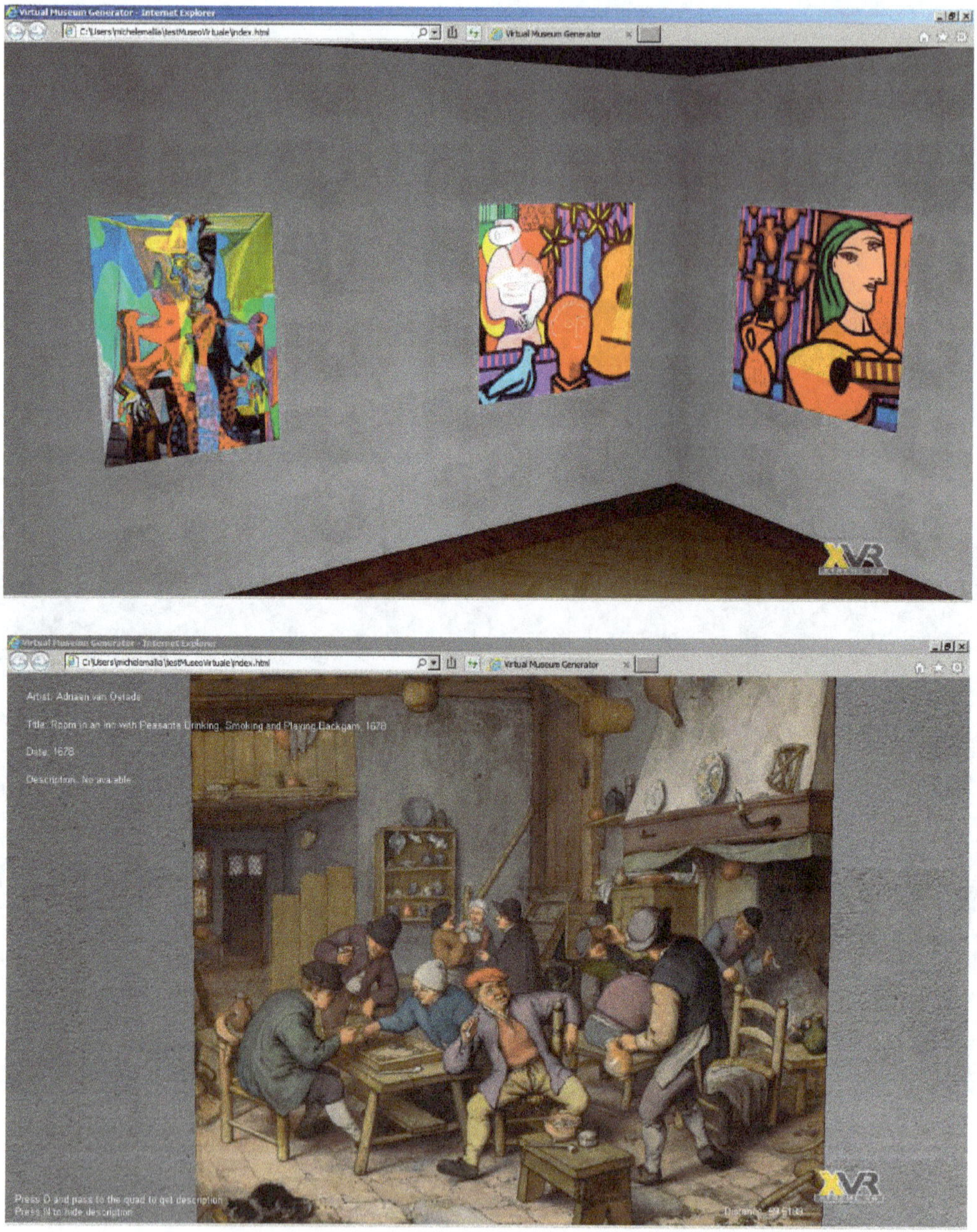

Fig. 5. Close-up view of a procedurally generated Picasso exhibition (top) Visualization of artist/artwork information automatically retrieved from metadata (bottom)

5 Architecture of the AR Museum

5.1 First Itinerary: Panels

The mobile augmented reality version of the procedural museum has been implemented as an Android app, using the Unity3D and Vuforia tools.

The application is based on four Android activities implementing the following functionalities:

- the home menu
- the interface to retrieve data from Wikimedia Commons (Fig. 6a, b)
- the interface to retrieve data from Google Images (Fig. 6c)
- a Unity-based activity managing the real-time AR application.

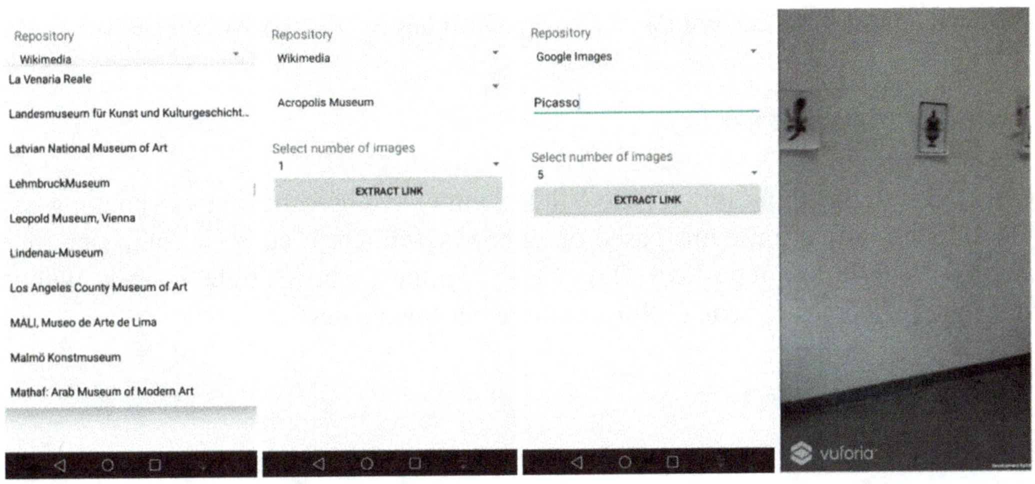

Fig. 6. Selection of the exhibition from Wikimedia (a), selection of parameters (b), free search on Google Images (c), picture of the real environment hosting the test AR exhibition

It can be seen that, with respect to the VR museum, in this case only two repositories are supported. The procedure of data retrieval and resource downloading is similar in many respects to the one used in the VR museum. Once the data has been collected from the various activities, the Unity3D graphical engine is started.

In this case, Unity3D is used in combination with Vuforia, a library allowing to easily marker-based augmented reality apps. Vuforia makes available to Unity an AR Camera and imports the defined set of markers as asset files. The Unity 3D scene is composed of quads on which markers are placed following a predefined order. Prior to the execution of the real-time application, each marker is associated to a certain downloaded resource. Once a marker is recognized, it will be substituted by the painting automatically associated to the marker ID.

Once the user points the device towards a marker placed in the physical scene (Fig. 4d), the associated painting is applied to the surface of the quad hosting it, modifying its size according to the proportions of the image. The user can then see the artwork appearing on the designated surface (Fig. 7).

Fig. 7. Selection of the exhibition from Wikimedia (a), selection of parameters (b), free search on Google Images (c), picture of the real environment hosting the test AR exhibition

6 Performance Test

Several runs of the application of the VR Museum have been performed, creating each time different virtual museums based on queries on different authors, composed of 30 paintings. The fastest repository (Fig. 8) was found to be Google Images, with an average of 27.06 s on average, Europeana being the slowest.

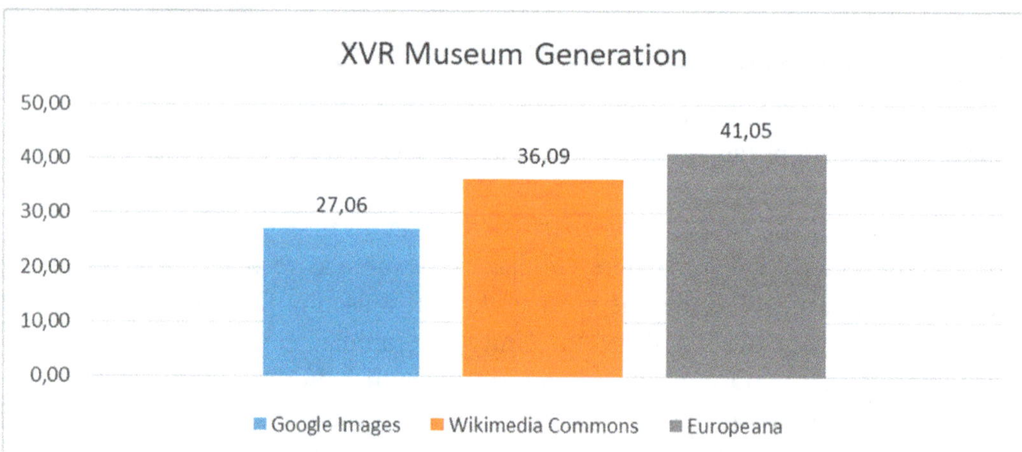

Fig. 8. Virtual Museum generation time by used repository

As for the average download time by single image, Wikimedia Commons was the fastest with 0.80 s per image on average (Fig. 9).

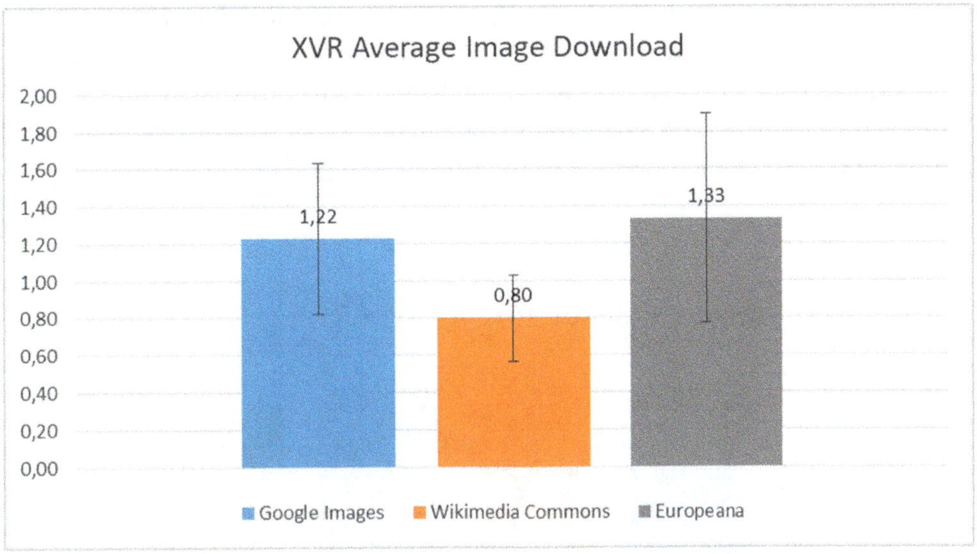

Fig. 9. Averaged image download time by used repository

7 Pilot User Study

To collect data for usability tests, questionnaires were drawn up subdivided into various sections ranging from the purely aesthetic aspect of the programs to the performative one. Questionnaires were distributed on a sample of twenty-five subjects. Three questions in particular sere aimed at evaluating, on a 7-point Likert scale, usability, quality of the cultural experience and the desire of reusing the application, with good results in these three respects in the case of the VR museum (Fig. 10).

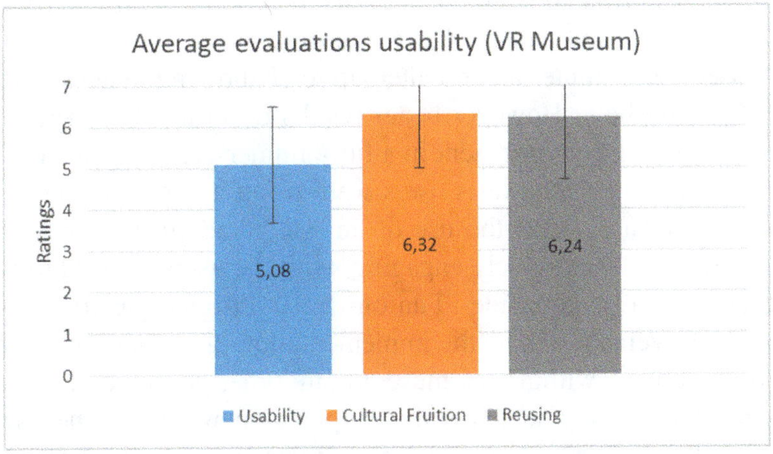

Fig. 10. Usability evaluation of the VR Museum experience

As far as the AR museum is concerned, results turned out to be extremely positive. All users find the augmented reality system suitable for a cultural experience; 92% of users confirmed that they want to reuse the application; 96% said they wanted to recommend this application to their friends; finally, 96% of users expressed the desire to see this type of technology adopted by museums (Fig. 11).

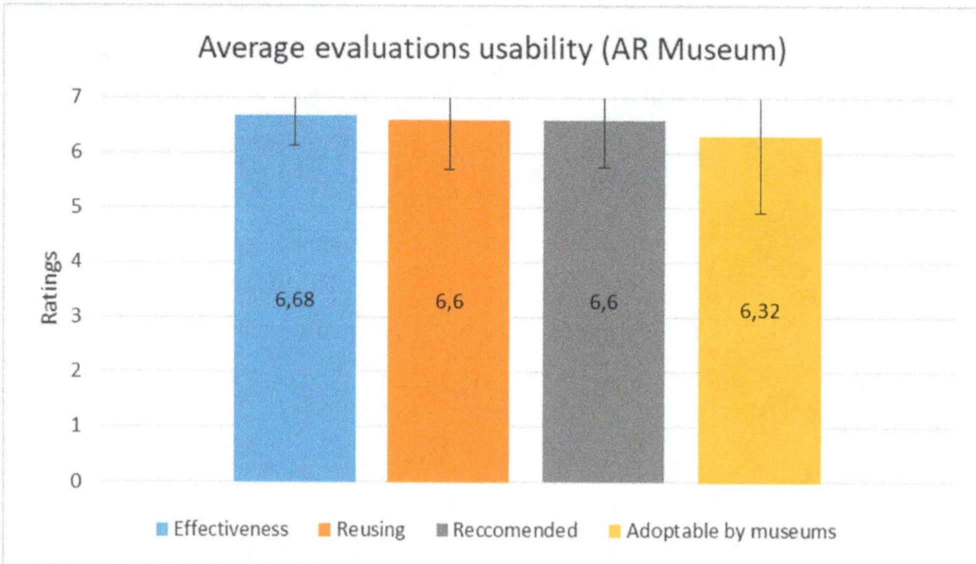

Fig. 11. Usability evaluation of the AR Museum experience

8 Conclusions

The obtained results show a good potential of the methodology adopted and of the pilot implementation sketched out and used in this study.

The VR museum constitutes a good alternative of showing images of paintings in a sort a virtual 3D slideshow. However better results in terms of engagement could be obtained by presenting the environment in a fully immersive setup such as an HMD or a CAVE, while in this first pilot tests users were using a desktop environment.

Particularly promising seems the use of an AR paradigm as it has aroused great curiosity and proved to be extremely engaging, with the users amazed to transform the environment they actually are inside in an on-demand digital gallery.

A possible improvement will be the implementation of a vocal interface to perform queries or some actions within the museum, in order to increase immersion. An interesting feature in the augmented reality application would be the use of a markerless implementation, in order to avoid a preliminary instrumentation of the physical space hosting the experience.

Acknowledgments. This paper is supported by European Union's Horizon 2020 research and innovation programme under grant agreement No 692103, project eHERITAGE (Expanding the Research and Innovation Capacity in Cultural Heritage Virtual Reality Applications).

References

1. https://www.vi-mm.eu/2018/01/10/the-vimm-definition-of-a-virtual-museum/
2. Bocchi, F.: The city in four dimensions: the Nu.M.E Project. JDIM **2**(4), 161–163 (2004)
3. Ponti, F.D., Guidazzoli, A., Liguori, M.C.: Virtual domestic environments and historical narration: a methodological hypothesis. In: EVA 2009 Florence, Conference Proceedings (2009)
4. Loscos, C., et al.: The museum of pure form: touching real statues in an immersive virtual museum. In: VAST, pp. 271–279, December 2004
5. Wojciechowski, R., Walczak, K., White, M., Cellary, W.: Building virtual and augmented reality museum exhibitions. In: Proceedings of the Ninth International Conference on 3D Web Technology, pp. 135–144. ACM, April 2004
6. Carrozzino, M., Bergamasco, M.: Beyond virtual museums: experiencing immersive virtual reality in real museums. J. Cult. Heritage **11**(4), 452–458 (2010)
7. Kiourt, C., Koutsoudis, A., Pavlidis, G.: DynaMus: a fully dynamic 3D virtual museum framework. J. Cult. Heritage **22**, 984–991 (2016)
8. Tecchia, F., et al.: A flexible framework for wide-spectrum VR development. Presence Teleop. Virt. Environments **19**(4), 302–312 (2010)

Digital Data, Virtual Tours, and 3D Models Integration Using an Open-Source Platform

Nicola Maiellaro(✉), Antonietta Varasano, and Salvatore Capotorto

Construction Technologies Institute, National Research Council of Italy, via Lembo 38/B, 70124 Bari, Italy
{maiellaro, varasano, capotorto}@itc.cnr.it

Abstract. The site of the 'Balsignano village' in Modugno (Italy), for some years has been the object of attention by scholars. Recently renovated, its valuation is nowadays the main objective for that Municipality. The aim of this article is describing our approach in integrating digital data, virtual tours and 3d models of the village elements to produce an interactive tool available on the internet, stimulating the desire to physically visit the settings. Our findings can be generalized to any context in which a link between a website and a physical site represent a challenge for low-budgeted Administrations.

Keywords: Virtual tour · Omni-directional cameras · 3D models
Multi-camera systems · Joomla

1 Introduction

The spatial documentation of cultural heritage sites using conventional surveying methods based on laser scanning and photogrammetry has been well established for conservation and restoration—see, for example, the summary of metric survey techniques for heritage documentation in [1]. Digital technologies have increased speed and completeness in that kind of survey, offering new opportunities to collect, analyzing and disseminate information [2], according to a project's scope timeline and budget constraints. However, due to the high costs of laser scanners, two approaches have been suggested for an intermediate documentation typology: the use of Virtual tours combined to Information Modelling [3] and the extraction of 3D structure from images captured from multiple viewpoints, utilizing different type of camera [4]. Moreover, the main focus of recent research is the visual, geometric, and textural characteristics of a single monument, while integration with other monuments and additional information —such as historical overview, detailed description, and location—are missing [5]. For example, a study on an exhaustive sample of 148 archaeology websites [6] shows that the 80% provides contextual information, 50% share data textually, using simple html pages or link to PDF document and only one website has virtual data in the form of an interactive map with data and image visualized in a callout [7]. In this article, we illustrate digital data, virtual tours and 3d models for representing selected objects located in 'Balsignano Village', integrated in a website with an intuitive interface (Fig. 1).

M. Duguleană et al. (Eds.): VRTCH 2018, CCIS 904, pp. 148–164, 2019.
https://doi.org/10.1007/978-3-030-05819-7_12

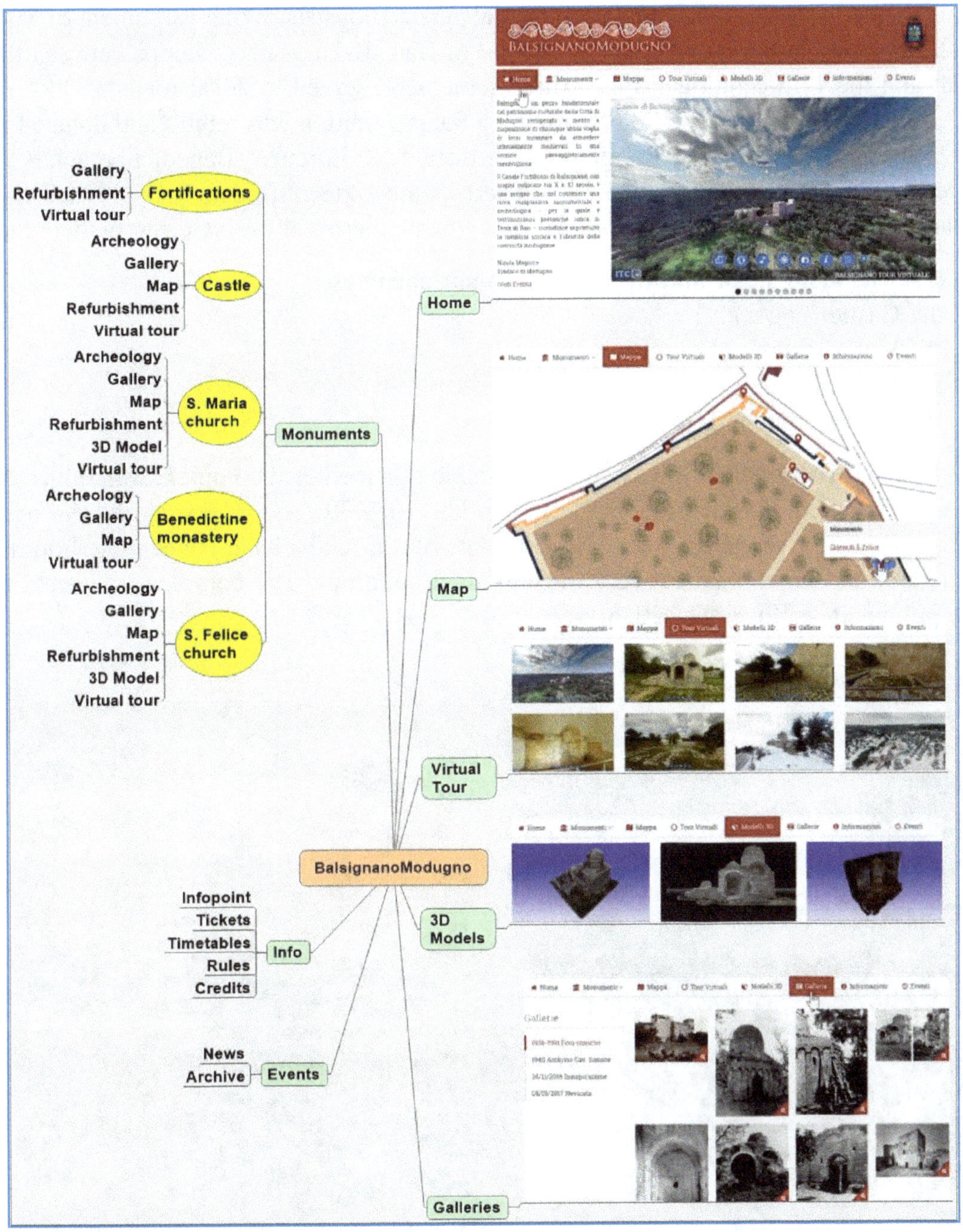

Fig. 1. The logical scheme of the website [8]: menu items (green background), Point of Interest (yellow background), and their contents (transparent background). (Color figure online)

2 The Case Study

The village, which is near a branch of the 'Via Traiana', owes much of its charm to the suggestive position in a context that has still preserved the natural appearance of the Apulian agricultural landscape, characterized by 'trulli', rock settlements, dry stone walls, areas for grapes pressing, natural ice storages.

The first historical documentation on Balsignano consists of one parchment of May 962, preserved at the Basilica of 'S. Nicola' of Bari. Balsignano develops between the 10th and the 11th centuries as a fortified settlement, served by local roads.

Destroyed a first time in 988 following a Saracen raid, it was rebuilt and donated in 1092 by the Duke Norman Ruggero to the distant 'S. Lorenzo' Benedictine abbey of Aversa. Finally, Balsignano was devastated in the sixteenth century by French and Spanish troops who contended for hegemony in southern Italy [9]. Currently there are:

- a substantial part of Fortifications, with slit openings;
- the Castle (Fig. 2);
- 'S. Maria' church (14th century);
- the Benedictine monastery;
- 'S. Felice' church (11th century).

In 1981, Balsignano, as exceptional example of a medieval complex, was subjected to the protection provided for by the Italian law 1089/39. The works carried out over the last twenty-five years, due to the constant lack of funds, have concentrated on the structural and functional recovery of individual buildings. The complex is opened to the public since November 2016.

Fig. 2. Virtual tour of the Castle – external side.

3 The Website Contents

The objectives pursued in the design and implementation of the website are:

- allowing users to explore the contents of the archive through the integration of this material into virtual tours and 3D models

- enhancing the sense of cultural presence, which can help to achieve the cultural aims of the project;
- ensuring accessibility and wider dissemination of the project.

In the following, we will describe the three main stages characterizing the development of any application [10]:

- documentation (gathering of information);
- representation (technical aspects of the digitization);
- dissemination (technical aspect about information and knowledge presentation).

3.1 Documentation

The primary source of documentation for the project were books [11, 12] and the photo and graph archives ('Galleries' in Fig. 1) of the Archaeological Superintendence of Puglia Region, the Architectural and Landscape Heritage Superintendence for Bari, BAT and Foggia, and the 'Simone' section [13] in the Picture Gallery 'Corrado Giaquinto' in Bari. Other valuable information was found on the Internet [9].

This significant amount of documents was selected to establish accurate references between sources and descriptions available in the representation output.

3.2 Representation

One of the factors considered in our work was to offer a visual feedback, improving the sense of presence. Thus, we followed two approaches, both image based, to produce virtual tours and 3d models.

Virtual Tours. Computer-generated representation of the real world are modeled through the personal perception of reality and are time-consuming using traditional Virtual Reality techniques. On the contrary, virtual tours are unbroken view of a whole scene surrounding an observer, giving a sense of presence [14].

The most common systems include a network of predefined viewing locations linked together to create various path.

They use a sphere projection in 'equirectangular' image having 2:1 width-high ratio, called 360-degree panorama.

There are many systems for acquisition of image suitable for building panoramas [15]. The most common systems include rotational single camera system: the panorama is created by stitching together several images (partially overlapping with each other for alignment purposes) taken by a rotating camera placed in an arbitrary viewpoint.

To hold up image quality at zooming, it is required to produce a high-resolution panorama, obtainable stitching images acquired through a telephoto lens equipped camera mounted on a rotating motorized mechanism.

The disadvantage of this concept is the long acquisition time and the need to edit images to equalize different exposures—especially outdoor—and delete moving objects, as walking people or moving cars.

To overcome these problems, we tested a multi-camera system made by assembling six fixed cameras in a prearranged angles pack specifically designed to capture the

360-degree scene (Fig. 3, left), encountering some problems with their assembling and synchronization; moreover it has a high cost to provide high-quality imagery.

Fig. 3. 360-degree systems: Commercial six camera spherical array specifically designed (left—source: Aerial Technology International, Oregon City, United States); Ricoh Teta Plus mounted on a telescopic rod in carbon fiber, with a cylindrical, low-radius, heavy base specifically designed to reduce its footprint (right).

An ultimate test was made using omni-directional cameras, having two back-to-back sensors and fish-eye lenses: Nikon Key Mission and Ricoh Teta Plus (Fig. 3, right), producing respectively 7744 × 3872 and 5376 × 2688 pixel panoramas.

Although the Nikon camera is newer, the quality of the panorama produced by the stitching firmware is lower than that of the Ricoh camera (Fig. 4).

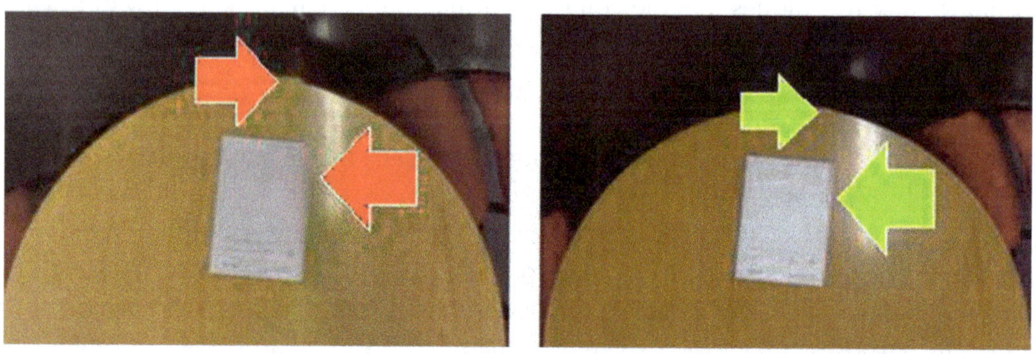

Fig. 4. Detail of panorama in the stitched area—laboratory test using two compact camera having two back-to-back sensors and fish-eye lenses. The results are poor for Nikon Key Mission camera (left) and good for the Ricoh Teta Plus camera (right)

We used the second one to shoot external panoramas instantly as that during a snowfall (Fig. 5), linked to a panorama produced using several shots from a camera mounted on a drone, to produce a virtual tour (Fig. 6).

Fig. 5. Panorama—firmware stitched—by Ricoh Teta Plus, during a snowfall.

Fig. 6. Virtual tour during a snowfall, based on two panoramas linked through hotspots in the floorplan or clicking on the 'drone' button: terrestrial view (left) based on panorama in Fig. 5; aerial view by drone (right).

Finally, we utilized for indoor panoramas a wide-angle lens equipped camera—mounted on a panoramic head—producing medium-resolution panoramas (10.000 × 5.000 pixel).

Panoramas are displayed on an interactive viewer, allowing their rotation, tilt, and zoom; most of them are just rotating images without further functionalities.

In the simplest application scenario, several individual panoramas are linked to each other using navigational hotspots to enter and exit scenes: when it is clicked in the panorama, the viewer is brought to the next panorama of the virtual tour.

To this end, we are now using AutoGarrow, a plug-in that allows the virtual tour navigation using the GPS coordinates of the camera generating panoramas.

To improve the significance of the virtual tour, the panoramas developed have been enhanced using the Kolor Panotour Pro software, embedding—among others—hotspots to access different types of digital media (Fig. 7) as well as functional keys (blue circle with icon and white perimeter to stand out on dark backgrounds) to open:

- the floorplan with the location of the user and navigational hotspot;
- a google map with navigational hotspot of the whole project;
- a window with project info;
- a window with an image gallery.

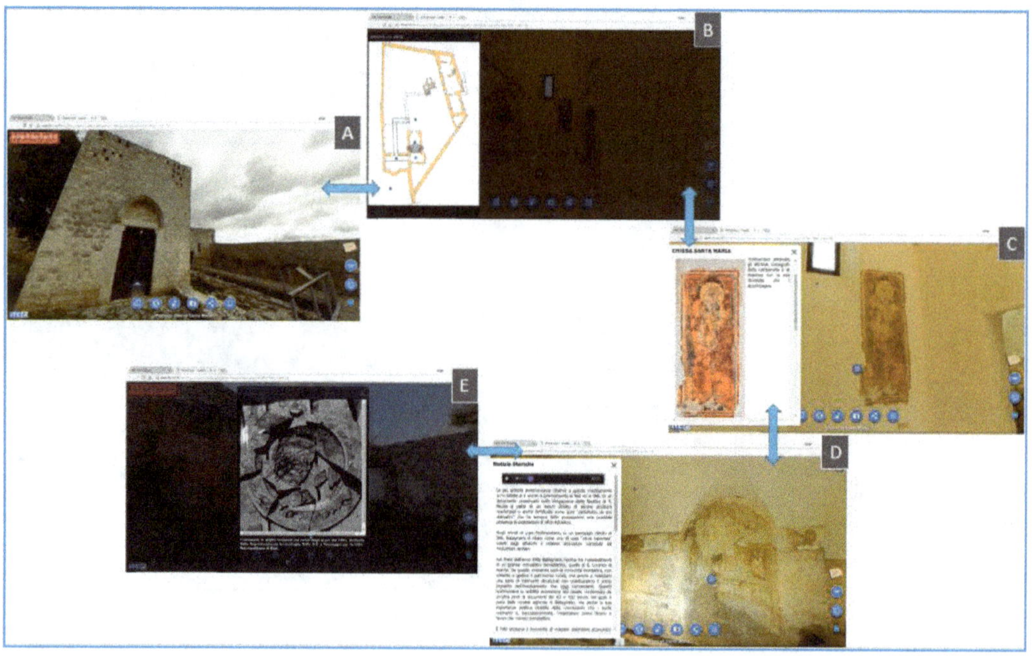

Fig. 7. Virtual tour of 'S. Maria' church organized into five linked panoramas: A. Main Entrance; B. Front nave (window on left: floorplan with hotspot); C. Back nave (window on left: info about the fresco); D. Lateral room (window on left: general historical info—text and sound); E. Rear outside view (window on center: historical image gallery).

3D Models. To navigate the virtual tour, the user can move between predefined viewing locations, which are linked together to create various paths as we have seen. To overcome this limited freedom of movements within the environment, 3D models of some buildings have been developed.

Many costly technologies, such as 3D scanning methods, are available for 3D digitization of cultural heritage artifact [16]. However, depending on the goal of the modeling, low-cost solutions hardware and software have been developed.

Fig. 8. The 3D model was obtained using SfM software by means of images by a camera mounted on an unmanned aerial vehicle (left) and by a multi-camera system ad hoc-developed (right).

The innovative 3D modeling procedure presented here was used to build the two churches model using a 'structure from motion' (SfM) software by means of images taken by the following cameras:

- Zenmuse X3 (CMOS sensor 12.4Mp; f/2.8; FOV 20 mm) integrated on an unmanned aerial vehicle 'Inspire 1' (Fig. 8, left) for the survey of remote objects (e.g., vaults and capitals) where physical access is delicate or impossible according [17];
- GoPro Hero3 + Black Edition (CMOS sensor 12Mp; f/2.8; FOV Ultrawide 17.2 mm, medium 21.9 mm, narrow 34.4 mm) mounted on a multi-camera system ad hoc-developed (Fig. 8, right) operated from the ground, to cover the entire targeted object.

The Multi-camera System. In this work, six camera were used, arranged on a carbon fiber rod in different height positions. The procedure provides for establishing a path along which to position the system every meter, so assuring a superimposition of 50%, acquiring synchronized images by each camera using a remote control.

To simplify the post-processing, the images acquired at each station point will be renamed according to whether it is an architectural survey around a monument (so-called 'convergent axis'), or a survey of a single facade (so-called 'parallel axis').

In the first case, the last photo of the first station must be followed by the first photo of the second station and so on forming a spiral path (Fig. 9, left).

In the second case, the last photo of the first station must be followed by the last photo of the second station and, proceeding backwards, resume again with the first photo of the next station, forming a serpentine path (Fig. 9, right).

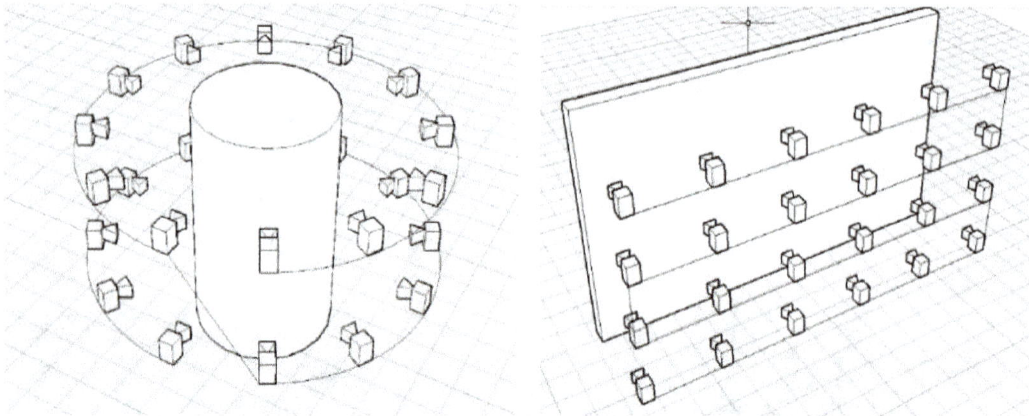

Fig. 9. Survey scheme with convergent axis (left), and parallel axis (right).

It should be emphasized that the sensor of the GoPro camera does not reflect the image quality standard required for a successful alignment process. This low quality is determined by the fisheye lens having a focal distance of 2.8 mm (equivalent in the camera reflex version to a 15.0 mm and therefore to a shooting range of 170°), installed on these cameras to shoot especially sports actions.

This wide-angle lens, despite having an excellent depth of field, has strong aberrations in the peripheral parts, prejudicing the process of recognizing homologous points. To reduce this problem, the frame of each camera is settled, through an internal menu, to the 'medium' value, so recording only the central part of the shot having reduced distortions. This operation, called 'cropping', reduces the final resolution to 7 Mp.

It should also be noted that the sensor on board these cameras belong to the range of economic sensors since each pixel has a size of just over 1.5 μ, far from the minimum 3 μ recommended for obtaining a good image. It is true that remaining below this threshold, due to the increase in electronic circuitry and the amplification of the signal applied to each pixel; as a result, a background noise disturbing the image quality is generated. For this reason, it is necessary to determine in advance the Ground Sample Distance (GSD) value corresponding to how much real surface is captured in each pixel.

GSD = pixel size × average shooting distance/focal length = 1.7 mm, where:

- the pixel size: 0.00154 mm (sensor width divided by the number of sensor pixels: 6.16 mm/4000);
- the lens focal length: 2.77 mm
- the average shooting distance: 3000 mm

The GSD value obtained at an average distance of 3 meters, even if acceptable, was slightly higher than the recommended value, which should usually not exceed 1.5 mm.

A solution to reduce the GSD value is to reduce the shooting distance, even if this involves a greater number of shots to preserve the overlap of 50% of the frames.

We made also a laser scanner survey to compare output and procedures, following the method already used [18]: the multi-camera is cheaper, requests basic skills and a reduced survey time; unfortunately processing time is very high using standard

Table 1. Scanner laser vs Multi-camera system

	Scanner laser	Multi-camera system
Equipment cost (Euro)	110,000	3,000
Total equipment weight (Kg)	60	2
Parts to be assembled	7	0
Acquisition process difficulty	Moderate	Low
Stations performed	25	250
Preparation times for each shot (minutes)	15	0
Acquisition time for each shot (minutes)	10	0.2
Total acquisition time (hours)	10	1.5
Shot hight (meter)	Up to 1.5	Up to 10
Data (GB)	34	9
Data management time (hours)	0	2
Processing time (days)	1	15
Software cost (euro)	10,000	3,000

workstation; on the other hand, using a laser scanner only at ground level, gross errors occur for covers and recessed area (Table 1).

The 3D model produced appears as a faithful reproduction of the scene respect to the laser scan cloud of colored dots (supplementary image acquisition and software are needed to transform it into a mesh).

To post-process the images, two SfM 3D reconstruction software were used: Photoscan Agisoft and Zephyr 3DFlow. In both software, while performing the self-calibration of the frames, their alignment did not give acceptable results.

Then we proceeded to calibrate the optics of the cameras using an application supplied with Photoscan (Agisoft Lens) that, by performing a thorough analysis on several shots to a grid pattern, generates a calibration file to be applied before alignment.

The 3D model obtained was then exported in 3DHop software, to be displayed in real-time and manipulated interactively (Fig. 10).

3.3 Dissemination

The goal was to find out how to develop an application accessible and able to combine all different types of data and output produced.

The dissemination tool is a multiplatform web site—described in the next paragraph—where users are interact with virtual tours and 3D models, with the support of text and sounds. Regardless of the order in which rooms are accessed, visitors are free to move around each environment, navigate the space and interact with it according to their own interests.

"You can't replicate that in VR, but you can give people a preview and understanding of what they would experience if they went to visit physically" says Abi Mandelbaum [19], CEO and co-founder of YouVisit (http://www.youvisit.com/), an organization that specializes in VR tours and works with more than 800 clients to drive

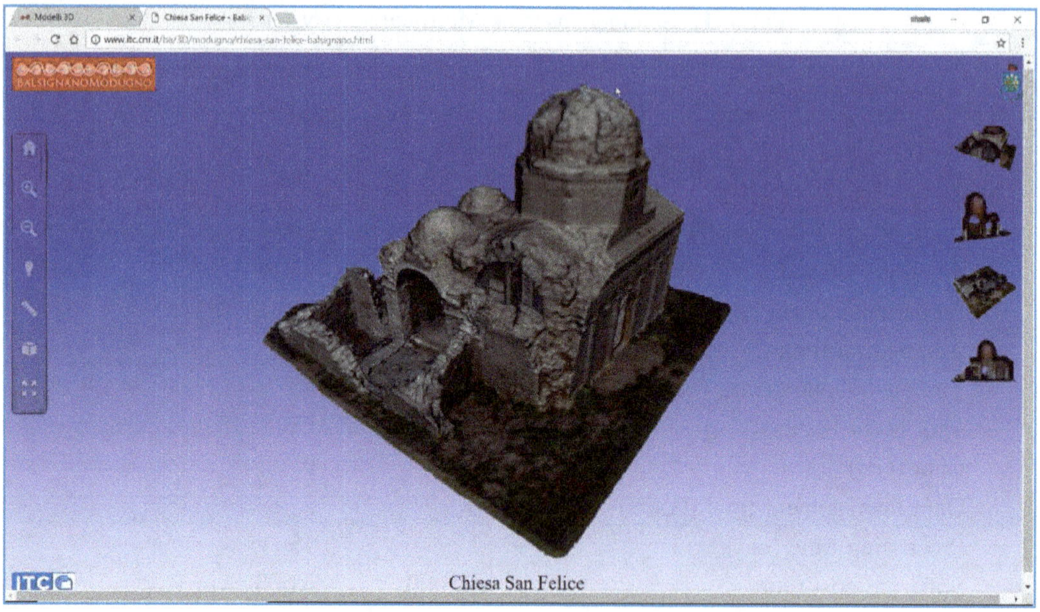

Fig. 10. 3D model displayed in real-time and manipulated interactively (3DHop software).

business results and engage consumers with interactive 360° experiences. The University of Massachusetts Amherst published a study on the effects the VR has on people and travel destinations. The research showed that "VR generates pleasant emotions towards the destination even though it's a new form of advertisement" and VR heightens the sense of presence by determining people's interest, since they can engage much more than they could just by reading a simple tour guide; pointing out that people were more likely to share their VR experience on social media and talk to their friends about it [20, 21].

4 The Web Site Implementation

'When designing a web site layout there are some common mistakes that often appear' [22, 23]. These mistakes cover not only design aspects but also general workflow tips that will get the job done nicely. We have supported the Municipality from concept through to post-implementation support of the web site; our goal was to not only provide a web solution but also to define features concretely, determine technology integration specifics, and prioritize anticipated future uses of the website to ensure that the system design is a scalable one.

The development process started with initial phase, 'ideation' [24]. During this phase, we worked with the Municipality to define the requirements for specific site functionality such as Virtual tours, 3D model, news, videos, social bookmarking, search, mobile device accessibility, and other such features. Designing a good website that combined strategic thinking and emerging technologies was a tricky balancing act to pull off.

In this step, the team needed to work with all stakeholders to gather as much information as possible about how they believed the web- site should be function. At first, the Municipality did not have a web hosting service that allowed us to make initial website accessible via Internet and seen by anyone in real-time, by facilitating cooperation between stakeholders. In this regard, we decided to adopt a platform to build the website (site builder) and make it accessible via Internet by authorized users.

On the wide spectrum of website building solutions, Wix was the right choice and it has allowed us to build an initial model of the website. This platform is beginner-friendly, has sleek designs, and boasts the easy drag and drop feature. Wix has become incredibly successful and has attracted over 103 million users to date; it has an extensive theme collection and many customization tools. Wix, with its users pre-designed theme (more than 500) [25], has allowed us to give an idea on how to arrange website content and to share the web-solution with the Municipality.

At a later stage, the aim was to have a clear understanding of what the layout needs would be when designing sections beyond the homepage. Identifying the goals for the website, the functionality needed and the skills and resources to manage it helped us determine the right kind of web design for needs. The cost associated with managed services of a web site (to make functional changes, structural/layout changes, design changes, content changes, monitoring, and backups) is hard for Public Administration to estimate, plan and maintain. In addition, if we add that, in the Italian public administration, it is very difficult to find someone with experience in software development or website building [26]. The cost associated rises: 'According to the DESI (Digital Economy and Society Index) in 2016 in Italy 48% of the workforce has insufficient digital skills (EU average 37%) on the basis of a 21% that has no digital competence and has never used the Internet (EU average 37%)' [27].

The web-design step goes through those problems that cannot be resolved through simply solution but rather through a good layout, a clear hierarchy and a content easily navigable. The first thing to do is to come up with a top-level framework that solves all the design problems. This framework is the User Interface (UI) that surrounds the content and helps the user perform actions and navigate through it. UI includes the navigation and components like sidebars and bottom bars.

Our goal was to build a site that could work not only in the ideal scenario, but also in the worst-case scenario. For instance, a user could be using a small screen and check the site when there is barely any content on it so it looks broken. In this phase, we have focused on the need to emphasize usability, but also provide an attractive web presence for the Municipality. 'Current best practices call for spending about 10% of a design project's budget on usability' [28].

In many contexts, such as the tourist domain, creating a website version for each resolution and new device would be impossible or at least impractical. After gathering, these needs we have chosen a Content Management System (CMS) platform, a web site authoring and administration tools that could provide a reliable, secure, and cost-effective content management solution to work more wisely and efficiently.

Therefore, even if Wix is designed and built specifically so it is easy for non-developers to use with ease, it is not an open source platform so its codes are not available to modify and may be some indirect costs involved, such as paying for external support. Today, free open source platforms to build a website are:

- Joomla, the biggest CMS platform, mostly used;
- Drupal, a great CMS;
- WordPress, the perfect choice for small content oriented websites.

One of the main advantages of CMS is that it enables non-technically minded users to create functional pages or upload and modify content themselves, without having to outsource the work to a webmaster, or understand programming languages such as HTML5 or PHP.

The team has developed the final website using Joomla, a flexible, reliable, mobile-ready and user-friendly platform.

Unlike WordPress, which is mainly a blogging and small website platform, and unlike Drupal which is meant mostly for big websites. In the field of web design and development, we are quickly getting to the point of being unable to keep up with the endless new resolutions and devices.

To make the most of the Joomla benefits, we have defined according to [29]:

- Technical requirements of website;
- Workflows, processes and procedures to creating, publishing and managing digital content of website;
- Who should have access to the CMS, and at what level.

During the templating, programming and customization phases, we have adapted the base technologies selected in the design phase; we have merged the graphical design with the functionality by creating a graceful template, including the custom programming (modules or components) with the chosen Joomla template.

In addition, we have implemented the 'JA Image Hotspot' module [30], allowing to integrate into the website a responsive map (Fig. 11). It is a flexible extension used for page rendering to obtain an interactive map from a static image, filling in information for a specific area and adding markers with title and description. The module resizes the web map automatically based on the width of the user's browser window, preventing the pixel references within the image map from pushing some hotspots off of the screen.

The software solution consists of a mix of flexible grids and layouts, images and an intelligent use of CSS media queries. As the user switches from their laptop to iPad, the website automatically switches to accommodate for resolution, image size and scripting abilities.

This advanced solution eliminates the need for a different design and development phase for each user device. In this regard, we have integrated a 'Responsive Joomla Template' into the website.

With Responsive Templates the necessity to swipe around to find hidden sidebars, zooming in and out to make the text comfortable enough to read simply falls off: it fit all possible devices that have an access to the web. After all, the look and feel of mobile version reflects the original website.

Fig. 11. The responsive web map in the website. The user can choose to display a tooltip (popover) when he clicks on the hotspot's position.

5 Conclusions

In our work, we developed an application that allows users to navigate the virtual representations and access the cultural resources in a dynamic way, according to their preferences and interests, thus experiencing 'Balsignano village' in an entertaining manner.

The application of digital techniques for the recording and visualizing the site of the 'Balsignano village' demonstrated how these tools can provide relevant and accurate information regarding the site's conservation as well as a posterity record in case of damage or further deterioration.

The proposed approach—interactive virtual tour and 3D models generated by images and as a whole constitutes an economic and practical alternative to the 3D scanner technology. Such integrated information can be beneficial both for accurate documentation and tourism.

It could be interesting to evaluate to what extent such an application can affect people's perceptions about 'Balsignano Village' and influence the will of actually visiting the place. Result of this evaluation could be useful to understand the power of virtual tours and 3d models on current tourism.

We have started to test 3D scenes reconstruction workflow using omni-directional camera Ricoh Teta Plus: it dramatically improves the performance of SfM software since the tracked interest points will not miss with a long base-line and sharp rotation [31].

Acknowledgments. This research was supported by the Municipality of Modugno (Italy) within the project 'Mu.S.A. – Must See Advisor'. We thank our colleagues from ITC-CNR who provided survey and outputs: Milella, N., Zonno, M., Battista, V., and Leandro, V.

Author Contributions. Maiellaro, N.: website project, testing, and 360 degree camera trials (Sects. 1, 2, 3); Varasano, A.: system architecture, and software development (Sect. 4); Capotorto, S.: 3D models (in Sect. 3).

References

1. Letellier, R.: Recording, documentation, and information management for the conservation of heritage places: guiding principles. J. Paul Getty Trust, Los Angeles (2007). https://www.getty.edu/conservation/publications_resources/pdf_publications/pdf/guiding_principles.pdf. Accessed 4 Apr 2018
2. Percy, K., Ward, S., Santana Quintero, M., Morrison, T.: Integrated digital technologies for the architectural rehabilitation & conservation of Beinn Bhreagh Hall & Surrounding Site, Nova Scotia, Canada. In: ISPRS Annals of the Photogrammetry, Remote Sensing and Spatial Information Sciences, vol. II-5/W3, pp. 235–241 (2015). https://www.isprs-ann-photogramm-remote-sens-spatial-inf-sci.net/II-5-W3/235/2015/isprsannals-II-5-W3-235-2015.pdf. Accessed 4 Apr 2018
3. Napolitano, R.K., Scherer, G., Glisic, B.: Virtual tours and informational modeling for conservation of cultural heritage sites. J. Cult. Herit. **29** (2017)
4. Bastanlar, Y., Grammalidis, N., Zabulis, X., Yilmaz, E., Yardimci, Y., Triantafyllidis, G.: 3D reconstruction for a cultural heritage virtual tour system. In: The International Archives of the Photogrammetry, Remote Sensing and Spatial Information Sciences, Beijing, vol. XXXVII, part B5, pp. 1023–1028 (2008). http://www.isprs.org/proceedings/XXXVII/congress/5_pdf/177.pdf. Accessed 4 Apr 2018
5. Koeva, M., Luleva, M., Maldjanski, P.: Integrating spherical panoramas and maps for visualization of cultural heritage objects using virtual reality technology. Sensors **17**, 829 (2017). http://www.mdpi.com/1424-8220/17/4/829/pdf. Accessed 4 Apr 2018
6. Freeman, M.A.: Not for casual readers: an evaluation of digital data from virginia archaeological websites. Master's thesis, University of Tennessee (2015). http://trace.tennessee.edu/cgi/viewcontent.cgi?article=4785&context=utk_gradthes
7. The Colonial Williamsburg Foundation, eWilliamsburg. http://research.history.org/ewilliamsburg/map.cfmTravel and Tourism Competitiveness Report (2015). http://www3.weforum.org/docs/TT15/WEF_Global_Travel&Tourism_Report_2015.pdf
8. Maiellaro, N., Varasano, A.: BalsignanoModugno (2017). http://www.casaledibalsignano.it. Accessed 4 Apr 2018
9. Macina, R.: Balsignano - dal degrado al recupero. Edizioni Nuovi Orientamenti (2012). http://www.pugliadigitallibrary.it/media/00/00/74/957.pdf. Accessed 4 Apr 2018
10. Addison, A.C.: Emerging trends in virtual heritage. IEEE Multimed. **7**, 22–25 (2000)

11. Balsignano, un insediamento rurale fortificato - Guida alla visita. Caggianelli, R. (ed.) Mario Adda Editore (2015)
12. Balsignano, un insediamento rurale fortificato - Archeologia, studi e restauri. Depalo, M.R., Pellegrino, E., Triggiani, M. (eds.) Mario Adda Editore (2015)
13. Fondo Simone. http://www.pinacotecabari.it/index.php/patrimonio-museale/patrimonio-fotografico/fondo-simone. Accessed 4 Apr 2018
14. Eiris, R., Moud, H.I., Gheisari, M.: Using 360-degree interactive panoramas to develop virtual representations of construction sites. In: LC3 2017: Volume I – Proceedings of the Joint Conference on Computing in Construction (JC3), 4–7 July 2017, Heraklion, Greece, pp. 775–782 (2017)
15. Popovic, V., Seyid, K., Cogal, Ö., Akin, A., Leblebici, Y.: Design and Implementation of Real-Time Multi-Sensor Vision Systems. Springer, Cham (2017). https://doi.org/10.1007/978-3-319-59057-8
16. Santos, P., et al.: CultLab3D—on the verge of 3D mass digitization. In: Proceedings of the Eurographics Workshop on Graphics and Cultural Heritage, The Eurographics Association, Aire-la-Ville, Switzerland, 6–8 October 2014, pp. 65–74 (2014)
17. Louiset, T., Pamart, A., Gattet, E., Raharijaona, T., De Luca, L., Ruffier, F.: A shape-adjusted tridimensional reconstruction of cultural heritage artifacts using a miniature quadrotor. Remote Sens. **8**, 858 (2016)
18. Maiellaro, N., Zonno, M., Lavalle, P.: Laser scanner and camera-equipped UAV architectural surveys. In: The International Archives of the Photogrammetry, Remote Sensing and Spatial Information Sciences, Volume XL-5/W4, 2015 3D Virtual Reconstruction and Visualization of Complex Architectures, 25–27 February 2015, Avila, Spain, pp. 381–386 (2015)
19. Mandelbaum, A.: Immersive Technology Expert. Co-Founder & CEO of YouVisit. https://www.linkedin.com/in/abimandelbaum. Accessed 13 May 2018
20. Griffin, T., Giberson, J., Lee, S.H.M., Guttentag, D., Kandaurova, M.: Virtual reality and implications for destination marketing. In: TTRA International Conference (2017). https://scholarworks.umass.edu/cgi/viewcontent.cgi?referer=&httpsredir=1&article=2103&context=ttra. Accessed 13 May 2018
21. Tussyadiah, L., Wang, D., Jia, C.H.: Exploring the persuasive power of virtual reality imagery for destination marketing. In: TTRA International Conference (2016). https://scholarworks.umass.edu/cgi/viewcontent.cgi?referer=&httpsredir=1&article=1180&context=ttra. Accessed 13 May 2018
22. Guglieri, C.: 23 steps to the perfect website layout (2017). https://www.creativebloq.com/web-design/steps-perfect-website-layout-812625. Accessed 4 Apr 2018
23. Spolan, S.: Common website design problems (2016). https://www.zivtech.com/blog/8-common-website-design-problems. Accessed 4 Apr 2018
24. Dam, R., Teo, S.: What is ideation – and how to prepare for ideation sessions (2018). https://www.interaction-design.org/literature/article/what-is-ideation-and-how-to-prepare-for-ideation-sessions. Accessed 4 Apr 2018
25. Wix Review 2017 – The Main Pros & Cons. Wix advantages and disadvantages (2017). http://www.wittythemes.com/wix-review. Accessed 4 Apr 2018
26. Rapari, G.: Una PA senza competenze digitali, Assintel: 'Prenda esempio dalle aziende' (2017). https://www.agendadigitale.eu/cultura-digitale/una-pa-senza-competenze-digitali-assintel-prenda-esempio-dalle-aziende. Accessed 4 Apr 2018
27. Carlizzi, D.N., Quattrone, A., D'Errigo, F.: Sblocco del turn-over: occasione per introdurre futuro nelle PA (2017). https://www.agendadigitale.eu/cultura-digitale/una-pa-senza-competenze-digitali-assintel-prenda-esempio-dalle-aziende. Accessed 4 Apr 2018

28. Nielsen, J.: Usability 101: Introduction to Usability (2012). https://www.nngroup.com/articles/usability-101-introduction-to-usability. Accessed 4 Apr 2018
29. Content management systems - Advantages of using a content management system. https://www.nibusinessinfo.co.uk/content/advantages-using-content-management-system. Accessed 4 Apr 2018
30. JA Image Hotspot (2018). https://www.joomlart.com/joomla/extensions/ja-image-hotspot-module. Accessed 4 Apr 2018
31. Song, M., Watanabe, H., Hara, J.: Robust 3D reconstruction with omni-directional camera based on structure from motion. In: Proceedings of the International Workshop on Advanced Image Technology 2018, 7–9 January 2018, Chiang Mai, Thailand (2018). http://www.iwait2018.org/Paper%20IWAIT2018/IWAIT2018_paper_105.pdf. Accessed 4 Apr 2018

Appropriate Control Methods for Mobile Virtual Exhibitions

Yue Li[1(✉)], Paul Tennent[2], and Sue Cobb[3]

[1] International Doctoral Innovation Centre, University of Nottingham Ningbo China, Ningbo, China
yueli@nottingham.edu.cn

[2] Mixed Reality Lab, School of Computer Science, University of Nottingham, Nottingham, UK
paul.tennent@nottingham.ac.uk

[3] Human Factors Research Group, Faculty of Engineering, University of Nottingham, Nottingham, UK
sue.cobb@nottingham.ac.uk

Abstract. It is becoming popular to render art exhibitions in Virtual Reality (VR). Many of these are used to deliver at-home experiences on peoples' own mobile devices, however, control options on mobile VR systems are necessarily less flexible than those of situated VR fixtures. In this paper, we present a study that explores aspects of control in such VR exhibitions - specifically comparing 'on rails' movement with 'free' movement. We also expand the concept of museum audio guides to better suit the VR medium, exploring the possibility of embodied character-guides. We compare these controllable guides with a more traditional audio-guide. The study uses interviews to explore users' experience qualitatively, as well as questionnaires addressing both user experience and simulator sickness. The results suggest that users generally prefer to have control over both their movement and the guide, however, if relinquishing movement control, they prefer the uncontrolled guide. The paper presents three key findings: (1) users prefer to be able to directly control their movement; (2) this does not make a notable difference to simulator sickness; (3) embodied guides are potentially a good way to deliver additional information in VR exhibition settings.

Keywords: Virtual Reality · Virtual exhibitions · Guide systems Mobile control

1 Introduction

The term 'Virtual Reality' (VR) was coined by Jaron Lanier in the late 1980s, defined as a three-dimensional, computer-generated environment, in which people can immerse, explore and interact [32]. Emphasising users' dynamic control of viewpoint, Brooks defines a VR experience as "any in which the user is effectively immersed in a responsive virtual world" [2]. VR has recently gained widespread

M. Duguleană et al. (Eds.): VRTCH 2018, CCIS 904, pp. 165–183, 2019.
https://doi.org/10.1007/978-3-030-05819-7_13

attention for research and applications with affordable headsets, such as the Oculus Rift and the HTC Vive. Both are tethered to high-end PCs with cables, with a wide 110-degree field of view and high-resolution displays. At the same time, several mobile VR devices have been well-received. Two typical examples are the Samsung Gear VR and the Google Cardboard. These are wireless, lightweight and low-cost options, but are essentially cases with lens arrangements for mobile phones. Therefore they suffer from two key challenges: first, the refresh rates and resolutions are restricted by the mobile phone platforms on which they are delivered - and while we can assume this issue will go away as the technology miniaturises, the second issue is more likely to persist: limited options are available to control the device. While equipment like the Gear or the Google Daydream offers handheld controls, the same does not apply to systems like Google Cardboard. As the cheapest and most available form of VR, it is worth considering how we might interact with and control experiences in this limited context.

Meanwhile, museum and cultural heritage exhibitions are shifting from being collection-based and communicating history with labels, to activity-oriented, engaging visitors to offer captivating experiences [12]. They are exploring the use of digital technology to attract visitors and to provide interactive experiences which are otherwise impossible with conventional museum technologies. Museums such as the Natural History Museum in London and the Acropolis Museum in Athens [16] are adopting VR technologies to create virtual exhibition experiences and apply AR technologies to develop augmented guide systems. In addition, Brown introduced a mixed reality system that enables a collaboration between onsite and online visitors [3]. The use of VR in an exhibition context essentially comes in two forms: (1) situated experiences where the VR equipment is set up in the gallery and visitors use that equipment to explore a curated exhibition. (2) At home experiences - often delivered on mobile phones allowing a user to either 'visit' an existing exhibition remotely or recreate a historical environment.

As mobile phone-based VR becomes increasingly ubiquitous and familiar, the prevalence of such home VR exhibitions is only likely to increase. In the light of this, we suggest that it is necessary to understand the way in which the interaction in such experiences should be designed given the constraints of limited control. To begin to address this, we created a simple virtual exhibition of famous paintings and performed a user study to question users' preferences about two aspects: movement control and access to additional information. The User Experience Questionnaire (UEQ) [18] and the Simulator Sickness Questionnaire (SSQ) [17] were adopted in the user study and interviews were carried out to discuss their preferences. The key findings of our research are (1) users prefer to be able to directly control their movement; (2) this does not make a notable difference to simulator sickness; (3) embodied guides may be a good way to deliver additional information in VR exhibition settings.

2 Related Work

Museums and cultural heritage exhibitions have traditionally been based on physical collections, providing static labels to communicate history and the story behind them. However, they are adopting activity-oriented presentations to engage visitors and offer more captivating experiences [12]. The deployment of digital technologies in the cultural heritage sector has significantly increased in the last few years, promoting the diffusion of culture by developing creative narratives to support education and recreation [34].

Researchers have investigated and exploited the immersive, interactive and imaginative nature of VR [5] to disseminate and present arts and humanities [7,8,11,14,25]. This includes the emergence of 'Virtual Museums', of which there are two main types [4]: one is the replication of an existing museum, which allows remote access to its digitalised exhibits; the other is the reconstruction of a lost archaeological site and activities that enables users to navigate and observe virtual objects, such as the Rome Reborn project [10]. Thanks to the recent advances in rendering techniques, the immersive systems could provide high-fidelity visualisations and simulate a virtual construction that is both physically correct and perceptually equivalent [15].

When immersed in a virtual environment, users need some navigation capability to be able to move around and explore the environment, just like they could walk around in the real world. Aside from 'walking' in VR by specifying a direction of movement, users can also teleport in VR, which could help reduce motion sickness by eliminating visible translational motion [1]. However, as teleporting is only afforded in the digital world, it could make the experience less natural. Synchronising real-world movements to VR is also feasible with external tracking sensors. This feature is usually supported by desktop VR equipment, however, becomes less feasible with mobile phone-based VR. Additionally, such systems also depend on the availability of a significant open physical space, which may be impractical for at-home use.

Similarly to physical exhibitions, it needs to be considered in a virtual exhibition whether and how to direct and maintain users' attention towards different exhibits. For example, whether the experience should be made a guided tour or a free look-around. The visiting experience varies when different navigation techniques are adopted. Previous designs reflecting navigation concerns include providing visual cues in the virtual environment, such as landmarks to help the user to know their location within the 3D environment [31]; use of map menus allowing direct movement to the selected site of interest that the user wants to go to [4]; or allow users move around freely in the environment using keyboard and mouse [6]. In many real-world museum experiences, visitors would find it difficult to navigate around the site without guidance. It is common practice for visitors to be shown a recommended visiting route by a tour guide, a map or an audio guide system. Similarly, a virtual museum visiting could also be a guided experience and the system could take over the movement control and automatically show the users around. However, surrendering the control in VR could contribute to the cause of simulator sickness when a moving visual imagery drives a compelling sense of self motion [19]. In addition, studies have shown that simulator sickness symptoms were reported at higher levels of passive viewing compared to active control over movement in the virtual environment [27].

Most guide information in virtual museums was presented in the form of 2D text and audio clips. They either stayed there as part of the scene or could be triggered by a button. Chittaro et al. [6] presented an embodied guide that assisting users with exhibit information in a virtual museum tour. Although the guide was programmed to give a tour that encompass objects in a certain sequence, which restricted users' control over the information, it has been shown that an embodied guide could contribute in drawing user's attention by providing visual cues [26], and help bring users more motivation and engagement [22].

Virtual museums used to adopt different control techniques for movement and guide information, yet the effect of different control methods on user experience has not been well studied. In addition, while complex systems with high computation efficiency allow more control capabilities with joysticks and tracking sensors, there is less control available on mobile systems and low-cost equipment. The control on these devices is supported by the buttons or touchpads that are embedded on the headset. In this paper, we propose that the application of AR object and marker recognition techniques could be used as an efficient supplementary control method that allows a mobile computing device to detect and track the augmented object. This may allow for interaction without the need for joysticks or controllers, which may work well for applications delivered on self-contained mobile VR platforms, where the headset is used as the sole input and interaction method. Meanwhile, using marker recognition is similar to hand gesture control, which could support more intuitive interactions than using controllers. As indicated in [21], incorporating movements and gestures in the real-world environment could be a more intuitive interaction approach for mobile VR scenes. In this paper, we describe an experiment using AR-inspired marker recognition as a stand-in for gesture control, without introducing extra sensors on the headset or users' hands. Using marker recognition could be a cheap alternative to allow certain control in the absence of external control devices, such as joysticks, particularly for mobile VR experience.

3 Experimental Virtual Museum

Figure 1 presents a matrix of different approaches that can be offered to users with regard to control over their movement and navigation within the VE and guide information. By *fixed movement* control, we refer to the situation where users are passively shown around and have little proactive control over movement, such as following a museum tour guide on a planned trajectory within a certain period. *Fixed guide* control refers to the case where users are given the information automatically, regardless of whether they have asked for it or not. This usually happens during a group visit, where a tour guide talks to the group and the user listens. A similar situation happens when users take a tour with a time-based or position-based audio guide system. The most common user

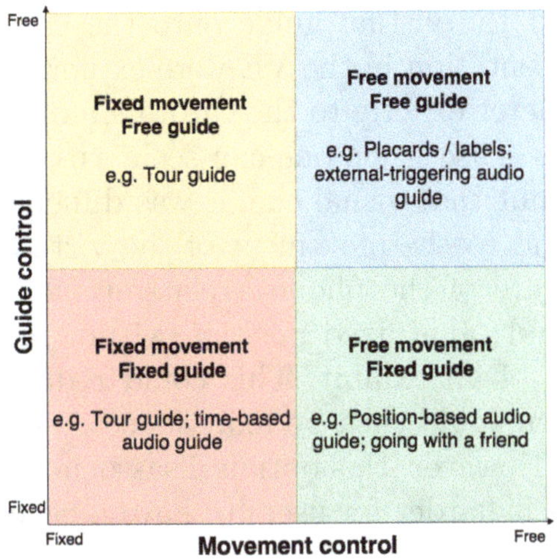

Fig. 1. Control matrix of different guide approaches

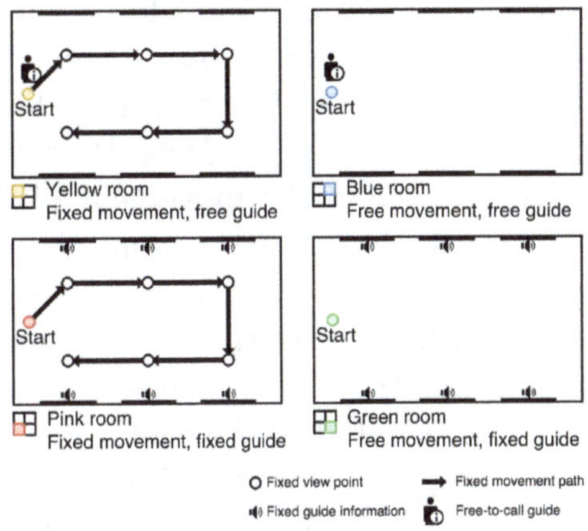

Fig. 2. Top-down room view with movement and guide controls settings (Color figure online)

experience in museums is free movement around the site with guide information provided by in-situ placards and externally-triggering audio guides. In Fig. 1 we have categorised these options as *free movement* and *free guide*, denoting options for allowing users to freely move around in a physical space and read or listen to guide information at will. As indicated in the matrix, tour guide and audio guide systems limit users' freedom of movement and guide control while more flexible options such as labels are usually less interactive.

In order to explore user preferences for these control options, we developed a very simple virtual museum as a low fidelity experimental set up, displaying famous paintings with a series of rooms - each of which offered a different combination of controls of both the users' movement and access to additional guide information. The experience was built in Unity and presented using a Samsung Galaxy S6 mobile phone in a Gear VR headset. The experience with different combinations of movement and guide controls was configured in four different rooms mapping to the control matrix (see Fig. 1), which we distinguished visually by four different colours (see Fig. 2).

3.1 Guide Design

One innovation tested in this study is the idea of embodying [9] audio guides as a virtual character, as shown in Fig. 4. Rather than have the virtual tour guide visible all of the time and leading the user around the VE, it can be called upon when required during the visit. For example, the virtual guide can appear when the user is looking at a museum exhibit to give the user information about the exhibit, but does not visually accompany the user as they move around the museum. The core design principle was that the guide could be 'carried around in the user's pocket' and taken out when needed to introduce the exhibits to users. To achieve this, we utilised an AR technique that recognised a code card held in the user's hand and augmented the virtual guide onto the card (see Fig. 3). Several designs for the guide presentation in the VE were explored. The initial implementation mapped the character exactly to the card, including both its position and orientation. This makes sense when one can see a virtual representation of one's hands. However, without that visual cue, it was difficult for users to relate the movement of their hand to the movement of the virtual guide, especially with the limited tracking rate of the phone's relatively slow processor. We also considered placing the guide at a fixed position within the world space, such as the left bottom corner of an exhibit. This could reduce the visual distraction as users' visual attention could then be more focussed on the exhibit located in the centre of the view. However, this option disassociated the virtual guide from the AR card - making it harder for users to have a clear mental model of how the guide works.

Ultimately we settled on mapping the guide to the position of the card but orienting it consistently vertically to the user's viewpoint, regardless of card orientation. A low-pass filter was applied to smooth its movement and avoid flickering that could be caused by a sudden change of the code card position and the hand. The character was further embodied with some natural movement animations, such as idling, looking/turning around and talking.

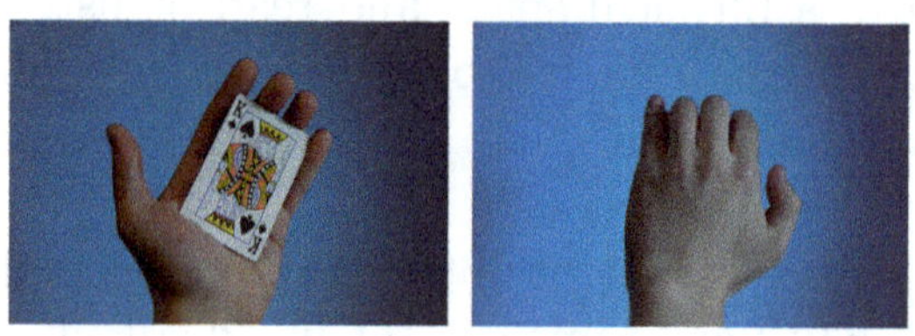

(a) Show card to trigger guide (b) Block card to dismiss guide

Fig. 3. Use code card to control virtual guide

Fig. 4. Virtual guide introducing *Starry Night* (https://www.mixamo.com)

3.2 Control Design

Guide Control. The guide's presence is triggered by the system recognising a code card (a proxy for actual hand gesture recognition). Once the code card is recognised, the virtual guide is presented at the place where the card is recognised. When the guide first appears, it is facing away from the user, allowing the users to 'show' the guide the exhibit that they would like to receive information about. Once the guide has recognised the exhibit, it turns to face the user and begins to talk. The user could adjust the position of the guide in the virtual room by moving the code card in the real world. The audio could be stopped by hiding the code card to dismiss the guide character, however simply looking away from the guide would not dismiss it - the action has to be deliberate (see Fig. 3). This is designed to alleviate the physical burden on the arm so that users do not have to hold the card all the time to keep the guide talking. It could also help prevent accidental stop of the audio information while wandering around in the room. In rooms with no guide control, the audio information is instead triggered automatically when users reached an exhibit and looked closely at it.

Movement Control. For the control of the movement around the VE, users were either moved on a fixed path (so-called 'on rails' movement) or had their own control of the movements by interacting with the touchpad on the headset as follows: a single tap to move forwards; swipe backwards to move backwards; single tap (again) to stop moving (see Fig. 5). However, the speed of movement was kept consistent at a walking pace that is slow enough to eliminate simulator sickness caused by fast-moving and ensure a clear focus at all times. For the experiment, the speed was set to 5.0f in Unity. The direction of movement is consistent with their head orientation, which is approximately their gaze direction. Using head movement for input has been shown to be an effective way as it is easy to learn and does not tire participants [13].

Fig. 5. Movement control

Fig. 6. Virtual room layout

3.3 Room Settings

The virtual art gallery developed for this study comprised a tutorial room and four exhibition rooms. The tutorial room and the exhibition rooms had the same virtual room layout. 24 paintings were randomly distributed in the exhibition rooms and each exhibition room had six paintings on the walls (see Fig. 6).

In the pink room, users were moved on a fixed path and audio information was automatically played when the user reached each exhibit. The system moved the user to the next exhibit once the previous audio information finished. The experience ended after the user had been taken to all of the exhibits in the room. Users could turn their head freely to look at the exhibits on the wall.

In the yellow room, users were moved on a fixed path. Users had control over the audio guide using the AR code card. The system auto-moved the user to the next exhibit after a fixed amount of time (5 s plus the audio length) at the previous exhibit. The experience ended after the user had been taken to all of the exhibits in the room.

In the green room, users had control over movement and were able to navigate themselves using the headset touchpad, but they had no control over the audio information. This was triggered automatically with a proximity detector. Any currently playing audio ceased when they moved close to another exhibit. Users were free to stay in the room for as long as they wanted and so they could finish the experience at any time.

In the blue room, users were able to navigate themselves using the headset touchpad. They also had control over the audio information in the same way as in the yellow room. Users were free to stay in this room for as long as they wanted and finish the experience at any time.

3.4 Technology Setup

The system was developed in Unity with the Vuforia AR platform. In this study, it ran on a Samsung Galaxy S7 and Samsung Gear VR headset (SM-R322). The graphics were displayed at a 60 Hz refresh rate and a 96-degree field of view.

A Vuforia *ImageTarget* was created for the camera to recognise and apply a 3D character on top of it. The virtual guide character followed the position of the code card in the real world while the rotation of the character was disabled. The movement was smoothed to avoid character flickering caused by sudden changes of card position. An idle animation was played by default; a turning back and talking animation were played when it detected an exhibit and started to introduce it. The triggering of the audio was implemented using a *Raycast* fired from the character's eyes. When the ray hit an exhibit, the character 'recognised' it and began talking.

The movement control was achieved by getting the inputs from the headset touchpad and updating the position of the main first perspective camera in accordance with input from the touchpad. With forward input, the system moved the user towards the direction that they were facing. The opposite direction was applied to the backward inputs. The moving speed was set to a constant at approximately walking pace.

The exhibits displayed in the virtual rooms were 24 paintings. 24 audio clips were recorded to describe the paintings and each audio clip lasted around 60s. In addition, four instructional audio clips were recorded to be played at the beginning of each exhibition room to remind the users of the controls that were available to them.

4 Methodology

4.1 Participants

In total, 10 participants (6 male, 4 female) were recruited from a pool of university students, after appropriate ethical review. The experiment was conducted with two groups (A and B). Participants in Group A experienced the pink room first, followed by the yellow room, green room and the blue room. Participants in Group B experienced the rooms in the opposite order. The study lasted approximately 1 h. Each participant was compensated for their time with a voucher.

4.2 Study Design

The aim of the study was to investigate users' preferences for the control of their movement and the control of the guide information in the virtual exhibition. The independent variables were the control of movement and the control of the guide information. The dependent variables were the user experience (measured by the user experience questionnaire), simulator sickness (measured by the simulator sickness questionnaire), and users' attitude towards the controls in the systems (discussed in a post-experience interview). The configuration of user control over movement and guide in each room were presented in Fig. 2. The sequence of room visiting order followed a pattern of increasing control for users in Group A and decreasing control for users in the Group B. Two pilot studies, one with an expert user and one with a naive user, were conducted to finalise system design details and questionnaire settings before recruiting participants.

Two questionnaires were used to measure users' experience and the simulator sickness. The User Experience Questionnaire (UEQ) [18] uses 26 pairs of contrasting attributes with a 7-point Likert scale to measure the attractiveness, perspicuity, efficiency, dependability, simulation and novelty of the system. The Simulator Sickness Questionnaire (SSQ) [17] has 16 items that allow users to report possible symptoms related to nausea, oculomotor and disorientation and evaluate the severity on four scales: none, slight, moderate and severe. A semi-structured interview was conducted to discuss users' preferences of controls and attitudes towards system interactions.

Considering the potential risk of motion sickness when being in the virtual environment, users were informed that they could remove the headset at any time during the study if they felt uncomfortable. No user made this request. In any case, users were required to take off the headset at the end of each experimental task and so they spent no longer than ten minutes wearing the headset at one time.

4.3 Procedure

At the start of the study, users were asked to read the information sheet and sign a consent form. An overview of the study was provided with screenshots to explain the room layout, menu settings, movement interactions, and guide information control. Headset fittings were adjusted and the tutorial room was used to allow users to get familiar with the interaction methods. When they were ready to start the experimental study, users in Group A started with the pink room whereas those in Group B started with the blue room. Users from both groups were required to explore all four exhibition rooms and fill in the two questionnaires for user experience and simulator sickness after exploring each room. During their explorations in the room, their head positions and the time duration were logged to monitor the exhibits they looked at and to analyse their points of interest. In addition, they were asked if there was anything they found interesting about the exhibits in each room, either from the audio information or their observations. After having explored all four rooms, they were asked to rank the rooms based on their preferences. A semi-structured interview was conducted to discuss their rankings.

4.4 Data Collection and Analysis

Quantitative data included the two questionnaire responses collected from the users after visiting each room, as well as the gaze data captured during their exhibition visits.

The original UEQ used a 7-point Likert scale evaluation for each item, where the middle value does not indicate any preferences. In addition, some items such as 'secure/not secure' did not apply to the context of this system. Therefore, we adapted the questionnaire to use a 6-point Likert scale and an additional 'Not applicable' option. Data collected from this questionnaire was analysed using Laugwitz et al. analysis toolkit [18]. The analysis transformed the 26 items and scores for the six evaluation scales were derived and compared with the benchmark, which contains data from 246 product evaluations with 9905 participant evaluations in total. For each scale, the benchmark classified a product into five categories: Excellent (10%), Good (10% to 25%), Above average (20% to 50%), Below Average (50% to 75%) and Bad (75% to 100%).

The SSQ results were analysed following Kennedy et al. scoring procedure [17]. The scores for each symptom are quantified as none (0), slight (1), moderate (2) and severe (3). The Total Severity (TS) score plus separate scores for three sub-scales: nausea, oculomotor and disorientation were derived by adding the corresponding symptom scores and applying a constant weight. The score values do not have particular interpretive meanings, but were used in comparison with scales based on the 1,100+ calibration samples provided by Kennedy et al. [17] (see Table 1).

Table 1. Descriptive statistics for SSQ scale provided by Kennedy et al.

	Nausea	Oculomotor	Disorientation	Total score
Mean	7.7	10.6	6.4	9.8
SD	15	15	15	15
Min	0	0	0	0
Max	124	90.9	97.4	108.6

Gaze information, inferred by a user's head position, was captured using a script that logged when the user looked at an exhibit. The data was stored in a list and written to `CSV` data files on the local storage of the mobile phone before users exited each room. This log file captured the identifier of the exhibit that the user was looking at, the absolute time when they faced towards the exhibit and when they looked away, as well as the duration of the gaze. The mean time that users spent in front of each exhibit were calculated and compared to the length of the audio information.

In the interview, users were asked to comment on their preferences for the different control methods in the rooms. A theme-based content analysis method was applied to analyse the interview transcripts [23], with top-level categorisation divided into two groups: (1) movement control and (2) guide control.

5 Results

After experiencing the four rooms, users were asked to rank the rooms from 1 to 4 based on their preferences, where 1 indicates the room that they enjoyed the most. The responses are shown in Fig. 7. It can be seen that most users preferred the blue room, where they had control of both movement and the audio guide information. The second preferred room was the green room, where they were allowed to move freely but the guide information was automatically triggered. The pink room with no control was ranked third and the yellow room, in which they had control of the audio guide but no movement control, was ranked last.

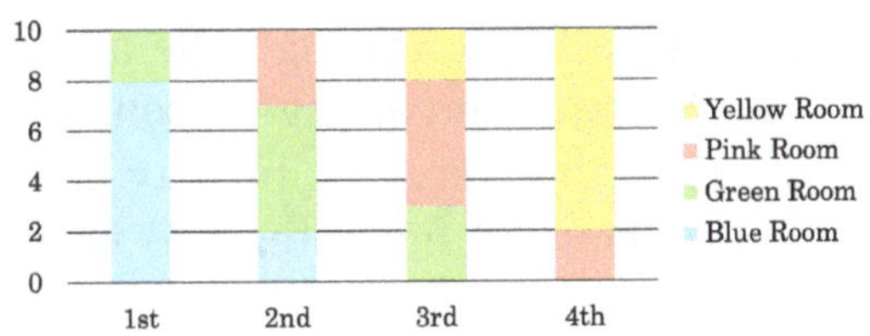

Fig. 7. Users' preference for room control (Color figure online)

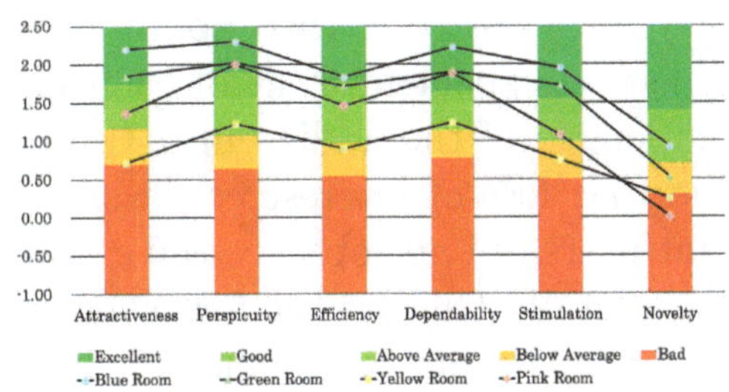

Fig. 8. User experience results (Color figure online)

A similar pattern of results was revealed by the UEQ (see Fig. 8): the blue room (free movement, free guide) created the best user experience, with most scales falling into the 'Excellent' category. Next was the green room (free movement, fixed guide) with slightly lower scores in each scale than the blue room. Although there was no control allowed in the pink room (fixed movement, fixed guide), users reported a good experience in general. The yellow room (fixed movement, free guide) yielded the lowest UEQ scores on most scales, with scores generally at, or below 'average'. In all rooms, the lowest rating was for 'novelty'.

Analysis of the SSQ indicated that in general, the total severity of symptoms reported in each room was below the Kennedy standard average (M = 9.8, see Table 1), except the yellow room. In addition, the blue room resulted in fewer reports of discomfort and sickness symptoms; whereas the yellow room had the highest sickness score (see Fig. 9). These results correlated with the results from the UEQ as well as the rankings provided by the users (see Table 2). Fewer sickness symptoms were reported in rooms with a better user experience in general. Meanwhile, an analysis of symptom change did not indicate a significant consistent increase or drop in sickness throughout the experimental period for either of the participant groups.

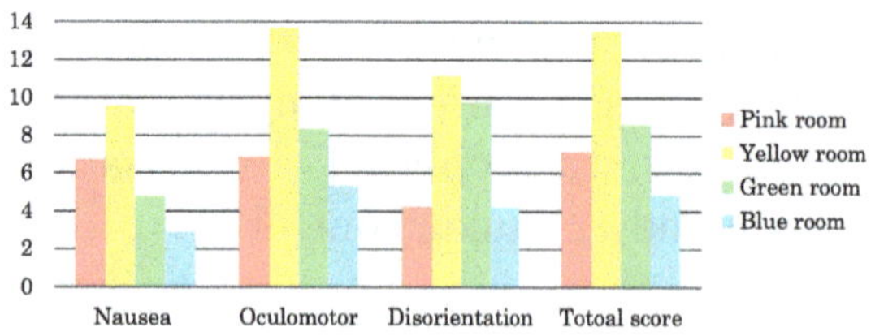

Fig. 9. Simulator sickness scores

Table 2. Correlations between the preference, UEQ and SSQ

	Rank	UEQ	SSQ
Rank	1		
UEQ	−0.994	1	
SSQ	0.861	−0.889	1

Figure 10 showed the average time users spent looking at an exhibit in relation to the length of its audio information. In the pink room and the yellow room, although users could look around freely and look at other places while situating in front of one painting, they were moved around by the system on a fixed path. Therefore, the time users spent in front of each painting was roughly the same as the audio length. While the time users spent looking at the exhibits was less predictable in rooms with free control over movement because they could linger longer in front of the paintings they were interested in and skip those they were less concerned about. However, it was worth noting that the average time users spent in front of each painting in the green room were shorter than the length of the audio clips. Leaving the exhibits half way through the audio due to a loss of interest could account for this. A more convincing reason was that users did not observe the exhibits they were not interested in, or may have accidentally triggered it for several seconds which they did not intend to view. Nevertheless, it was included when deriving the average viewing time. These cases were significantly reduced in the blue room and false positive results were avoided because it required intentional triggering of the audio. The audio was triggered when the system detected the user facing an exhibit. Therefore the audio would start again if the user remained in front of it - something users commented on and they disliked. When this happened, they would usually leave and move to another exhibit. Being unable to stop the audio information did not permit them to appreciate the exhibits without listening to anything. It was one of the reasons given in the interview to explain why they preferred the blue room (with a control of the audio guide information) over the green room.

Users suggested in the interview that they preferred to have control of their movement because they would like to move freely in the exhibitions, decide the order of visit and take their time. When they were moved on a fixed path, they felt that they were forced to look at the exhibits and listen to them.

"The last one (blue room) was my favourite. I could take my time. Some pictures I wasn't very interested in but I want to look at it without having to hear it."

"Once the audio starts, I feel like I have to stay."

Users considered the guide as a vivid embodiment of the audio information. They preferred to take control of the audio guide information and decide when to start or stop it, rather than having the audio triggered automatically.

"I like the robot, it looks interesting and funny. But in the green room, it just comes with the voice and I don't know where the voice comes from."

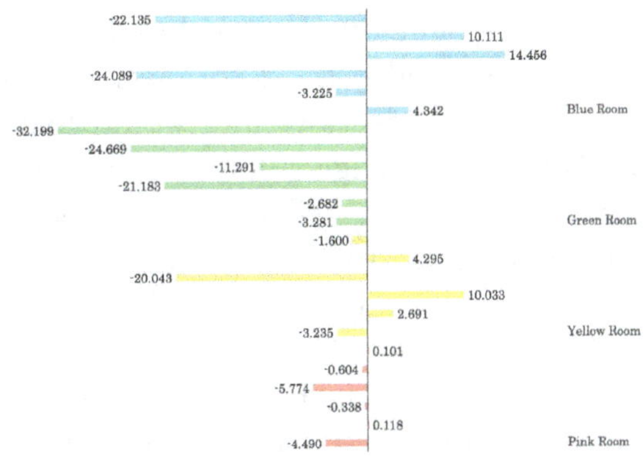

Fig. 10. Average time spent in front of each painting compared with the audio length (Color figure online)

"I wasn't a fan of the audio starting straight away."

In general, no significant sickness symptoms were reported and users enjoyed the VR experience. Some slight discomforts were raised regarding the movement directions and potential discomfort can result from the time of use and the headset design.

"(I) felt pretty comfortable in the headset, that's definitely fine. Didn't feel nausea or any of the stuff."

"When I was faced to the picture, it moves me from the left to the right and I don't feel very well."

"The headset generally was good and convenient because the time of viewing each room was not too long, it was just about right. Because if it's more than that you may feel discomfort even if you have too many exciting stuff."

6 Discussion

In this section, user preferences for the exhibition rooms and their attitudes towards the control over movement and guide are discussed. Comments on simulator sickness that could be caused by the interaction design are also presented with a view to supporting future system designs for virtual exhibitions. The quantitative data from UEQ and SSQ indicated that rooms with both movement control and audio guide control provided better user experience and caused less sickness or discomfort.

6.1 Movement Control

In general, most users said that they preferred the control of their own movement, allowing them to choose their order of viewing and take their time.

As for the method of control over movement, users commented that "it is easy to pick up" and "the interaction is quite intuitive". However, one user suggested setting swiping forwards to move forwards as it provides a better mapping between the direction of movement on the touchpad and in the virtual room. It was observed that other users also tried to control movement in this way, especially after they did a backwards move and would like to go forwards. The reason for selection of 'Tapping' to trigger forward movement was because the directions on the touchpad were not visible to the users. However, this comment and observed behaviour suggested that a more intuitive system based on direction may be preferable. From an ergonomics point of view, the design of the movement control should consider the natural mappings and the conceptual model user might have in mind [20,24], but at the same time, the affordance, visibility of control and the learning cost should be taken into consideration [33].

Some restrictions on the types of movement made available with a touchpad control were discussed in the interview. For example, in a real-world exhibition, users may look at an exhibit and navigate from one side of it to the other - and it happens quite often. The direction we are looking at is not always consistent with the direction we are walking towards. However, the movement direction in the virtual world is dominated by the user's head direction, which is roughly the gaze direction. Therefore one cannot move from side to side in this system. One possible implementation of this feature could be to use a gyroscope to adjust positions through head tilting. However, the effect of this needs to be explored as a disconnection between the movement direction and the facing direction could be an inducer of simulator sickness [19]. Another issue raised was about the distance between the user and the exhibit. In the real world, a guardrail or at least a warning sign would prevent users from going too close to an exhibit. However, there is no concern of the exhibits being damaged or stained in the virtual world, users are allowed to go as close as they like. One user commented that the downside of this is "it is unnatural to go too close to the painting, we are like in search of pixels in there". It was also suggested to slow down the movements when one becomes close to the exhibits. Given the lack of resolution in VR environments, it is arguably desirable to be able to move close to the object than one might in the real world.

Meanwhile, as a digital representation, the virtual world could offer more possibilities than the real world [28]. Users identified some features that the system could possibly have, such as having a zoom-in function to allow observing the paintings in even more detail. In addition, it was asked if the navigation could be designed in a way that looking at a painting for several seconds would automatically move the user position close to that exhibit. This is currently the most widely used approach for menu selection in VR systems. A dot in the virtual world indicates the object to be selected and a loading bar is usually presented along with it to provide an instant visual feedback. The users may have proposed these interaction approaches deriving from their experience of picture viewing and game navigations, which indicates these interaction approaches could be accepted if adapted to the virtual world.

A natural and intuitive way of interaction should consider the potential mental model of users and the visibility of the control, as well as the learning cost in the system context. Although the virtual movements have many restrictions compared to the movements in the real world, it offers many possibilities of interaction approach as a digital representation, and it is known that there is a relationship between methods of movement and simulator sickness in VR settings [19]. In the rooms with no movement control (pink and yellow), users were moved on a fixed path, on part of which users were moved from left to right. It was reported that this caused some instances of discomfort. This is entirely understandable as the moving direction was inconsistent with the direction they were looking and sensory disconnect is a well-known cause of simulator sickness [29]. Additionally, some users commented that after they finished the sessions, they did not know the orientation with respect to the room they were sitting in. Of course, room-scale movement provided by systems such as the HTC Vive sidestep many of these issues, however many current VR systems, especially those delivered on mobile phone platforms are unlikely to provide such facility in the near future.

In this study there does not appear to be a difference reported levels of simulator sickness symptoms between rooms where the user is moved (fixed path) and rooms in which the user controls their own movement (free path), possibly because the movement is fundamentally similar in both cases - being a smooth translation of position. It would be interesting to compare between full 'on rails' movement, controlled free movement, and the so-called 'room scale' movement as epitomised by the HTC Vive system.

6.2 Guide Control

The guide acted as an embodied controller of the audio information for the exhibits. Generally, users would like to have their own control of an audio guide because there were cases where they found it annoying that they could not stop the audio information or the audio started straight away. When being asked about their real-world museum and gallery visiting behaviour, some considered the museums and galleries places for knowledge and they would like to acquire information where possible; while many suggested they would like to take their time looking at the exhibits and may only look for information when they are interested in them. In particular, some deemed art appreciation to be a personal experience and would feel bothered when people keep talking and introducing exhibits to them. Therefore, they preferred to take their own control of the audio guide and decide when to trigger and stop the audio information.

As for the guide character, analysis of the interviews indicated that users favoured it for the following reasons. First, the look of the character was interesting; and the animations added some semblance of 'intelligence' to it. In addition, they considered the character as an embodiment of the audio guide, which explained why and how they are receiving the audio information and informs them where the voice is from [9]. Moreover, some assumed the guide was an artificial intelligence because it could 'recognise' the painting the user was situated in front of and started talking to them. The idea that even a simple embodied guide suggests intelligence stands as an indicator that there may be a place for *actually* intelligent agent-based guides, which could converse more dynamically with the user, such as those virtual humans described in [30].

When listening to the audio information, some users preferred to dismiss the guide character while the audio is playing. They found the character distracting because when it was in the view and animated, they were more inclined to look at it. Similar situations could occur with the real-world tour guide or expert as well - but of course, this does not offer the option of dismissing them as easily! When a person is talking to you, a natural social interaction is to look at his eyes to show attention. Providing users with the flexibility of keeping or excluding the guide character in the view could suit for different requirements and enhance the user experience in general.

In addition, the embodied interaction in the guide control was shown to have a positive impact on the user experience. Dourish introduced tangible and social computing in [9]. Tangible computing is concerned with physical interaction in an augmented environment and it uses computation as part of the physical world; while social computing uses social understandings of interaction to enhance the interaction with computation. Dourish argued that both exploit the sense of familiarity to smooth the interaction and are founded on the same idea based on the embodiment. In this study, the audio information was presented to the users through the animated guide character, which involved users' proactive interaction with the physical marker and fit with users' mental models about the guide's activities in an exhibition. The embodied interaction that users are familiar with could enhance their user experience and contribute to the engaged participation and comprehension of the digital content.

7 Conclusion

In this paper, we have presented a simple study to look at aspects of user control related to movement and audio-guides in VR exhibitions. An indication of the results suggested that users prefer to have control over both movement and the audio guide. However, an increase of control does not necessarily result in an enhancement of user experience or a decrease in simulator sickness symptoms. When users were moved on a fixed path, they would prefer to have everything automatically controlled, instead of them taking control of the audio information alone. From the interviews, we surmise that users would prefer to walk freely and decide their own order of visit in an exhibition. They would ask for information about an exhibit when they are interested in it and they find it overwhelming and annoying when being automatically provided with all information about every exhibit. When they take a second visit, they would like to look at the exhibits without having to hear about anything. Therefore, having control of both the movements and the audio guide is preferred.

We have also shown that there may be benefits to providing an embodied virtual guide, with users generally reacting positively to its presence, while appreciating the control of being able to call or dismiss it at will. We were surprised by the amount of 'intelligence' users attributed to the guide.

The key contributions of this paper are as follows:

- Experimental evidence that users prefer the direct control of movement in VR exhibitions, but there is no notable difference in simulator sickness between these conditions.
- An example of the use of an embodied virtual guide, which suggests that this may be a good alternative way of providing users with information in VR exhibitions, different to traditional audio guides or labels.
- Experimental evidence that users would prefer the option to dismiss supporting information at will.

Acknowledgements. This work was carried out at the Mixed Reality Lab (MRL). The authors acknowledge the financial support from Ningbo Education Bureau, Ningbo Science and Technology Bureau, China's MOST and The University of Nottingham. The work is also partially supported by EPSRC grant no EP/L015463/1.

References

1. Bozgeyikli, E., Raij, A., Katkoori, S., Dubey, R.: Point & teleport locomotion technique for virtual reality. In: Proceedings of the 2016 Annual Symposium on Computer-Human Interaction in Play - CHI PLAY 2016, pp. 205–216 (2016). http://dl.acm.org/citation.cfm?doid=2967934.2968105
2. Brooks, F.P.: What's real about virtual reality? IEEE Comput. Graph. Appl. **19**(6), 16–27 (1999). https://doi.org/10.1109/38.799723
3. Brown, B., MacColl, I., Chalmers, M., Galani, A., Randell, C., Steed, A.: Lessons from the lighthouse: collaboration in a shared mixed reality system. In: Proceedings of the SIGCHI Conference on Human Factors in Computing Systems, pp. 577–584. ACM (2003)
4. Bruno, F., Bruno, S., De Sensi, G., Luchi, M.L., Mancuso, S., Muzzupappa, M.: From 3D reconstruction to virtual reality: a complete methodology for digital archaeological exhibition. J. Cult. Heritage **11**(1), 42–49 (2010). https://doi.org/10.1016/j.culher.2009.02.006
5. Burdea, G.C., Coiffet, P.: Virtual Reality Technology, vol. 1. Wiley, Hoboken (2003)
6. Chittaro, L., Ieronutti, L., Ranon, R.: Navigating 3D virtual environments by following embodied agents: a proposal and its informal evaluation on a virtual museum application. PsychNology J. **2**(1), 24–42 (2004). 10.1.1.98.137
7. Ch'ng, E., Gaffney, V., Chapman, H.: From product to process: new directions in digital heritage. In: Digital Heritage and Culture: Strategy and Implementation, pp. 219–243 (2014)
8. Ch'ng, E., Stone, R.J.: Enhancing virtual reality with artificial life: reconstructing a flooded European mesolithic landscape. Presence Teleop. Virt. Environments **15**(3), 341–352 (2006)
9. Dourish, P.: Where the Action Is: The Foundations of Embodied Interaction. MIT Press, Cambridge (2004)
10. Frischer, B.: The rome reborn project. How technology is helping us to study history. OpEd **10**, 1–5 (2008). http://www.romereborn.virginia.edu/romereborn2documents/papers/FrischerOpEdfinal2.pdf

11. Gaucci, A., Garagnani, S., Manferdini, A.M.: Reconstructing the lost reality archaeological analysis and Transmedial Technologies for a perspective of Virtual Reality in the Etruscan city of Kainua. In: 2015 Digital Heritage, pp. 227–234. IEEE, September 2015. https://doi.org/10.1109/DigitalHeritage.2015.7419502, http://ieeexplore.ieee.org/document/7419502/
12. Ghose, S.: Rethinking Museums: the emerging face of story-telling museums. University of Victory Legacy Art Galleries, pp. 1–4 (2014). http://www.maltwood.uvic.ca/cam/publications/other_publications/Text_of_Rethinking_Museums.pdf
13. Giannopoulos, I., Komninos, A., Garofalakis, J.: Natural interaction with large map interfaces in VR. In: Proceedings of the 21st Pan-Hellenic Conference on Informatics - PCI 2017, vol. Part F1325, pp. 1–6. ACM Press, New York (2017). https://doi.org/10.1145/3139367.3139424, http://dl.acm.org/citation.cfm?doid=3139367.3139424
14. Giloth, C.F., Tanant, J.: User experiences in three approaches to a visit to a 3D Labyrinthe of Versailles. In: 2015 Digital Heritage, vol. 1, pp. 403–404 (2015). https://doi.org/10.1109/DigitalHeritage.2015.7413914
15. Gutierrez, D., Sundstedt, V., Gomez, F., Chalmers, A.: Dust and light: predictive virtual archaeology. J. Cult. Heritage **8**(2), 209–214 (2007). https://doi.org/10.1016/j.culher.2006.12.003
16. Keil, J., et al.: A digital look at physical museum exhibits, pp. 685–688 (2013)
17. Kennedy, R.S., Lane, N.E., Berbaum, K.S., Lilienthal, M.G.: Simulator sickness questionnaire: an enhanced method for quantifying simulator sickness. Int. J. Aviat. Psychol. **3**(3), 203–220 (1993)
18. Laugwitz, B., Held, T., Schrepp, M.: Construction and evaluation of a user experience questionnaire. In: Holzinger, A. (ed.) USAB 2008. LNCS, vol. 5298, pp. 63–76. Springer, Heidelberg (2008). https://doi.org/10.1007/978-3-540-89350-9_6
19. LaViola, J.J.: A discussion of cybersickness in virtual environments. ACM SIGCHI Bulletin **32**(1), 47–56 (2000). https://doi.org/10.1145/333329.333344. http://portal.acm.org/citation.cfm?doid=333329.333344
20. Mayhew, D.J.: Principles and Guidelines in Software User Interface Design. Prentice-Hall Inc., Upper Saddle River (1992)
21. Mountain, D., Liarokapis, F.: Interacting with virtual reality scenes on mobile devices. In: Proceedings of the 7th International Conference on Human Computer Interaction with Mobile Devices & Services - MobileHCI 2005, p. 331 (2005). https://doi.org/10.1145/1085777.1085851, https://www.researchgate.net/publication/250425912_Interacting_with_Virtual_Reality_models_on_mobile_devices
22. Mulken, S.V., André, E., Müller, J.: The Persona Effect: How Substantial Is It? In: Johnson, H., Nigay, L., Roast, C. (eds.) People and Computers XIII, pp. 53–66. Springer, London (1998). https://doi.org/10.1007/978-1-4471-3605-7
23. Neale, H., Nichols, S.: Theme-based content analysis. Int. J. Hum.-Comput. Stud. **55**(2), 167–189 (2001). https://doi.org/10.1006/ijhc.2001.0475
24. Norman, D.A.: The psychology of everyday things. In: Basic Books (1988)
25. Reunanen, M., Díaz, L., Horttana, T.: A holistic user-centered approach to immersive digital cultural heritage installations. J. Comput. Cult. Heritage **7**(4), 1–16 (2015). http://dl.acm.org/citation.cfm?doid=2669619.2637485
26. Rickel, J., Johnson, W.: Task-oriented collaboration with embodied agents in virtual worlds. In: Embodied Conversational Agents, pp. 1–29 (2000). http://www.isi.edu/isd/VET/eca00.pdf

27. Sharples, S., Cobb, S., Moody, A., Wilson, J.R.: Virtual reality induced symptoms and effects (VRISE): comparison of head mounted display (HMD), desktop and projection display systems. Displays **29**(2), 58–69 (2008). https://doi.org/10.1016/j.displa.2007.09.005
28. Sutherland, I.E.: The ultimate display. In: Proceedings of the Congress of the International Federation of Information Processing (IFIP), pp. 506–508 (1965). https://doi.org/10.1109/MC.2005.274, http://citeseer.ist.psu.edu/viewdoc/summary?doi=10.1.1.136.3720
29. Tennent, P., Marshall, J., Walker, B., Brundell, P., Benford, S.: The challenges of visualkinaesthetic experience. In: Proceedings of the 2017 Conference on Designing Interactive Systems, pp. 1265–1276. ACM (2017)
30. Valstar, M., et al.: Ask alice: an artificial retrieval of information agent. In: Proceedings of the 18th ACM International Conference on Multimodal Interaction, pp. 419–420. ACM (2016)
31. Vinson, N.: Design guidelines for landmarks to support Navigatiion in virtual environments. In: Proceedings of the SIGCHI Conference on Human Factors in Computing Systems (May), pp. 278–285 (1999). https://doi.org/10.1145/302979.303062, http://dl.acm.org/citation.cfm?id=303062
32. Virtual Reality Society: Who coined the term "virtual reality"? https://www.vrs.org.uk/virtual-reality/who-coined-the-term.html. Accessed 4 Apr 2017
33. Wickens, C.D., Hollands, J.G., Banbury, S., Parasuraman, R.: Engineering Psychology & Human Performance. Psychology Press, New York (2015)
34. Wyman, B., Smith, S., Meyers, D., Godfrey, M.: Digital Storytelling in Museums: Observations and Best Practices. Curator Mus. J. **54**(4), 461–468 (2011). http://doi.wiley.com/10.1111/j.2151-6952.2011.00110.x

Exploring European Cultural Heritage Using Conversational Agents

Octavian M. Machidon[1(✉)] and Ales Tavcar[2]

[1] Transilvania University of Brasov, Brasov, Romania
octavian.machidon@unitbv.ro
[2] Jozef Stefan Institute, Ljubljana, Slovenia

Abstract. The semantic web and open data paradigms are gaining momentum in recent years and more information is being published online following the linked data principles. This enables easy access and processing of data by external services. An example of such services are intelligent conversational agents that provide to the users the ability to interact with a computer system in natural language. Such communication is much more intuitive and facilitates the use of complex services to less skilled users (e.g., elderly) or users with disabilities (e.g., visually impaired) thus providing to these groups access to the huge amount of information stored in the semantic web or specific online services. In this paper, we present a proof-of-concept conversational agent able to provide information about the European cultural heritage and display stored digital content from the Europeana database.

Keywords: Cultural heritage · Conversational agent
Natural language interaction

1 Introduction

One of the most dynamic fields of research nowadays is the intuitive human-computer interaction through the development of intelligent agents. In order to provide users with efficient methods to interact with computer systems, intelligent agents with two key features have been developed: natural language communication and knowledge handling [1]. Conversational agents (CAs) are an innovative mechanism to enable verbal interaction with humans and a computer system. Although their understanding of natural language for a general application is still limited, it is possible to design and tweak an efficient agent for a specific target domain. Moreover, their knowledge base can be well-defined and fueled by the huge amount of data existing on the World Wide Web.

Although technologies for enable conversation are getting adopted in more and more domains, applications for interactions and content delivery in the cultural heritage domain are not as widespread as we would expect. The majority of such systems is developed specifically for museums and exhibitions as virtual guides and are limited to specific content and intended to be used by museum visitors. There is a noticeable lack of applications for content delivery from the cultural heritage domain to the general public.

M. Duguleană et al. (Eds.): VRTCH 2018, CCIS 904, pp. 184–194, 2019.
https://doi.org/10.1007/978-3-030-05819-7_14

In recent years, publicly available data on the web has known a tremendous growth in nearly every domain, even cultural heritage. The available semantic data for this domain can provide to heritage communities new methodologies and support the development of specific applications for both the expert users and general public, to access heritage collections, create online digital libraries of cultural artefacts, navigate and interact with these online resources (search and retrieve data). Also, Semantics in cultural heritage may help overcome other specific issues like handling the multidisciplinary nature of the analytical data available in this field of research. Information about an artefact may come from different data sources and be in various formats, which raises difficulties in the process of efficient knowledge extraction and interlinking data sources, issues that can be solved by applying semantic web technologies.

In this paper we present a prototype version of a web-based conversational agent that can interact with users in natural language and can assist them to explore the European cultural heritage. The agent implements a simple conversational mechanism, which is based on the Google Assistant platform [3]. The mechanism for detecting the users' intent is based on keywords and entity recognition. The knowledge base for this agent is Europeana, a digital cultural library, museum and archive, offering public access to millions of digital objects from thousands of contributing heritage collections all across Europe. This digital library embraces the principles of the Semantic Web in the structure of its data model, which enables an improved integration in applications providing recommendations or assistance based on its knowledge base.

The rest of the paper is structured as follows: Sect. 2 provides a short background on conversational agents, highlighting other existing implementations. Section 3 presents the Europeana digital library and its API that is being interfaced by the agent. Section 4 presents the implementation details of the web interface and a short qualitative evaluation of system. We conclude this paper with Sect. 5, where also some future research directions are highlighted.

2 Related Work

Due to their intuitive interfaces and features, CAs are being credited to bring on several key assets regarding the interaction effects they have on the human users [3]. Natural language interaction capabilities make CAs very promising instruments for enhancing user access to the Web of Data, since they can provide the desired information in a friendly, natural language conversation.

CAs are being used in a variety of areas, with many applications benefiting from their particular features. Some applications are in the field of virtual cultural heritage, where CAs are deployed as virtual guides for various heritage sites, either in the real-world or in virtual environments [4–6]. These implementations have the potential not only to entertain and engage visitors but also to contribute to the learning process by offering personalized feedback, answering questions, storytelling, etc.

Other applications of conversational agents are in adjacent areas such as education (for instruction and training) [7, 8] in the form of question answering systems where such implementations are highly used and thus needed (for example supporting access to large data sets like encyclopedias, in libraries or cultural institutions) [9], for informational purposes (automated customer service, e-commerce) [10], tourism [11], municipalities [2], and many other fields.

The Semantic Web is being credited as particularly useful for exploratory search queries, in which the user has only a glimpse of what exactly he is searching for and during the interaction with the semantic data he develops further insights, leading to the accumulation of knowledge about the inquiry subject [12]. This incremental approach is can be applied by having turn-taking dialogues with conversational agents - as a natural interaction scenario for human users engaged in exploratory semantic searches [13].

The first implementations involving conversational agents for accessing Web information were prior to the development of the Semantic Web. They were targeting improved web navigation by offering an interface capable of accepting search queries in the form of natural language questions instead of the traditional menu-driven navigation and keyword search [14]. Since then various systems were deployed exploiting structured data available on the web [1, 14–16].

3 The Europeana Public Digital Library and API Access

The Europeana project is one of the major international projects based on the synergy between cultural heritage and the Semantic web. Europeana is Europe's digital cultural library, museum and archive, offering public access to millions of digital objects from thousands of contributing heritage collections all across the European Union, via a multilingual interface [17] The creators of Europeana state that it should not be regarded merely as an accumulation of digital object representations, but instead its purpose should be that to enable the generation of knowledge pertaining to cultural artefacts [18].

Thus, the current efforts targeting Europeana are focused on the development of the technological solutions, data models and functionalities needed in order for it to transcend beyond a classic digital library and towards an interactive knowledge provider. In this context, Europeana is being regarded [18] as a complex aggregation of digitalized cultural artefacts and rich contextualization data, all in the process of being embedded in a Linked Open Data architecture [19].

The key mechanism for accessing the stored data is a public API (Application Programming Interfaces). Europeana offers an extensive interface for both end users and content providers, in an effort to enable cultural heritage entities (institutions and private developers) to build their own applications by integrating the functionalities of the Europeana DLMS (Digital Library Management System) or even extend them [20]. This unique framework for accessing Europe's cultural heritage is being used in an increasing number of projects that are built around the Europeana API and are run by various cultural heritage institutions [21].

In this context, this paper aims to provide an evaluation of the usability and quality of the large amount of structured cultural heritage content that is digitized in Europeana. The API used in this paper for the evaluation is the Europeana REST API based on HTTP calls, with the response information being returned in the JSON format. An Europeana Search API call is basically an HTTP request in a specific format sent to the Europeana API service URL located at:

https://www.europeana.eu/api/v2

There are 4 methods for search and retrieve actions using the Europeana API, among which 2 in particular have been used given the requirements of the present application: *search* and *record*. The *search* method returns a list of records found within the Europeana repository according to the specified search parameters. The HTTP request for a search is done at the following URL:

https://www.europeana.eu/api/v2/search.json

Any HTTP request to the Europeana API must include in the URL string a query string parameter names *wskey* that is used for authentication. The *search.json* API method allows for several other query string parameters to be included in the URL for filtering the search results according to the user's needs. The key parameters are *query*, which specifies the search term(s) and *qf*, which provides facet filtering query. Besides these, several other parameters enable filtering of the results according to various factors (copyright status, thumbnail present, and others). A basic example of a search API request URL is:

https://www.europeana.eu/api/v2/search.json?wskey=xxxx\&query=mona+AND +lisa

In the above example, the search query will provide a response with records containing both words mona and lisa. Moreover, it is possible to limit the search to a specific data field by providing its name using a predefined syntax. For example, searching for objects whose author is Leonardo da Vinci is performed using the following syntax who:"Leonardo da Vinci":

https://www.europeana.eu/api/v2/search.json?wskey=xxxx&query=who: "Leonardo+da+Vinci"

Other data fields that can be used in a query are: *title*, *who*, *what*, *when*, and *where*. This provides to the user the ability to create complex queries that retrieve specific cultural objects. In this paper we limited our queries to the data fields *what* that describe the type of the object (paintings, pottery, statues, etc.) and *who* to search for the object's author.

The other Europeana API search method used is *record*, which retrieves detailed information about a single record within the Europeana repository. A generic HTTP request for a *record* method call is done at the following URL:

http://www.europeana.eu/api/v2/record/[recordID].json

The *record.json* API method needs prior knowledge of the Europeana record's ID string, which needs to be included explicitly in the URL like in the following example:

http://www.europeana.eu/api/v2/record/9200300/BibliographicResource_ 3000052917527.json?wskey=xxxx

The response of a record-type HTTP API request contains an object representing the EDM (Europeana Data Model) metadata record in JSON format. This object includes information specific to that particular record, among which the Europeana Collection which it belongs to, the record title, location, time of creation, EDM Dataset name, information about when the record was created in the digital library.

4 Web-Based API Interface

In order to facilitate a user-friendly interaction and communication in natural language with the Europeana database we designed a simple web interface, where the user can input a query, the back-end analyses the text, based on the query data constructs the request, and sends it to the Europeana API.

4.1 Implementation

The whole Web application was implemented using Django, a high-level Python Web framework. Django follows the MVC paradigm, where the model (M) represents the data (usually stored in a database), the view (V) is the representation layer of the app (HTML Web app), and the controller (C) controls the flow of information between the model and the view and implements business logic. Django enables rapid and reliable development.

The front-end of the application (see Fig. 1.) was created using Bootstrap and custom JavaScript code. The application is divided in two parts: (i) the top part allows to interact with the CA in natural language and displays part of the conversation history; (ii) the bottom part presents the search results in a structured way (see Fig. 2.). The communication with the back-end CA is implemented through AJAX calls, where JSON objects are exchanged.

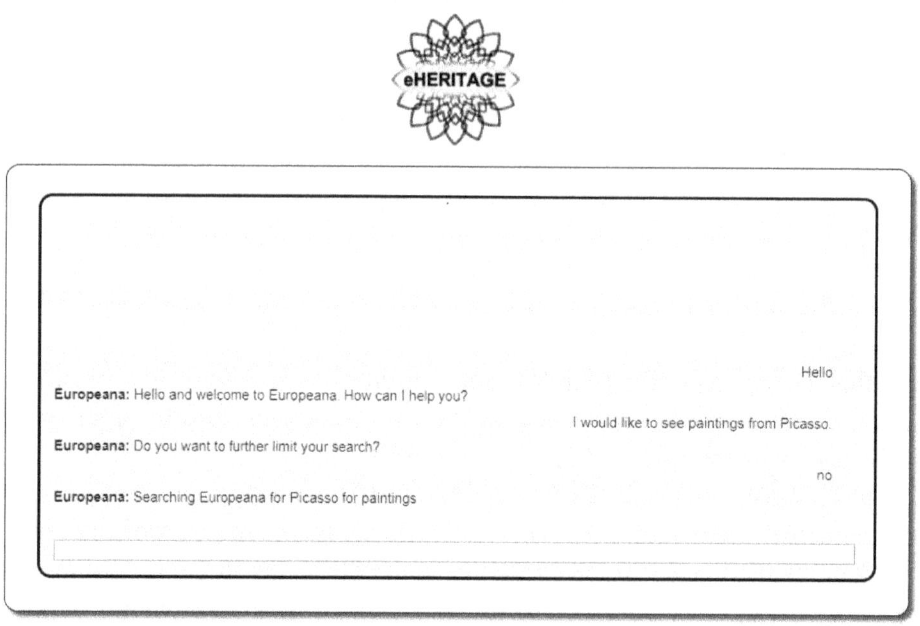

Fig. 1. A Simple chat web interface to access the Europeana API.

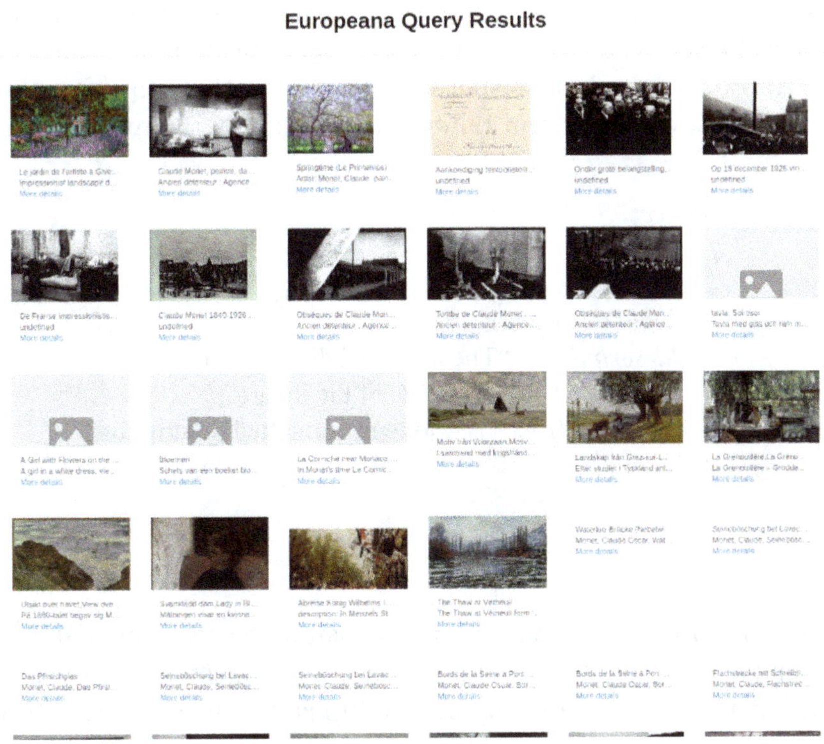

Fig. 2. Retrieved images for the query Monet paintings.

The input data is sent as a JSON object containing three fields: (i) question, where the query of the user is stored; (ii) userID, containing the ID of the current user to track the conversation; timestamp, that holds the time of the request. The JSON is processed in the back-end functions. The simple CA is created using the Asistent platform [2]. The platform supports the creation, management and use of virtual assistants. It is developed as a Software as a Service and is thus accessible through API calls. The platform is composed of several modules that provide answers to questions The most important modules are: (i) keyword-based answers; (ii) dynamic answering using RSS feeds or CSS selectors; (iii) indexing library to provide answers from structured data; (iv) applications that provide additional functionality to end-users. As a proof of concept we limited our search to the artwork type paintings or pictures and well-known authors in the prototype application. Communication with the Asistent platform is implemented using the API call:

/ask (HTTP GET method) using input parameters:

- *question:* The query from the user
- *context:* The context within the question was stated

The answer is provided as a JSON object containing four fields: (i) *answer*, providing the textual response of the CA; (ii) *ID*, the serial number of the answer; *URL*, a website that is associated with the response and (iv) *data*, that contains a JSON object with a list of artwork obtained from Europeana. The JSON is structured as follows:


```
{
"listSelect":
  {
  "items": [{
    "title": "Artwork title",
    "description": "The provided description",
    "imageURL": "The URL of the image",
    "formattedText": "A longer, formatted description"
    },...
  }
}
```


The data filed is used to construct the bottom part of the application, the gallery-like list representation (see Fig. 2). Selecting a specific element opens up a full-screen overlay showing a basic card providing more information linked to the selected object.

4.2 Evaluation of Search Results

A simple evaluation was performed based on the relevance of the search results and the perceived usefulness. We limited our search to paintings and/or images from five famous painters (Giotto, Monet, Picasso, Rembrandt, van Gogh) to ensure the presence of relevant artwork in Europeana. For each author, the first 100 results obtained from Europeana, that should be the most relevant, are analyzed qualitatively by obtaining user feedback from two questions: *Q1: CA provides appropriate search results based on the input* and Q2: *Interacting with CA is easy and flexible*. The two questions are graded with a number from 1 to 5 according to his perception of the statement (1 - totally disagree, 2 - partially disagree, 3 - neutral, 4 - partially agree, 5 - strongly agree). Next, a quantitative analysis is performed to obtain the ration of relevant results in the first 100 hits.

The next three figures present part of the search results for different search queries. Figure 2. Shows the retrieved images for the paintings of Monet query. Only part of the results are actual paintings or images of paintings, there are some documents linked to the painter, photographs from various events and also some objects, that are relevant, but missing the appropriate image. Out of 100 hits 42 objects can be regarded as relevant and they are not ranked in the order of importance.

Next, in Fig. 3. objects obtained from Europeana for paintings of van Gogh are listed. In this query, a higher ratio of relevant results was obtained (67 out of 100), but ranking by importance is again missing, which lowers the perceived quality of results. As before, among the results we can see images of documents, book and journal covers and not relevant portraits of the painter. There are less objects missing the image field; however, they are still present.

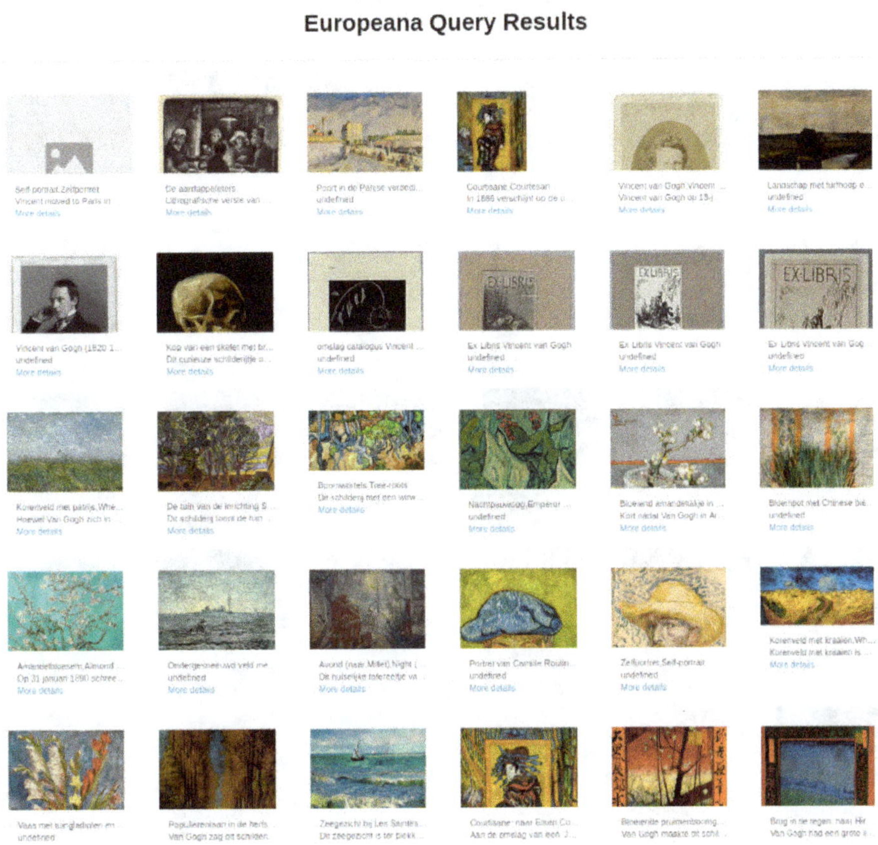

Fig. 3. Search results for the query van Gogh paintings.

Finally, in Fig. 4. part of the search results for Picasso paintings are listed. In the first 100 hits, 37 objects are tagged as relevant, which is, as in Fig. 2., a rather low value of relevant hits. There is a high ration of photographs of Picasso among the results, which is expected since he is a contemporary artist that died in 1973. We noticed that his most important artworks are missing in the results, which again points to a poor ranking mechanism provided in Europeana. As can be seen in Fig. 4. several objects missing the image field are present among the results, even though some of them represent relevant artwork of Picasso.

Table 1 provides a summary of the quantitative and qualitative evaluation. Q1 was evaluated for each author, while Q2 addressed the overall usability of the system and is thus represented with a single number. The numerical evaluations for Q1 and Q2 are averaged and rounded to the first decimal number. As it can be observed, the evaluation of the relevance did not score high values, which means that users did not find the obtained search results to be useful. Contrary, they found the CA to be easy to use and flexible (average 4.3 out of 5.0). The relevance ratio of artwork in the first 100 hits is presented in the last row. Except for van Gogh, the values are rather low, which is in line with the user evaluation from Q1.

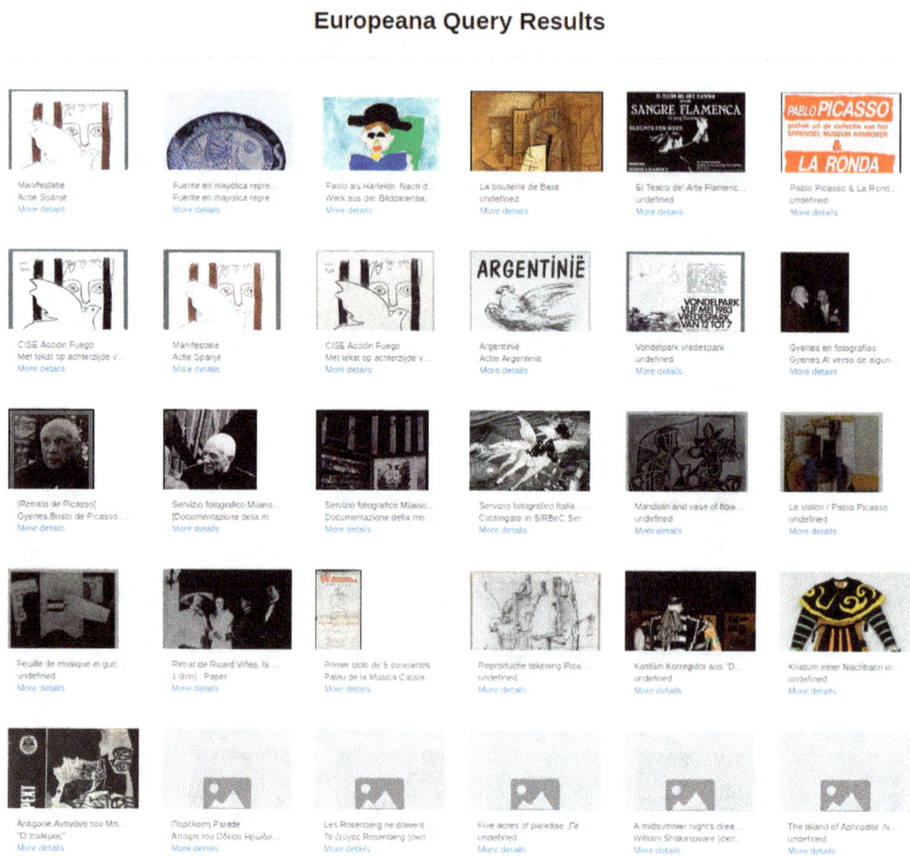

Fig. 4. Search results for the query Picasso paintings.

Table 1. Evaluation summary.

	Giotto	Monet	Picasso	Rembrandt	Van Gogh
Q1	2.6	3.0	2.9	2.8	**3.4**
Q2	**4.3**				
Relevance ratio	35%	42%	37%	46%	**67%**

The implication is that the Europeana API does not provide relevant results based on the search queries, which limits its usability. There is a need to provide an efficient ranking or scoring mechanism to improve the relevance of the search results.

5 Conclusions and Future Work

In this paper we presented a proof-of-concept of a web-based application implementing a conversational agent that enables communication in natural language with the user and provides an intuitive interface to the Europeana database, a digital cultural library which provides public access to millions of digital objects from thousands of contributing heritage collections all across the European Union. Within the application, the user can search for paintings and images of specific authors.

The evaluation of the search results highlighted a major issue linked to the Europeana database. The lack of a ranking measure that would rate search results based on the popularity or importance of the artwork results in a rather poor relevance of the top search results. This gives to users the perception of poor understanding by the CA and limited usability of the system to provide relevant results to search queries.

Future research efforts will address the aforementioned issue and will focus on finding the appropriate solutions for improving the quality and format of the responses to user queries. By applying machine learning and linking additional data from external resources (e.g. Wikipedia) to design an evaluation function that would rank the artwork obtained from Europeana and display the top 50 best ranked results will greatly improve user acceptance, usefulness and increase the perceived intelligence of the conversational agent. Learning will be performed on the textual meta-data associated to each record and by introducing decision rules that qualitatively evaluate a specific record. In addition, computer vision methods could be applied to the graphical element of the record set to identify the most relevant record by comparison among them or with data from external sources.

References

1. Francisco, J.S., Carlos, B.: VOX system: a semantic embodied conversational agent exploiting linked data. Multimed. Tools Appl. **75**(1), 381–404 (2016)
2. Jernej, Z., Damjan, K., Ales, T., Mihai, D.: Virtual assistant platform. Informatica **40**(3), 285–290 (2016)
3. Foster, M.E.: Enhancing human-computer interaction with embodied conversational agents. In: Stephanidis, C. (ed.) UAHCI 2007. LNCS, vol. 4555, pp. 828–837. Springer, Heidelberg (2007). https://doi.org/10.1007/978-3-540-73281-5_91
4. Bickmore, T., Pfeifer, L., Schulman, D.: Relational Agents Improve Engagement and Learning in Science Museum Visitors. In: Vilhjálmsson, H.H., Kopp, S., Marsella, S., Thórisson, Kristinn R. (eds.) IVA 2011. LNCS (LNAI), vol. 6895, pp. 55–67. Springer, Heidelberg (2011). https://doi.org/10.1007/978-3-642-23974-8_7
5. Kopp, S., Gesellensetter, L., Krämer, Nicole C., Wachsmuth, I.: A conversational agent as museum guide – design and evaluation of a real-world application. In: Panayiotopoulos, T., Gratch, J., Aylett, R., Ballin, D., Olivier, P., Rist, T. (eds.) IVA 2005. LNCS (LNAI), vol. 3661, pp. 329–343. Springer, Heidelberg (2005). https://doi.org/10.1007/11550617_28
6. William, S.: Lessons learned from virtual humans. AI Mag. **31**(1), 9–20 (2010)
7. Arthur, C.G., et al.: AutoTutor: a tutor with dialogue in natural language. Behav. Res. Methods **36**(2), 180–192 (2004)
8. Jayfus, T.D.: PECA: pedagogical embodied conversational agents in mixed reality learning environments. In: AIED, p. 957 (2005)
9. Victoria, L.R., Yimin, C., Lynne, M.T.: Artificially intelligent conversational agents in libraries. Libr. Hi Tech **28**(4), 496–522 (2010)
10. Bing, X., Pan, Z.G., Yang, H.W.: Agent-based model for intelligent shopping assistant and its application. In: The first Conference on Affective Computing and Intelligent Interaction, Beijing, pp. 306–311. Citeseer (2003)
11. Čereković, A., et al.: Implementing a multi-user tour guide system with an embodied conversational agent. In: Liu, J., Wu, J., Yao, Y., Nishida, T. (eds.) AMT 2009. LNCS, vol. 5820, pp. 7–18. Springer, Heidelberg (2009). https://doi.org/10.1007/978-3-642-04875-3_7

12. Ian, D.: In favour of (more) intelligence in the semantic UI. In: Proceedings of the Sixth International Workshop on Semantic Web User Interaction (2009)
13. Philipp, C., Stefan, K.: Accessing the web of data through embodied virtual characters. Semant. Web **1**(1, 2), 83–88 (2010)
14. Eduardo, M.E., Víctor, L., Juan, L.C.: A framework for designing closed domain virtual assistants. Expert Syst. Appl. **39**(3), 3135–3144 (2012)
15. Ulli, W., Alexa, B., Ipke, W.: Digital fruits for lunch: feeding embodied conversational agents with Wikipedia knowledge. Postersession at the Interdisciplinary College (2011)
16. Ulli, W., Alexa, B., Ipke, W.: Interfacing virtual agents with collaborative knowledge: open domain question answering using wikipedia-based topic models. In: IJCAI, pp. 1896–1902 (2011)
17. Jon, P.: Think culture: Europeana. eu from concept to construction. Electron. Libr. **27**(6), 919–937 (2009)
18. Stefan, G.: Knowledge = informatio in conyext: on the importance of semantic contextualisation. In: Europeana white paper, vol. 1, pp. 1–19. Berlin School of Library und Information/Humboldt Universitat zu Berlin (2010)
19. Antoine, I., Bernhard, H.: Europeana linked open data–data. europeana. eu. Semant. Web **4**(3), 291–297 (2013)
20. Cesare, C., Stefan, G., Sjoerd, S.: Not just another portal, not just another digital library: a portrait of Europeana as an application program interface. IFLA J. **36**(1), 61–69 (2010)
21. Vecchio, P., Mele, F., De Paolis, L.T., Epicoco, I., Mancini, M., Aloisio, G.: Cloud computing and augmented reality for cultural heritage. In: De Paolis, L.T., Mongelli, A. (eds.) AVR 2015. LNCS, vol. 9254, pp. 51–60. Springer, Cham (2015). https://doi.org/10.1007/978-3-319-22888-4_5

Restoration and Digitization

"I Went to America to See Ancient Italian Paintings": The Problem of the Re-contextualization of Artworks Uprooted from Their Original Settings

Grazia Maria Fachechi[1(✉)], Antonella Guidazzoli[2], Daniele De Luca[2], Maria Chiara Liguori[2], Luigi Verri[2], and Giovanni Bellavia[2]

[1] Urbino University, Urbino, Italy
grazia.fachechi@uniurb.it
[2] VisitLab, Cineca Interuniversity Consortium, Casalecchio di Reno, Italy
visitlab@cineca.it

Abstract. The paper aims to explore new methods of re-contextualization of artworks in their original settings, based on 3D reconstruction and 3D Web, through a case-study. It concerns a cycle of Medieval frescoes, detached from the walls of a monastery in Umbria, Central Italy, altered by numerous and some very recent renovations. At the present, the fragments of the cycle of frescoes are preserved in various museums, mostly in the United States.

Keywords: Italian Medieval frescoes · American museums · 3D reconstruction 3DWeb · Digital Heritage

1 Introduction

"Sono andato in America per conoscere molte antiche pitture italiane": the important Italian art historian Lionello Venturi wrote these words in his introduction to two volumes, titled *Pitture italiane in America*, published by Ulrico Hoepli Editore in Milan in 1931, and dedicated to many artworks from Italy that ended up across the ocean. At the enthusiasm he discovered, unexpectedly but happily, of the love for Italian art demonstrated by American collectors, Venturi also discovered many questions about the "plucked flowers" and the problem of the de-contextualization of artworks uprooted from their original settings and sold on the art market, which, on the one hand, had increased the phenomenon of collecting and connoisseurship, and on the other, had led, in many cases, to the loss of any sense of the provenance of the works themselves, all now exhibited in museums [1]. Historical research attempted, over the course of the last decades, to close some of the gaps created between artworks and their provenance, often enabling a complete sense of the original context, which new 3D technology allows us to visualize, going well beyond written description or simple graphic recreation, leaving future generations with an effective memory of culturally

M. Duguleană et al. (Eds.): VRTCH 2018, CCIS 904, pp. 197–205, 2019.
https://doi.org/10.1007/978-3-030-05819-7_15

complex systems, now fragmented and no longer accessible, while the interaction between the Humanities and Digital Heritage continues to solicit deeper reflections and new knowledge.

This paper presents the results of a multi-disciplinary project linking Humanities to Digital technologies (started from a preliminary survey of artworks uprooted from Medieval religious buildings in Central Italy [2]), that aimed to virtually piece together a dispersed cultural heritage, restoring its overall physiognomy by putting it into its historic and historic-artistic context and by creating suitable traditional and multi-media tools, which enables the works of art to be enjoyed as though they were still all together in the same place, in their original layout

2 The Frescoes of the Monastery of S. Maria Inter Angelos

The cycle of frescoes of the Clarissan monastery of St. Maria inter Angelos, called Le Palazze, located very close to Spoleto, in Umbria, Central Italy, was created by an anonymous Maestro, which we call the "Maestro delle Palazze". It is of such high quality that another important Italian art historian, Roberto Longhi, described it as "la splendida serie duecentesca", whereas other critics referred to individual parts of it as "outstanding examples of thirteenth century Italian art".

In the 1920s, the majority of the frescoes were removed and purchased by American collectors, and now are preserved in five museums on the East coast of the United States [3]: the Museum of Fine Arts in Boston (MA), the Glencairn Museum in Bryn Athin (near Philadelphia-PA), the Fogg Art Museum at Harvard University in Cambridge (MA), the Wadsworth Atheneum Museum of Art at Hartford (CT), and the Worcester Art Museum at Worcester (MA).

The technique employed to remove the frescoes, known as *lo strappo*, that is the removal of only the upper surface of paint, made possible to remove, many years later, also the second layer still visible on the walls of the monastery. In 1964, in fact, these 'second detachments' of the five frescoes earlier detached, and one of the frescoes not yet detached, were removed from the walls, and are now exhibited in the National Museum of the Duchy of Spoleto, with other two scenes found in another room, on the lower level of the monastery, representing the *Enthroned Madonna and Child with Saints Clare and Francis*, and the *Crucifixion* [4].

In the end, the bond between text and context was lost forever. We are not just talking about a physical de-contextualization, meaning the separation of the frescoes from the architecture and, as a consequence, the musealization (an operation often very useful, since it makes the works of art better preserved), but also about a cultural de-contextualization, meanings a fragmentation (the cycle is not united anymore), and a dispersion in places far from the original place. Since we all agree that every work of art should be understood in its context, with our project we intended to recreate the original context for these fragments.

Today nothing remains on the walls, save a few small, evanescent traces of the frescoes. We don't even have any written evidence about the monastery at the time when the frescoes were painted, and the only description of the cycle before the removal of the frescoes, written by Raimond van Marle [5], is vague. Fortunately, we have a few historical photographs of the monastery before the 'second detachments' were detached, and, of course, we have the frescoes.

As we said, the frescoes were originally painted in two different rooms of the monastery, on two levels, one above the other. The most interesting room is certainly the upper room (see Fig. 1).

Fig. 1. Monastery of St. Maria Inter Angelos, upper room, eastward, and its 3D reconstruction (on the right).

In the upper room, the frescoes represent stories about the Virgin and the Passion of Christ. The sequence began on the south wall, moving eastward, which now reveals only infinitesimal signs of plaster and pigments. Based on a historic photograph taken when the room was used as a hayloft and before the second detachment was removed, we can virtually restore, with certainty, the two scenes on the east portion of the south wall: the *Annunciation*, to the right, and the *Nativity*, to the left. The virtual reconstruction of the scene of the *Nativity* is based on the photograph found by Francis Henry Taylor in the file cards of the Worcester Museum, which he published in 1932 [6]. The image was taken when the fresco was still *in situ*, and thus prior to its removal and subdivision into various parts, only a few of which have survived to this day and are now in four different American museums. The black and white image, virtually repositioned on the wall, was used as a base for the application of color reproductions of the fragments that survived the subdivision of the image by the antiques market. This scene of the *Nativity* contains also the representation of the *Adoration of the Magi*. The position of the Magi appears designed to create a sort of continuity with the adjacent wall, a condition often found in wall paintings from the Byzantine world. Unfortunately, no traces remain of the portion to the right of the east wall. Maybe this area was once covered by an *Enthroned Virgin and Child*, with the Magi kneeling before them.

The narrative continued on the north wall, where the traces of the pigments are more evident. This wall was occupied, to the left, by *The Last Supper*, and, to the right, by the *Derision of Christ* (the scene in the room detached later respect to the other scenes). The narrative ended with the *Crucifixion*, in the left part of the eastern wall. In the room there were other two frescoes, that seem "independent" from the cycle we just mentioned: on the left, a *Crucifixion*, on the right, *The Second Coming*, maybe painted later, after the earthquake occurred in 1298 at Spoleto. This event and anxieties about the turn of the century, in other words trepidation about the coming of the end of the world and the imminent arrival of the Day of Judgment, at a time when calamities were considered punishment for human errors, offers a plausible explanation for these two scenes. What's more, here, for the first time in an eschatological context, we find a depiction of the *Mater omnium*, the very first representation of this iconography. This monumental figure, whose accentuated verticality evokes the bell tower of a church or town hall, welcomes the entire community beneath her mantle. The intermediary between sinners and a judging God, here the Virgin Mary is also to be seen as a bulwark against calamities and natural disasters [7].

For the study of the frescoes at Le Palazze, based largely on traditional methodologies, the use of digital technologies proved fundamental, since they consented a 360° exploration of space and a vision from different points of view, raising new questions and subsequent new intuitions and stimulating continuous attempts to express the indissoluble nexus between the frescoes and their place of origin. Above all they permitted a reunification – ideal, to be sure – of the fragments distributed in different museums. This dream was caressed during the past century by the directors of the Glencairn Museum and the Worcester Art Museum when, within their possibilities, the one attempted to purchase the fragments of frescoes from Le Palazze held by the other.

3 3D Spaces for Cultural Environments

Virtual environments are widely recognised as great opportunities in Cultural Heritage for research and communication [8–11] and 3DWeb is their natural ally. A fruitful tool for Cultural Heritage on-line outputs has been achieved in the past thanks to, for example, Multi User Virtual Words for cultural and educational aims [12, 13] and, at present, there are some considerations about merging virtual worlds and 3DWeb [14]. 3DWeb is a very simple solution for users: no specific applications to be downloaded, no plug-in to be installed, just a common recent browser and an average device are needed. In an approach aiming at developing the audience for Cultural Heritage contents, the Web option can be considered as the most viable and effective one and 3D environments have received a significant help by 3D Web.

VisitLab Cineca is engaged since the late Nineties in the development of Digital Heritage applications and deployed its first 3D environment online as part of the "Certosa Virtual Museum in Bologna" project in 2004 [15]. At the time, the virtual versions of two existing monuments, dedicated one to the Bolognese dead soldiers of the Great War and the other to the partisans fallen during the liberation war of the World War II, were created for a semi immersive stereoscopic fruition in Cineca Virtual Theatre. Thanks to a proprietary plug-in, called Exhibit 3D, the two virtual environments were delivered for a desktop and an online navigation and linked to a large database about the people and the events commemorated by these two monuments and their related ossuaries. However, the Exhibit 3D plug-in not only required an installation, in order for the 3D environment to be navigated, but also implied a licence to be paid, reasons why these 3D applications were, at some point, discontinued.

In recent years VisitLab tested some open source 3D players, such as X3DOM and Blender Game Engine [16], landing, in the end on Blend4Web (https://www.blend4web.com), an Open Source framework well integrated with the software Blender (https://www.blender.org/), used at the Lab as the main 3D modelling software since 2010. Blend4Web framework has been mainly used in order to achieve the online visualisation in projects such as Terrae Motus (https://hpc-forge.cineca.it/files/visit_reggiacaserta/public/demo_01/terremotus/terremotus.html) [17] or MUVI - Museum of Daily Life in 20th century Italy (http://muvi.cineca.it/) [18]. In those projects the applications were delivered for online fruition and, in both cases, along with a cardboard version, developed as an offline application. The final HTML file was created in a non automatic way matching the JSON + BIN export from Blender, the Javascript used for creating the interactions, the CSS file and Uranium.js for the physics. We will see in paragraph 4 why in the "Le Palazze" project a comprehensive HTML file was preferred instead.

4 The 3D Application for "Le Palazze"

The 3D reconstruction of the upper room of the monastery has been performed using Photoscan (http://www.agisoft.com/), starting from a photographic campaign suitable for photogrammetric reconstructions, and refined in Blender (www.blender.org). The room, used at present as a conference room and furnished with easily movable pliable chairs, enabled a straightforward acquisition campaign (see Fig. 1). The lower room, on the contrary, is now in use as a warehouse, preventing therefore a photogrammetric reconstruction and forcing a 3D modelling directly in Blender (see Fig. 2).

Fig. 2. Monastery of St. Maria Inter Angelos, lower room, eastward, and its virtual reconstruction (on the right).

After the setting of the photos of the frescoes dispersed among the different museums, the real-time navigation of the virtual environments has been implemented in Blend4Web (www.blend4web.com).

Blend4Web is a framework that, thanks to the integration of WebGL libraries inside the latest browsers, enables visualisation and interaction with 3D environments exported from Blender. Blend4Web does not need a plug-in and is programmable in JavaScript. For the application developed for the present project no JavaScript was used, preferring a direct export from Blender to the Web through the add-on in Blend4Web. This same add-on makes available in Blender logic nodes, that can be used managing the camera movements inside the scene (Fig. 3). In any case, by using Blender API's and JavaScript it is possible to create more complex movements and interactions.

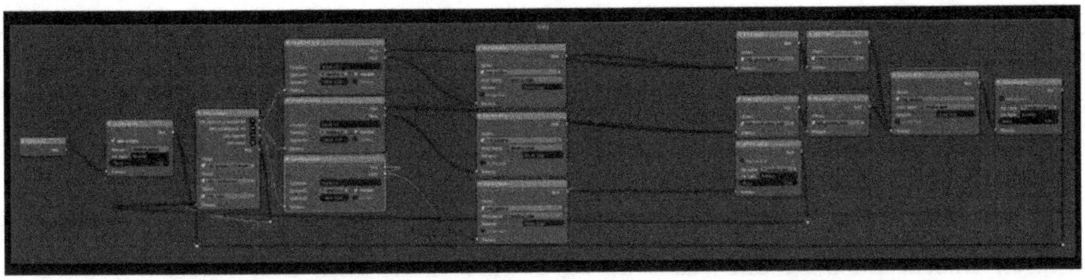

Fig. 3. Blender: node tree created to trigger the information panel by clicking on the info icons.

For the development of the app two nodes sufficed: "switch select" and "move camera". The first one, that consents to track the selection of an object in the scene, holds a list of clickable objects, that is, for both rooms, a series of tiles on the floor. With "move camera", instead, when an object is selected with the mouse, the node moves the camera by using two fictitious objects functioning as "destination" and "look at". "Destination" gives the point of arrival of the movement; "look at" directs the view of the camera.

The mesh was simplified in order to optimise the high-poly photogrammetric 3D model for a real-time navigation. The process was implemented in Blender thanks to a retopologizing of the high-poly mesh towards a low-poly model, with a number of polygons low enough to enable a smooth navigation inside the virtual reconstruction.

Further on, the transfer of the color information coming from the textures of the high-poly model was performed in Blender with the bake to textures technique. The technique needs a precise superimposition of the two models (high and low poly), the creation of a UV mapping by unwrapping the model, a source texture - from which to copy the information, and a destination canvas texture, where to copy the new colour information on the low-poly model.

5 A Simple 3D Web Application for an Off-Line Distribution

As before said, for the final publishing the 3D application was exported as a single comprehensive HTML file including geometries, the scene, the logics of the user's interactions and the libraries of the framework. As an all-in-one application it can be easily distributed. In our case this led also to the possibility of linking the application to other HTML pages through simple links: a 2D HTML page introduces the applications, explains the navigation modalities and enables the access to the two 3D reconstructed environments at Le Palazze - the main hall and the lower chapel, prepared as two comprehensive HTML files. The Blend4Web solution with the HTML export enables the user to visualise the application on whatever recent browser without the need of installing anything on its own device. Furthermore, by choosing Blend4Web, it is possible to rely upon very good final performances on mobile devices, on a wide selection of possible interactions inside the virtual world, a very good physics engine and an excellent reliability [19].

The navigation solution adopted for Le Palazze, user friendly in its simplified interface, was selected in order to be easily used by art historians, the preferred audience of the publication, and other researchers in humanities, that are not yet too versed in navigating virtual environments. Therefore, instead of a point and click system, a simplified version with hot spots was preferred. The movement is possible among large squared areas on the floor and is further helped by a minimap with an orthogonal view of the squares on a side of the window.

A JSON + BIN export would have enabled wider customisation options and more complex interactions. In our case, however, the main aim, that foresaw letting the viewer perceive the space and the relocated works of art in their pristine setting, was achieved with a more simple and slender solution.

6 Conclusions

The 3D reconstruction, based on the data collected through traditional historical research focused on various aspects (iconographic, stylistic, technical), finally shows the frescoes in their original settings, trying to help the scholars to understand the purpose of the complex original decorative program, until now pretty confused.

The 3D reconstruction will also have a certain impact on the use of the monastery as a monument, now stripped of the images that once completed it, and on the images themselves, the frescoes preserved in the museums, far from the monument to which they once belonged, both finally reunited.

The next step foresees the analysis of feedbacks of the users and the virtual restoration of the frescoes.

Acknowledgements. The authors wish to thank Alessandro Rivalta.

References

*Whereas the study presented here is a joint project undertaken by the scholars who signed the paper, the sections entitled "Introduction" and "The Frescoes of the monastery of S. Maria inter Angelos" are the work of Grazia Maria Fachechi exclusively.

1. Venturi, L.: Pitture italiane in America, p. XVII and passim, Hoepli, Milano (1931)
2. Fachechi G.M.: Dal complesso al frammento, dal testo al contesto: a proposito di opere d'arte umbro-marchigiane dei secoli XI-XIII. In: Neri Lusanna E. (ed.) Umbria e Marche in età romanica: arti e tecniche a confronto tra XI e XIII secolo, pp. 297–308, Ediart, Todi (2013)
3. Di Carpegna, T., Fachechi, G.M.: The Palazze Frescoes. A Tale between Umbria and America, pp. 195–209. Gangemi Editore International, Roma (2017)
4. Toscano, B.: Il Maestro delle Palazze e il suo ambiente. Paragone 25, pp. 3–23 (1974)
5. Van Marle, R.: The Development of the Italian Schools of Painting, I, p. 407. Nijhoff, The Hague (1923)
6. Taylor, F.H.: Rainaldictus Fresco Painter of Spoleto. Bull. Worcest. Art Mus. **22**, 78 (1932)
7. Fachechi, G.M.: From the Monastery to the Museum and Back. Le Palazze at Spoleto, from Fragmentation to Virtual Reconstruction. In: Di Carpegna, T., Fachechi, G.M. (eds.) The Palazze Frescoes. A Tale between Umbria and America, pp. 57–131, Gangemi Editore International, Roma (2017)
8. Barcelo, J., Forte, M., Sanders, D. (eds.): Virtual Reality in Archaeology (BAR International Series S 843). ArcheoPress, Oxford (2000)
9. Roussou, M.: Virtual heritage: from the research lab to the broad public. In: Niccolucci, F. (ed.) VAST 2000 Euro Conference. BAR International Series, vol. 1075, pp. 93–100. Archaeopress, Oxford (2002)
10. Lercari, N., Shiferaw, E., Forte, M., Kopper, R.: Immersive visualization and curation of archaeological heritage data: Çatalhöyük and the Dig@IT App. J. Archaeol. Method Theory (2017). https://doi.org/10.1007/s10816-017-9340-4
11. Bekele, M., Pierdicca, R., Frontoni, E., Malinverni E.S., Gain, J.: A survey of augmented, virtual, and mixed reality for cultural heritage. J. Comput. Cult. Herit. **11**(2), 1–36. https://doi.org/10.1145/3145534
12. Urban, R., Marty, P., Twidale, M.: A Second Life for Your Museum: 3D Multi-User Virtual Environments and Museums, Archives and Museum Informatics (2007)
13. Huang, Y.-C., Han, S.R.: An immersive virtual reality museum via second life. In: Stephanidis, C. (ed.) HCI 2014. CCIS, vol. 434, pp. 579–584. Springer, Cham (2014). https://doi.org/10.1007/978-3-319-07857-1_102
14. Bakri, H., Allison, C., Miller, A., Oliver, I.: Virtual worlds and the 3D web – time for convergence? In: Allison, C., Morgado, L., Pirker, J., Beck, D., Richter, J., Gütl, C. (eds.) iLRN 2016. CCIS, vol. 621, pp. 29–42. Springer, Cham (2016). https://doi.org/10.1007/978-3-319-41769-1_3
15. Borgatti, C., et al.: Databases and virtual environments: a good match for communicating complex cultural sites. In: SIGGRAPH Proceedings 2004. ACM, Los Angeles (2004)
16. Baglivo, A., Delli Ponti, F., De Luca, D., Guidazzoli, A., Liguori, M.C., Fanini, B.: X3D/X3DOM, blender game engine and OSG4WEB: open source visualisation for cultural heritage environments. In: 2013 Digital Heritage International Congress (DigitalHeritage), Marseille, pp. 711–718 (2013)

17. Felicori, M., et al.: Reggia di Caserta: un Patrimonio in Rete. In: Conferenza GARR 2016 - The CreActive Network - Selected Papers, Firenze, 30 novembre-2 dicembre 2016, pp. 111–114. Associazione Consortium GARR (2017). ISBN 978-88-905077-6-2. https://doi.org/10.26314/garr-conf16-proceedings-19
18. Chiavarini, B., Liguori, M.C., Verri, L., Imboden, S., De Luca, D., Guidazzoli, A.: On-line interactive virtual environments in Blend4Web. The integration of pre-existing 3D models in the MUVI-Virtual Museum of Daily Life project. In: Cappellini, V. (ed.) EVA 2017 Proceedings, Florence, 10–11 May 2017. Firenze University Press, Florence (2017)
19. Prakov, A.: Blend4web vs Unity: WebGL Performance Comparison 21 October 2016. http://www.blend4web.com/en/community/article/280/

Non-physical Painting Restoration in Improved Reality

Marko Aleksić[1(✉)] and Vanja Jovanović[2]

[1] Ayako Studio, Jurija Gagarina 166A/51, 11000 Belgrade, Serbia
markoaleksic81@gmail.com
[2] Tehnoart Beograd, Svetog Nikole 39, 11000 Belgrade, Serbia

Abstract. How to restore a painting when physical and chemical alteration of the painted layer has not yet reached a final stage and is partly caused by unknown ageing processes? Can we make a painting look restored without any physical intervention on it? We encountered this problem in the course of conservation treatment of paintings of the famous Serbian Cubistic and Informalist painter Lazar Vozarević. In the period of 2015–2017, the "Lazar Vozarević" Gallery, based in Sremska Mitrovica, carried out a large project of conservation and restoration of Vozarević's paintings from different periods. The conservation and restoration treatment was successfully carried out on all paintings but one, a painting from his Informal period, entitled "Untitled" (1961). Due to its physical deterioration, the painting could not be successfully restored using conventional well-established methods. We came to a decision to propose a virtual restoration treatment which would be conducted in a mixed reality environment. In strictly controlled light condition, an exact virtual retouch would be projected onto the canvas, so that the result would be a unique installation, which would emphasize and unify both the original painting and its virtual counterpart.

Keywords: Virtual restoration · Virtual retouch · Improved reality

1 Introduction

How to restore a painting when physical and chemical alteration of the painted layer has not yet reached a final stage and is partly caused by unknown ageing processes? Can we make a painting look restored without any physical intervention on it? We encountered this problem in the course of conservation treatment of paintings of the famous Serbian Informalist painter Lazar Vozarević (Merenik 2010; Trifunovic 1998; Stanojević 2013). In the period of 2015–2017, the "Lazar Vozarević" Gallery, based in Sremska Mitrovica, carried out a large project of conservation and restoration of Vozarević's paintings from different periods. The conservation and restoration treatment was successfully carried out on all paintings but one, a painting from his Informal period, entitled "Untitled" (1961) (Fig. 1).

An integral part of the paint layer consists of two copper plates that were tinted with dark thin coating to fit the tonality of the painting. The plates were firmly attached (using nails) but in some places a bit disconnected from the surface to which they are

M. Duguleană et al. (Eds.): VRTCH 2018, CCIS 904, pp. 206–214, 2019.
https://doi.org/10.1007/978-3-030-05819-7_16

Fig. 1. Lazar Vozarević "Untitled" 1961, Gallery "Lazar Vozarević", Sremska Mitrovica

bound. The material that was used for the "application" of copper plates in the surface layer of the painting, a kind of filler, was cracked and unstable. The color of the paint layer was degraded, discolored and missing in some places.

The building where the painting was located within, the Lazar Vozarević Gallery, was built in the first half of the twentieth century. It was poorly maintained and showed visible signs of damage to the structure and traces of humidity influx. The building has never had acclimatization; it has large window surfaces and lacks insulation. Typically, this type of exhibition spaces are exposed to sudden, significant changes in temperature and relative humidity, which lead to mechanical damage to the paintings such as cracking. In addition, during the reconstruction of the Gallery, the collection was stored in inadequate conditions; paintings were kept in piles and exposed to daily rise in temperature due to the presence of two windows on the eastern side of the storage.

However, the existing damage to the surface of the painting is evidently not only the consequence of effects of microclimate conditions, but also of the techniques and materials used. Analysis of the combination of adhesives, pigments and dyes used on the painting, confirmed the existence of changeable pigments, in particular lithol red, which is not only highly light-sensitive but also chemically unstable and sensitive to heat. This made the painting additionally susceptible to environmental conditions and mechanical damage, at the level of the paint layer (Standeven 2008). These underlying causes and the extent of the deterioration would have demanded exhaustive treatment, the use of toxic compounds (Artigas 2009) and a near-complete restoration with similar materials and techniques. This was considered invasive and hazardous. The alternative was to restore the pristine state of the painting virtually, concealing the damage of the painted layer without physical intervention on the painting itself (Stenger et al. 2016; Janke and Riedl 2010).

The question posed was how can we make the painting look restored? At present, there is a multitude of tools and specialist knowledge, to create a near-identical digital copy of the original painting and to perform a virtual restoration. To achieve this, the painting could either be 3D scanned or acquired by photogrammetric technique, obtaining a highly precise 3D mesh with realistic texture. Lacunas and damage to the paint layer could be remodeled in the generated model's geometry, with colors corrected on the texture. The result would be a realistic digital counterpart of original painting's appearance. The created model can be presented in a tailor-made software application or in a web browser, allowing it to be observed and valuated. Most importantly, the painters' original idea and painting's artistic significance can be preserved and conveyed. This virtually restored replica cannot be exhibited within the museum as a single undivided work of art, as the original and its digital representation will always be separate items in confrontation with each other, whether the digital representation is presented in graphical (printed) form or as an on-screen video. One could argue that this is nonetheless a legitimate solution. Its greatest benefit is that it would not disrupt or compromise the paintings integrity and authenticity. But, the question was raised, if we could go one step further, can we improve the painting's appearance by using its digitally restored replica? If we were to create an augmented reality application for mobile devices, we could present digitally restored version of the painting to the visitors. After observing the original painting, one could download the AR application and through mobile device observe the painting restored. This solution demands that spectators have powerful devices and that the light conditions in the exhibition room can be precisely measured and reproduced in the AR application, for the best quality experience. Other issues with this solution are the targeting of the painting, as it is a two-dimensional object. The technology needs to be user friendly enough for regular museum visitors to use it without the need for additional training.

2 Resources and Comparison

The initial idea was further developed by studying the conservation work performed on Mark Rothko's Harvard Murals, where the painting's appearance was successfully altered by means of a projected compensation image as an integral part of the restoration process. Rothko's murals had suffered significant color fading and alterations that were virtually restored by software controlled light conditions and a fine-tuned color compensation image that was projected onto it. In fact, there turned out to be similarities between Rothko's mural and the Lazar Vozarević's painting, in terms of the pigments and techniques used.

Comparing the colors used for the painting of Lazar Vozarević with those of Rothko's murals, it was concluded that both used lithol red. Representative Raman spectra were collected on the selected samples from the painting "Untitled". Due to high spatial resolution, micro Raman spectroscopy was employed to identify lithol red synthetic organic pigment (Vandenabeele et al. 2008). In the literature there is clear evidence of lithol red fading due to sunlight (Standeven 2008). Having this in mind, careful attention was paid to Raman spectra collection on the paint that contains lithol red, especially to the used power of illumination.

Firstly, physical conservation treatment was carried out to stabilize the paint layer on Vozarević's painting. Based on the test results of the cleaning exercise, dirt from the paintings surface was removed with distilled water, while the copper plates were cleaned with artificial saliva. The new ground was applied on the damaged areas, which was identically structured to the relief of the original one. Retouching was performed with watercolor paints and completed with MAIMERI® Restaurocolours - pigments with ketone-based resin and selected hydrocarbon solvents, with retouching varnish (J. G. VIBERT retouching varnish; LEFRANC & BOURGEOIS: with acrylic and ketone resin, quick drying petroleum; contains the most resin with 25% dry extract after drying) between them (Jovanović 2012). Both retouching techniques were done in the tratteggio, using vertical lines in different colors. Degraded areas on the surface of the paint layer were not retouched. Although the conservation and restoration activities were carried out successfully, it was evident that the color fading was still highly visible.

Secondly, the virtual restoration treatment was initiated. It was to be conducted in a mixed reality environment, where virtual retouch would be projected onto the painting's surface, in controlled light conditions. The difference to Rothko's murals is that Vozarević's painting has a more three dimensional geometry, which means that the image projection could not have just one direction, since it would not cover all surfaces and would create highly contrasted shadow areas around bump feathers. Also, the decision was made not to use software algorithms for the real-time calculation of the compensation image, but rather to create an exact virtual retouch to be used as a projection under strictly controlled light conditions in the exhibition space, so that the result would be an installation that both emphasizes and unifies the original painting and its virtual counterpart.

3 Proposal for the Virtual Restoration in Improved Reality Process

The virtual restoration project was divided into two phases:

1. Real to virtual – A process of obtaining the exact spatial information of the painting, as well as information on the paint layer's color and characteristics, i.e. full digitalization of the painting to enable the restoration work in the virtual environment.
2. Virtual to real - Extracting the virtual retouch and implementing it in the real world environment by projecting it onto the painting's surface. The aim was to create a visual experience that made the painting look fully restored and without physical damage.

3.1 Real to Virtual

To implement this idea, an exact digital copy of the painting needs to be created. This means collecting all the spatial and color information that can be recovered, with the highest possible precision and in a visually adequate sense. Geometrical and spatial information of the painting is needed because the paint layer is not flat, two copper plates are attached in the paint layer and are an integral part of the composition. In addition, the paint layer doesn't have the same thickness throughout the surface, since the artistic strokes are applied freely and unevenly. Therefore, the visual data collection process has to collect the maximum level of output quality to achieve the desired results. Therefore, the visual data collection process has to meet minimal requirements needed to achieve the desired results.

The initial facts and requirements were:

- The painting's dimensions are 160 cm (width) × 58 cm (height) (area of interest - 9280 cm^2);
- The painting has to be an integral part of exhibition;
- Light conditions in the painting's environment need to be strictly controlled, to match the virtual compensation retouch.

In order to keep the same light conditions within the exhibition space physical barrier has to be constructed to obstruct light sources that cannot not be controlled (sunlight from windows, distant light sources, etc.). The barrier has to leave enough space for the visitors to observe the painting without getting too close. Within the gallery exhibition space a suitable niche was found in a short corridor that connects the collections from painters cubistic and informal period. The space is adequate for the set-up of controlled light conditions and the size of the space is suitable for visitors to see the painting, without separating the painting from the rest of the collection (Fig. 2).

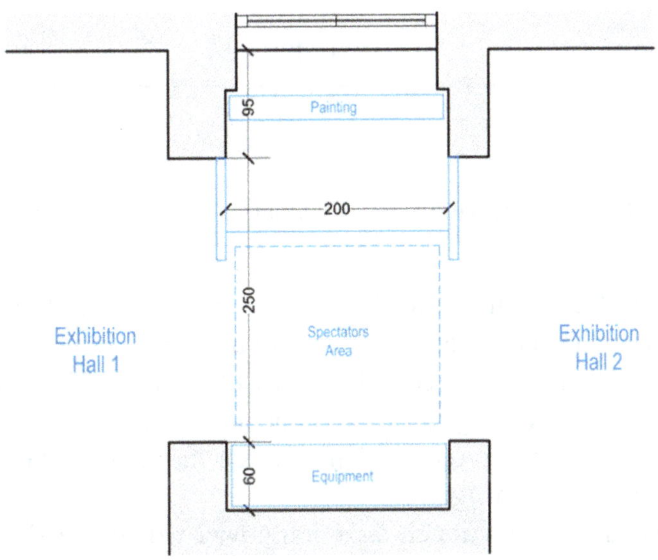

Fig. 2. Exhibition area and spatial set-up

The next step was choosing the projection resolution. We considered the Full HD projectors (1920 × 1080 px) and Ultra HD projectors (3840 × 2160 px). Ultra HD projectors offer up to 0.4 px/mm of line resolution of the projected image, while Full HD 1 px/mm. To attain the best projection quality, UHD projectors were the first choice as they provide a higher resolution image. However, after some initial tests, it was concluded that Full HD projector offers satisfying results at the minimum viewing distance of around 2 m, taking into account the painting's details which are not very sharp and applied with thick strokes. Even at this lower resolution the projector will have an adequate amount of over 2 million pixels projected onto the painting's surface. The projection image size resolution was set to 1920 × 696 px. Because of the paint layer's uneven surface it was decided to project the image from two separate sources, the combination of which would create a united projection, with even lighting on the entire surface of the painting. The projectors will be positioned behind the spectators and above the painting's top level at an optimal angle. A very small area of the painting cannot be lit this way and will be lit with compensating white LED light, acting as ambient light inside the installation (Fig. 3).

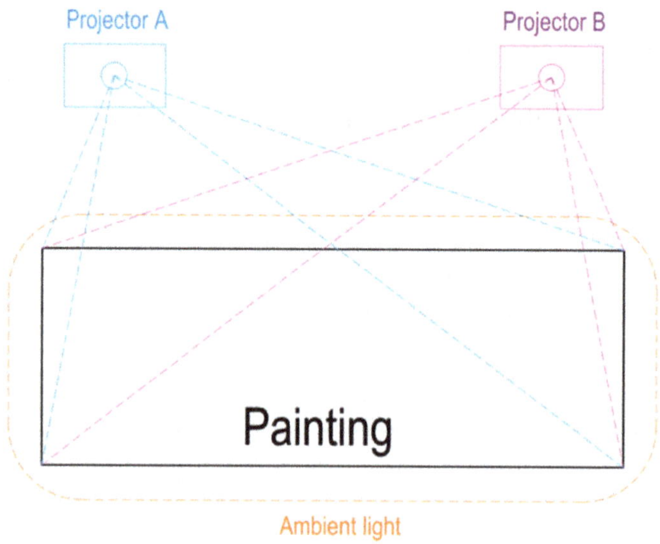

Fig. 3. Schematic view of virtual retouch installation

The final set-up of the virtual retouch will use 3 main additive light sources: 2 from projectors and 1 from the general ambient light, in uneven amounts. In other words, the illumination of the painting's surface will consist of around 20% from white ambient light and 40% from each of the projectors. Some areas (such as the sides of the bump feathers) will be lit from one projector only, which means the projectors have to be strong enough to emit enough light.

A crucial question was how much radiation power would actually be emitted onto the painting. For a conclusive answer to this question, a preventive conservation specialist would have to be consulted. Before a final decision on the project's approval is made, the exact value of emitted power has to be measured, its influence on the paint layer and the chemical processes inside the pigments analyzed, in order to determine the exact amount of power, light intensity, and safe time duration of single continuous projection per day, month and year. With the potential detrimental effects of the projection in mind, it was proposed to turn the projection automatically on only when visitors approached, while setting strict time limits on the maximum allowed duration (example, just 8 h per day).

The relatively small projection image size of 1920 $\times$ 696 px makes the virtual retouch technology widely applicable. The 3D digital model of the painting that will be created will have a higher resolution, making it suitable for other digital-only applications. It will be an exact 3D document of the present state of the painting. To acquire the data, close-range photogrammetry is a chosen method, because of its high-density models and high quality texture maps, and because the process of spatial and color information is simultaneous. The targeted 3D model mesh size is 10 points on 1 mm^2, with the same texel density. With the production of high density 3D models with regular mesh grid and rectangular UV map, the first phase of the project will be finished.

3.2 Virtual to Real

The next phase moves the work into the digital realm. The UV map of the 3D model of the painting will be fully flattened, with some little distortions on the bump area, which is inevitable in all 3D models with uneven surfaces. By working with very large-scale texture maps, the appearance of these errors can be minimised to the point of invisibility. The virtual restoration is the next step in the process, creating a layer of retouch in the same manner and colors as it would be created in a regular restoration treatment. This can be carried out in rasterized image editing software such as Adobe Photoshop or Gimp. To ensure the quality of the work, it must be carried out by skilled conservation professionals (Fig. 4).

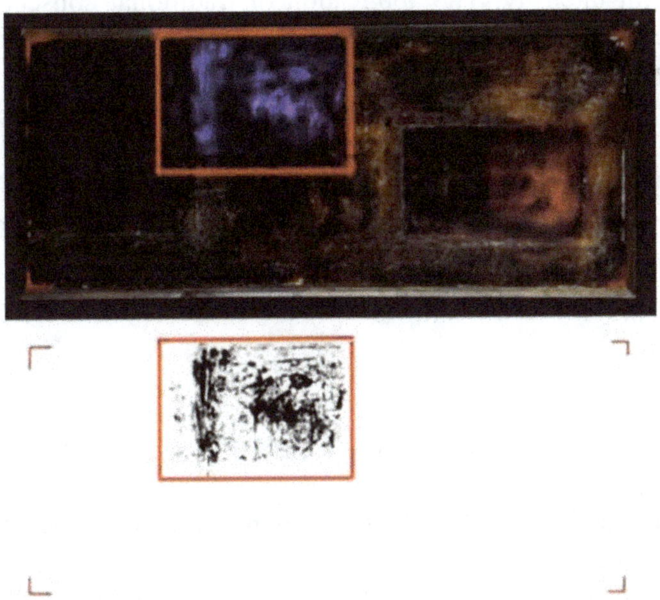

Fig. 4. Virtual retouch test area and example of projection image

While the work on digital retouch is being performed, testing and measurement of the distortions of the projected images should start. Like all devices with optical lenses, projectors have some distortion of image output. This is especially significant in this case, as the image is being projected at an angle. It is crucial for the projected image to perfectly match the painting's surface in order to prevent blurry and inadequate results. To optimise the projector's positions, curvature of the image projection (curvilinear projection) needs to be determined, as well as the perspective distortion. The resulting image of the distortion patterns need to be applied on a final virtual retouch image to compensate for all the perspective bending, so that projection geometrically matches the painting's surface.

The resulting images have to be fine-tuned with chromatic additive matching of the virtual retouch and lightness. This fine-tuning can be embedded directly into the color channels (RGB). The lightness of each projection image will be determined by mutual adjustment and with the consideration of ambient light. The last adjustments will be done on site when the installation is put into place.

4 Conclusion

The aim of this research was to show that the causes and processes of deterioration can only be properly understood when an appropriate conservation treatment is combined with a long-term preservation strategy that focuses on a historical-critical analysis of objects involved, while performing a detailed scientific study of the materials used.

In the case of Lazar Vozarević's painting, entitled "Untitled", extensive mechanical damage to the paint layer and lithol red fading had developed, due to inappropriate storage and the continuous exposure to fluctuations in temperature, relative humidity and especially light intensity. The application of traditional conservation techniques was limited. The restoration project focused on a promising new alternative to conventional preservation methods: virtual restoration. It raises important questions on the future of this hybrid digital approach as an alternative to conventional restoration treatments.

We would like to express our gratitude to Ognjen Kovačević, conservator at the Central Institute for Conservation in Belgrade, for his contribution to this research and for his help in writing the article.

References

Merenik, L.: Umetnost i vlast. Srpsko slikarstvo 1945–1968 (Art and Power. Serbian painting 1945–1968). Fond Vujičić, Belgrade (2010)

Trifunović, L.: Od impesionizma do enformela (From Impressionism to art informel). Nolit, Belgrade (1998)

Stanojević, Đ.: Slikanje Lazara Vozarevića ili traganje za identitetom. Živopis **7**, 179 (2013)

Standeven, H.A.L.: The history and manufacture of lithol red, a pigment used by Mark Rothko in his Seagram and Harvard Murals of the 1950s and 1960s. Tate Papers **10**, 1–8 (2008). http://www.tate.org.uk/download/file/fid/7323

Aleksić, M., Pendić, J.: Fotogrametrijsko snimanje muzejskih predmeta. In: Aćimović, M., Jovanović, S. (eds.) Preporuke za stvaranje I upravljanje digitalnom foto-dokumentacijom u institucijama zaštite kulturnog nalеđa. Centralni institute za konzervaciju, Beograd (2015)

Artigas, G.: Exhibition of Gustavo Artigas in galleria Hilario Galguera in Mexico. http://www.galeriahilariogalguera.com/nueva/index.php?id=91. Accessed 20 Apr 2018

Stenger, J., Khandekar, N., Raskar, R., Cuellar, S., Mohan, A., Gschwind, R.: Conservation of a room: a treatment proposal for Mark Rothko's Harvard Murals. Stud. Conserv. **61**(6), 348–361 (2016)

Janke, M., Riedl, N.: Missing piece of 16th-century mural recreated virtually. The Art Newspaper (2010). http://www.theartnewspaper.com/articles/Missing-piece-of-16th-century-muralrecreated-virtually/21757

Vandenabeele, P., De Paepe, P., Moens, L.: Study of the 19th century porcelain cards with direct Raman analysis. J. Raman Spectrosc. **39**, 1099–1103 (2008)

Jovanović, V.: The conservation of Petar Lubarda's painting prisoner – challenges and results. Public paintings by Edvard Munch and his contemporaries. Change and conservation challenges. In: Tine, F. (ed.) Proceedings International Conference in Oslo, pp. 325–333. Archetype Publications, London (2012)

Cultural Tourism

Improving Dissemination and Localization of Cultural Heritage Through Multimedia Maps - The Case of Lipari Island

Nicola Maiellaro(✉), Antonella Lerario, and Antonietta Varasano

Construction Technologies Institute, National Research Council of Italy, via Lembo 38/B, 70124 Bari, Italy
{maiellaro, lerario, varasano}@itc.cnr.it

Abstract. Most of the maps in tourist information websites show only the position of the Points of Interest (PoIs)—providing sometime a link to a webpage—making choices difficult. Multimedia maps, instead, could support users in satisfying the traveler needs giving links to information about the PoIs. The developed application supports improved connections between documents and the places they refer to because the user could select PoIs to visit through previews of its multimedia documents. PoIs could also be filtered through their categories and types, accessibility status and time line, thus improving the system usability. This article describes a multimedia map developed as sample for the Lipari Island, the largest of the Aeolian Islands (in Sicily), inscribed in the UNESCO World Heritage List.

Keywords: Multimedia map · UNESCO · RESTful web service
GeoJSON

1 Introduction

The World Economic Forum identified [1] two main categories of users: 'over 60' and 'Millennials'. The former practice non-seasonal tourism, requiring accessible services and high quality standards; the latter are particularly interested in cultural experiences even in less known destinations, regardless of the level of services. Moreover, 95% of travelers use digital resources not only to book but also to search for information, plan the trip and share their experiences [2].

Although there are many websites containing a great amount of information, it is not easy to find proper and tailored information satisfying various traveler needs, due to a poor attention to the potentiality of interactive maps gathering and sharing multimedia information. Most of the maps in tourist information portals show only the position of the Points of Interest (P.o.I.s), sometime with a link to a webpage.

Multimedia maps, born with the development of the personal computer since the 1980s [3], interact with multimedia documents through mouse clicks on hypertext links available in 'hot-spots' [4]. Another way, providing descriptions details (in hypertext format), photo, and video—organized in three tabs in the callout—has been suggested in [5] but now not available online [6].

M. Duguleană et al. (Eds.): VRTCH 2018, CCIS 904, pp. 217–233, 2019.
https://doi.org/10.1007/978-3-030-05819-7_17

In our novel approach, multimedia documents and P.o.I.s are linked in bidirectional way: the user could start selecting a P.o.I. in the map and access its multimedia data through their previews (in order to select the objects to visit), or viewing the multimedia documents available in the map and select the owner P.o.I. to visit.

In order to reduce the great deal of time and efforts to produce this kind of maps—unfamiliar to many—an authoring system has been developed, using two sets of files with info about P.o.I.s and the related multimedia documents.

2 The Case Study

Lipari, the largest of the Aeolian Islands in Sicily, is an outstanding testimony of the processes of generation and destruction of islands due to volcanic phenomena, still underway in other islands of the archipelago such as Stromboli and Vulcano. The whole archipelago was inscribed in the UNESCO World Heritage List in 2000, as remarkable example of the coexistence of two types of eruption (Vulcan and Strombolian), and can be considered as a constantly evolving archaeological park, enriched with naturalistic areas. 'Wild' areas can hardly be found in the whole Aeolian archipelago; the actual landscape is the result of a close intertwining of man and nature, of the natural environment and a millenary human work [7]. The succession and overlapping of anthropic activities over time ended up marking this territory in negative sense, starting from the chaotic building development in the '60s up to the growth of tourism-related activities, especially in coastal areas, with often-irreversible effects leading to a differentiation among the Aeolian Islands. Lipari and Vulcano can be considered as being in their mature stage as tourist destination; Lipari, in particular, though having a weaker volcanic component, has undergone mass tourism more than the other islands thanks to its closer connection with the rest of Sicily and to the higher level of its accommodation facilities. The latter, anyway, faced with the recent explosion of over-tourism in the summer, is now struggling to bear such burden in a context where general services turn out inadequate even for residents [7].

Tourism, precious in the critical post-war period, is by now one of the two main causes for the environmental deterioration of the whole archipelago, and of Lipari in particular, due to its unrestrained and disharmonic development. The other cause is to be found in the current climate changes, in relation to the extreme vulnerability of coasts, determining a sensible and progressive rise in the relative sea level and the subsequent gradual submergence or flooding of valuable archaeological and cultural sites along the coasts, such as the port and the Church of 'Anime del Purgatorio'.

In this respect, the flooding scenarios outlined up to 2100 [8] are undoubtedly alarming. Such situation suggests the opportunity to protect this endangered material heritage from within an organic view, such as UNESCO can ensure. The designation in the WHL can potentially prove decisive also in relation to economic development, through tourism-related activities: the current local offer is still focused on the conventional 'sun-sea-and-sand' segment and on a young target, and it is not fitted for a demand referred to the volcanic area [9]. However, although recognizing the extreme fragility of coastal zones, new promotion strategies still head towards them, by proposing thematic or geo-tourist itineraries [10], without sensibly impacting in terms of flow de-seasoning, which is instead more and more necessary [7, 9].

Much research work has been carried out, in general, on the effects of WHL designation on heritage management and on territorial development [11–16]. Among them, and with specific reference to tourism, some are of the view that the UNESCO 'brand' in itself can have only indirect impacts and that the inscription in the List is not sufficient, alone, to exert long-lasting effects [9].

On the basis of the 'public good' nature of UNESCO heritage and of the analysis of the performance observed in the Aeolian Islands [17], it derives that the main determiner for a correct territorial development is the whole of virtuous processes that are concretely triggered upstream and downstream of the designation, i.e. preparatory and subsequent to it, bringing about the production of further public goods [18]. More specifically, the effectiveness of the UNESCO recognition is linked to the site's ability to activate creative processes in different sectors.

Creativity is, then, an essential factor for the positive development of a UNESCO site. Actually, this is an element that marks the evolution of WHL recognition criteria, gradually shifted along the years from historic and artistic value to the consideration of immaterial culture, up to the current focus on the relation between heritage and local community and on creativity.

In our vision, knowledge plays a key-role in this virtuous relationships between material (physical resources) and intangible (the ways communities relate to them) culture, even more for a threatened heritage as is the case with the Aeolian Islands. Alongside with heritage, also knowledge on it requires careful protection and promotion, and the tools designed to support it can effectively generate creative processes.

Indeed, creativity can be expressed also in the ways residents and visitors define and plan their visit experiences based on knowledge available. More specifically, tools conceived for interactive use facilitate, on one hand, knowledge acquisition, concretely realizing one of the basic principle of the current UNESCO perspective: the 'transmission' – especially in intergenerational sense [7] -, of heritage. On the other hand, interactive tools, enriched with multimedia content, support creativity in the establishment of relationships between users and resources, by allowing personal approaches in the planning of visits, the selection of resources, the definition of physical or thematic paths combining them and, ultimately, in the logics of appropriation of their meanings.

Furthermore, giving more visibility to unknown inland resources alongside with coastal sites through the use of tools able to connect - though not physically - heritage and people, also lets unexplored resources come to light, rebalancing and rewriting the overall predominant image of a region.

Within the framework of the project 'Mu.S.A.—Must See Advisor', we have developed multimedia demonstration maps on the cultural heritage of Matera and Lipari, included in 'Mirabilia—European Network of UNESCO Sites' project managed by the Chamber of Commerce of Matera. The project started in 2012 as a joined initiative of thirteen Chambers of Commerce in Italy; it is committed to the promotion of unexpected places of historical, cultural, and environmental importance in the UNESCO World Heritage Sites [19].

Currently the map of the general catalogue of cultural assets developed by the Ministry of Heritage and Cultural Activities and Tourism of Italy [20] does not contain any point of interest in Lipari (Fig. 1).

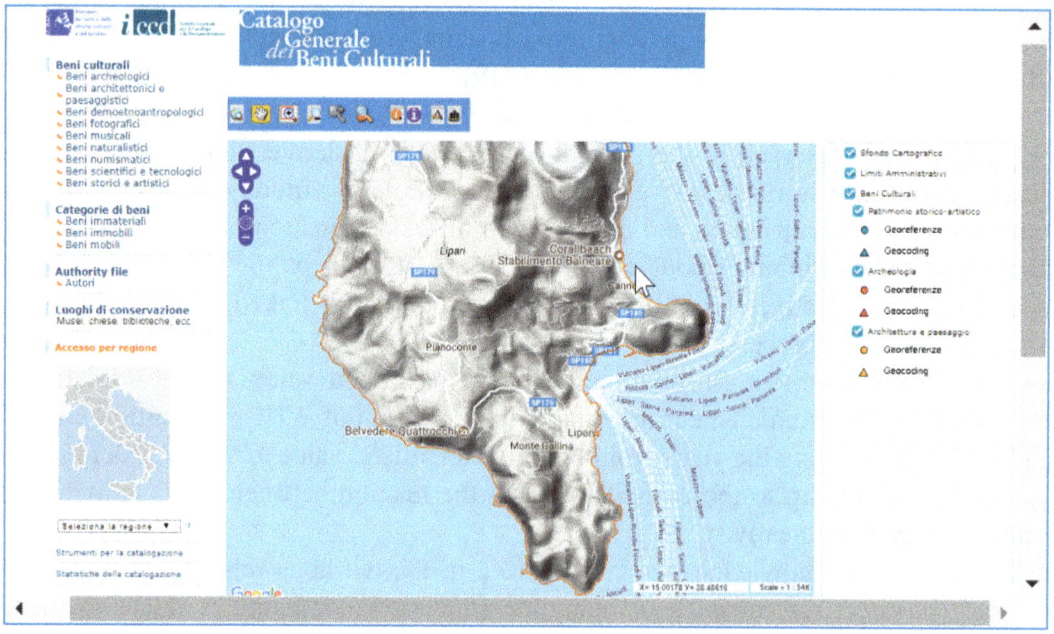

Fig. 1. General catalogue of cultural assets – Lipari Island [20]

The map of Parks, Museums, Galleries and Archaeological Areas developed by the Department of Cultural Heritage and Sicilian Identity [21] shows a single point of interest: the Regional Archaeological Museum 'Bernabò Brea' (Fig. 2).

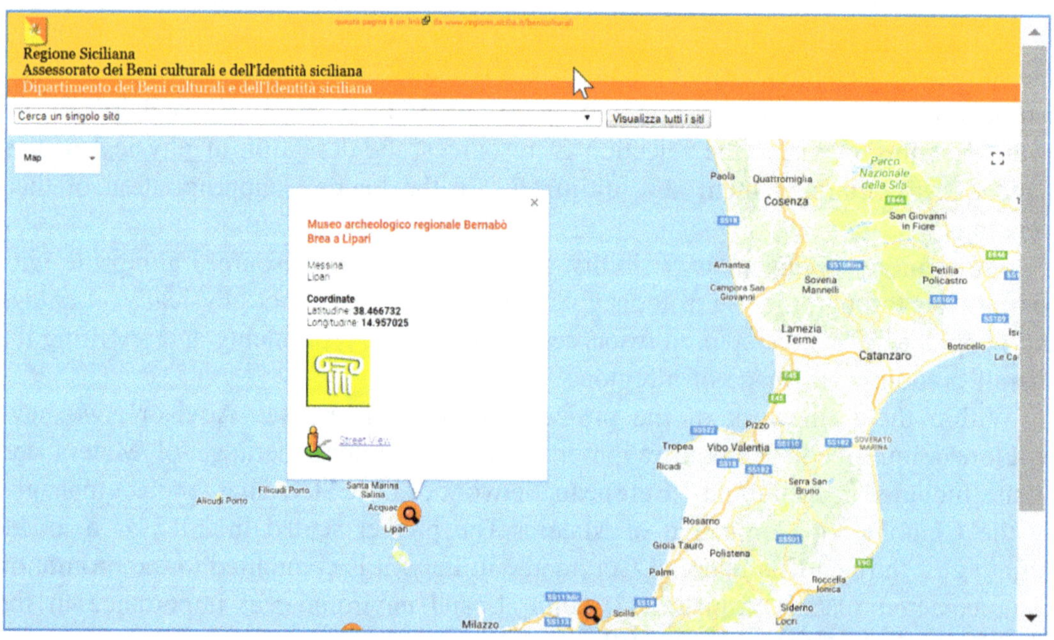

Fig. 2. Map of Parks, Museums, Galleries and Archaeological Areas in Lipari Island [21]

The official website of Lipari [22] has a static map with the following P.o.I.s, described in different webpages: the Castle of Lipari, the Cathedral, the Norman Cloister, the Aeolian Archaeological Museum and the Diana's Park (Fig. 3).

Fig. 3. Monuments in Lipari Island [22]

In the maps there is therefore very little information on P.o.I.s in Lipari, although there are 44 archaeological areas listed in the 'Aeolian Islands UNESCO Management Plan' [23] localized in detail scale (Fig. 4) and in a map in 1:10000 scale (Fig. 5).

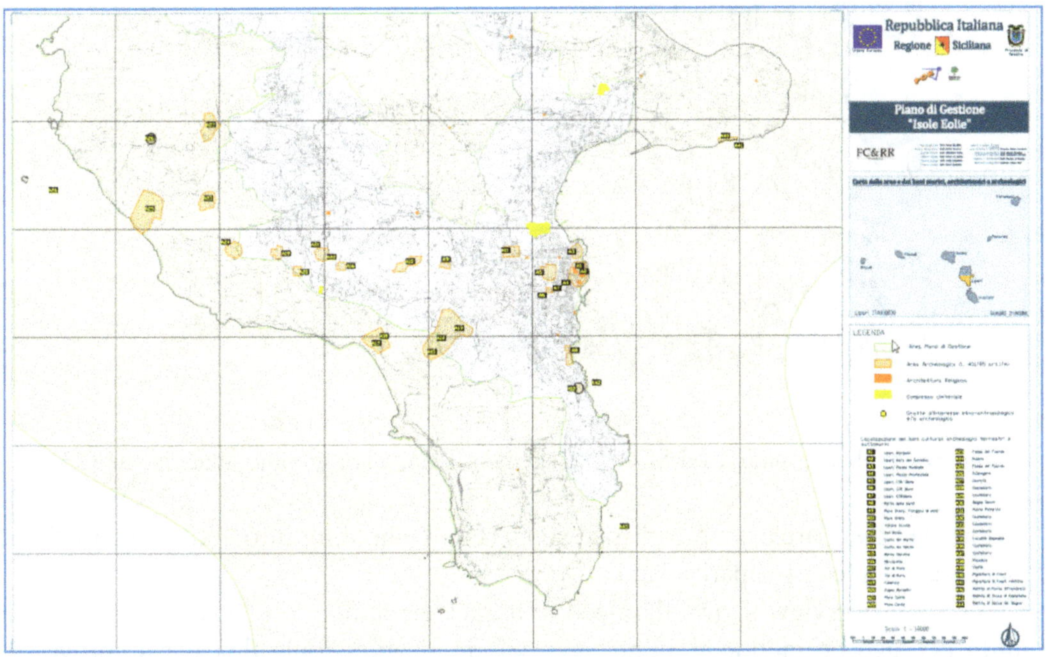

Fig. 4. Map of the historical, architectural and archaeological areas and assets of the 'Aeolian Islands' Management Plan

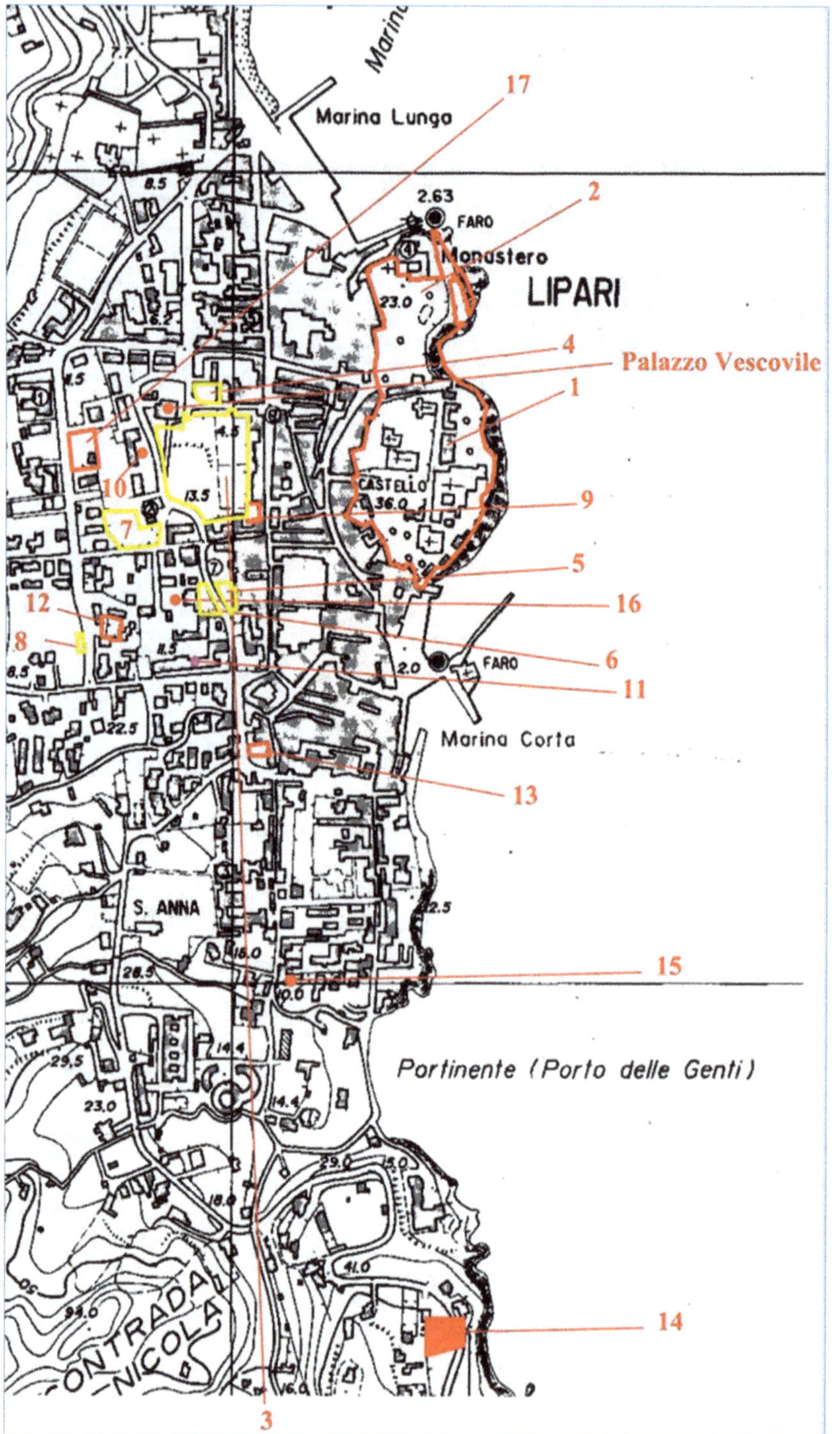

Fig. 5. Aeolian Islands UNESCO Management Plan, Cartographic attachments [23]

Moreover there are a couple of road signs (Fig. 6) holding info about historical and archaeological sites of Lipari Island.

This short overview shows the need to attract the attention of institutions towards cultural heritage promotion through new communication tools that can improve the visit experience. To this end, using only information available on-line, a multimedia

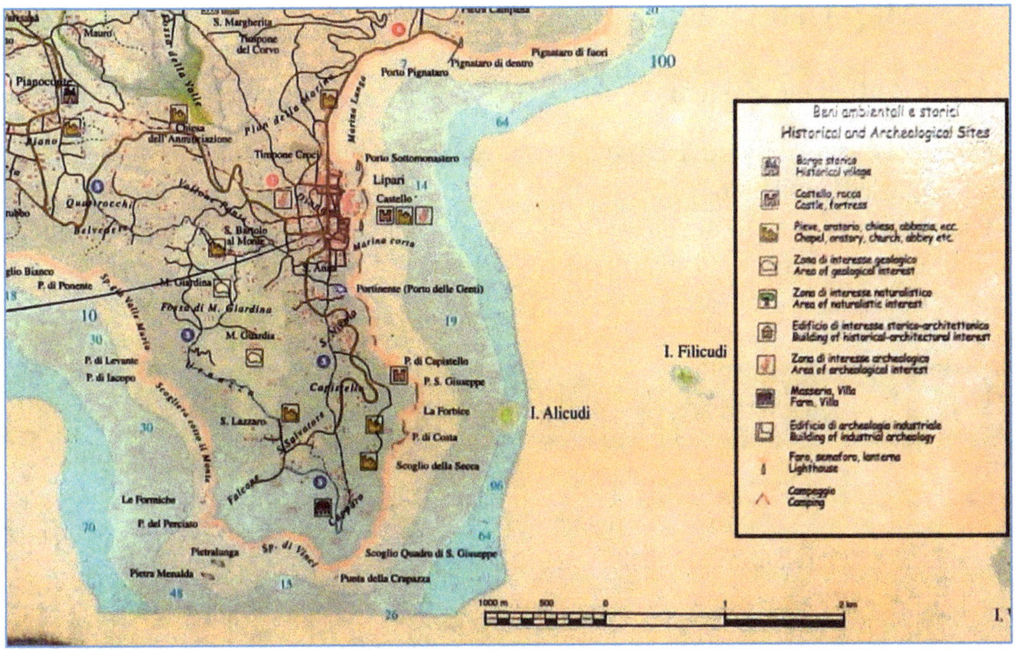

Fig. 6. Road sign (detail): Lipari Island—Historical and Archeological Sites

map of natural and cultural P.o.I.s of Lipari Island has been developed (Fig. 7). In order to give an example of the interactive map potential, the P.o.I.s have been grouped in five Categories and, for the case of the category 'Archaeologic site', in four Types.

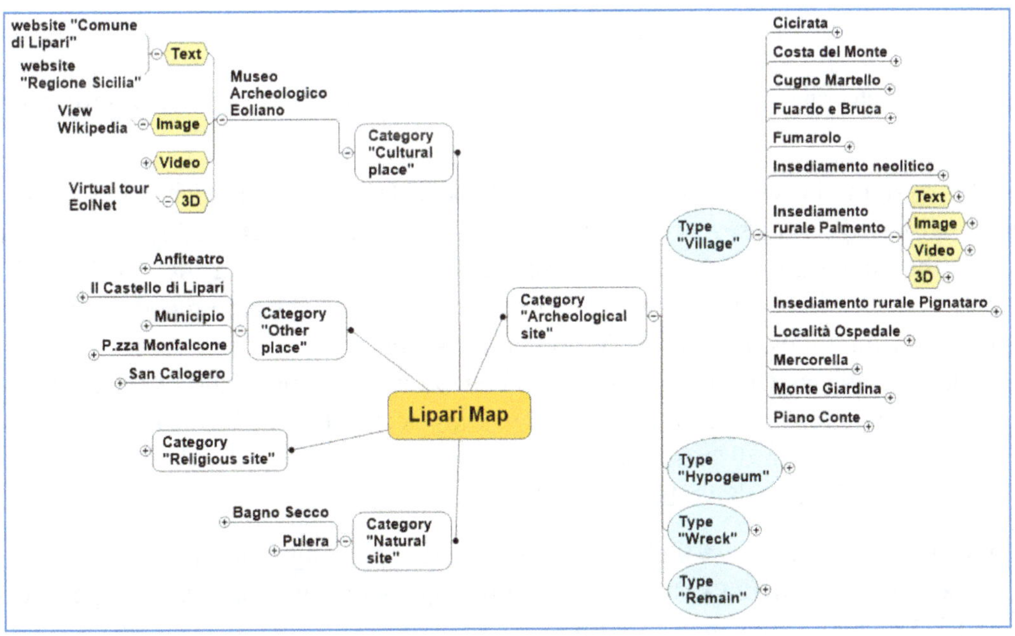

Fig. 7. Lipari Map overview: P.o.I.s grouped in Category (in transparent rectangular topic) and Type (in light blue oval topic); each P.o.I. has its own documents (in yellow hexagonal topic), grouped in Text, Image, Video, and 3D. (Color figure online)

3 The Map Generation

3.1 The Authoring System

In the last few years, cloud-based services have been playing an important role in large-scale web-based applications.

The authoring system developed (Fig. 8) is a practical and exhaustive example of cloud-based service for data management and integration.

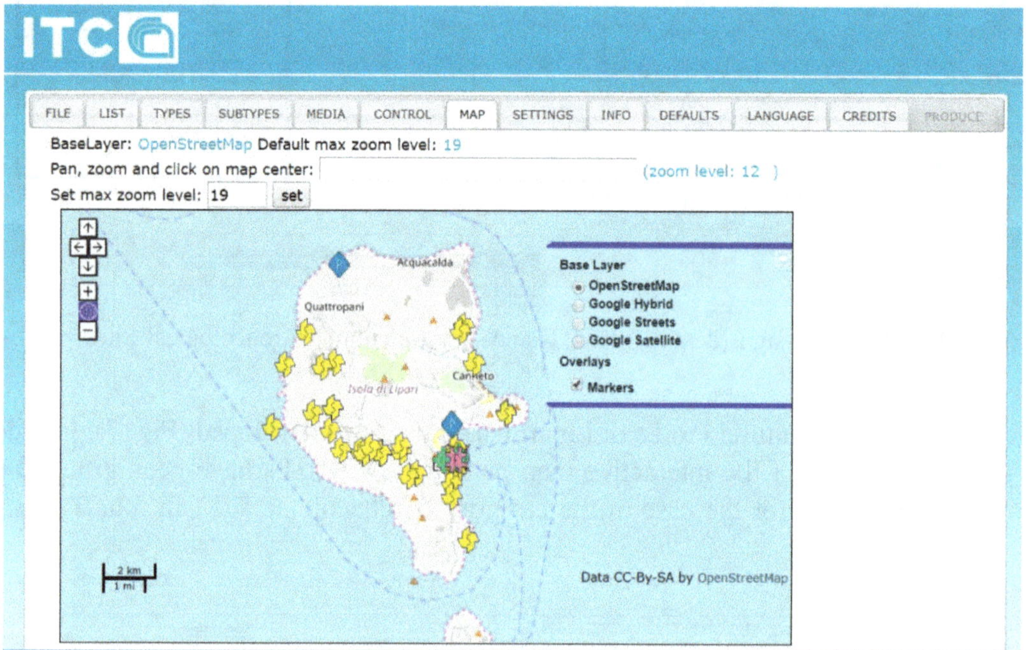

Fig. 8. The authoring system for multimedia map production: tab 'map' for preview/settings.

This system allows developers to import local data from spreadsheets file format into cloud-based services. As result, cloud data can be easily integrated to own website. Indeed, the authoring system enables users to upload tabular data files in the 'DBF' format, even if it is possible easily to extend the ability of system upload functions to import extra file types, such as CSV and spreadsheets.

Automatically and during end-user upload procedure, the authoring system supports the integration of data by performing joins across tables that may also contain different data stored in discrete files.

At present, the data have been stored in two files:

- a spatial set (P.o.I.s List file), including latitude and longitude of each P.o.I.;
- a document set (Media List file), including objects (grouped by text, image, video, and 3D content) contained in P.o.I.s.

This system has the ability to aggregate the data and provides multiple ways of visualizing the data using a map and a HTML table (DataTable).

The map provides geospatial visualization of information by create a marker on each location/P.o.I. so that users can analyze and understand the relationship between data and geographic location. The HTML table provides an immediate option to visualize, modify and analyze data.

The storage aggregate automatism, carried out in accordance with the entity-relationship (E-R) model, builds and verifies the entities or 'items' of an aggregate [24], making a JSON data store. The E-R model of the authoring system is the result of systematic analysis in recent years. We applied E-R principles to the physical modeling of JSON data store, which is non-relational in nature and its relationships are implicit.

Entities are characterized not only by implicit relationships, but also by additional properties (attributes) and identifiers (primary keys) need to aggregate data.

An aggregate consists of four entities (see Fig. 7): Category, Type, P.o.I., Media Object (text, image, video, and 3D). It compares the data in the P.o.I. List file with the Media List file to ensure that the interconnectedness of entities, relationships and their attributes are completely aligned, synchronized and meshed together with their cardinality [25].

All functions for serving as user interaction purposes are implemented in JQuery, where visualizations are interactive and dynamic based upon user's requests and DataTable jQuery plugin [26], integrated into the system, is a perfect choice in order to accomplish this task.

DataTable supports client side searching, sorting, pagination (client/server side) through ajax/html request and exposes a lot of functionalities for server side processing, such as any list data (table) can be converted to JSON format, without any issues, and send it as Ajax response.

Using the command 'Produce' in the authoring system, the end-user can quickly and easily create an attractively formatted web page, even if he is not familiar with HTML coding. After creating a web page and producing a multimedia map as a 'Single-Page Application' (SPA), which is a different way of building HTML5 applications from traditional web page development [27], the end-user can post it to an Internet or intranet location.

A SPA is one web page that works inside a browser and does not require page reloading when the end-user interacts with the app, so that JSON data are combined with reusable template to create views that make up the SPA's User Interface (UI) [28].

Instead of spreading the functionality of the multimedia interactive map across a collection of separate web pages with hyperlinks among them, a single root page has been defined: the application uses the JSON data to update the page dynamically, without reloading it and separates the UI library and the data.

3.2 The Map Architecture

While the potential of SPA is promising, implementing them can actually be tricky due to search engine optimization (SEO). Search engines are still the most popular way to discover new products and find information. The SPA interactive map (see http://www.itc.cnr.it/ba/map/LPR/) runs AJAX [29] calls and client-side scripts (Javascript) while search engines do not run scripts within pages, so, today SPA-based map is not completely indexed by search engine crawlers and it is necessary that all AJAX requests in web application can also be requested by static links [30]. Google is claiming to be able to index website content generated using JavaScript [31] and saying it will crawl and render AJAX-based websites as they are [32].

Today, effective ways to find and access existing datasets distributed across a range of repositories are increasing requested. Therefore, our research is focusing on improving the discoverability of data; part of this will involve using information about how data is searched for (search terms, location, etc.) via web application and making data easier to interpret and use across different formats; visualizations and APIs will be also key to maximizing its beneficial use and impacts.

Over the past few years, single-page web applications and their frameworks have gained huge popularity. The SPA solution has been adopted for its main advantage of improving the web surfing of the multimedia interactive map on mobile; it is able to:

- Affect the positioning and the discoverability of data on the web, since the usability on mobile devices is now a ranking factor.
- Support rich client-side functionality that does not require reloading the page as users take actions or navigate between areas of the app.
- Load more quickly, fetching data in the background, and individual user actions are more responsive since full-page reloads are rare.
- Run in a disconnected mode, making updates to a client-side model that are eventually synchronized back to the server once a connection is re-established.
- Concentrate all content in a single page, which is useful when we are targeting very precise queries.

The SPA solution is fast and user-friendly; it supports RESTful APIs and enables the distribution of the processing workload between the server and client computers. Finally, it is much easier to convert such web application into a mobile one.

The multimedia map is built on client-side JavaScript web application framework based on the model-view-controller (MVC) software architectural pattern and utilizing server side RESTful web services to provide desktop-like rich browser interfaces.

This architecture is designed on the service-orientation design principles of reusability, simplicity, extensibility, thus causing a clear separation of component responsibilities compare to 'traditional web application architecture'. Ajax and RESTful Web services naturally fit with each other and leverage widely available web technologies and standards, such as: HTML, JavaScript and XML/JSON [33]. For this system, there is absolutely no need to install or configure any other component to enable effective interaction between Ajax front ends and RESTful Web services. In fact, RESTful Web services provide Ajax with an application-programming interface (API) to deal with the interactions with resources on the server. Furthermore, Google Maps API is integrated in the application for rendering geospatial data within a web browser and for accessing rich mapping features and it is 'optimized' for smartphones with a set of APIs developed by Google, which allow communication with Google Services and their integration to numerous other services.

4 The Map Interface

The desktop map interface has three main components: 'Menu', 'Callout' and 'Sidebar', which are closed in the default status (Fig. 9) to maximize the map, and opened on user action (Fig. 10). P.o.I.s are visualized on the map through markers with unambiguous colors [34], with different shapes and image according to category/type.

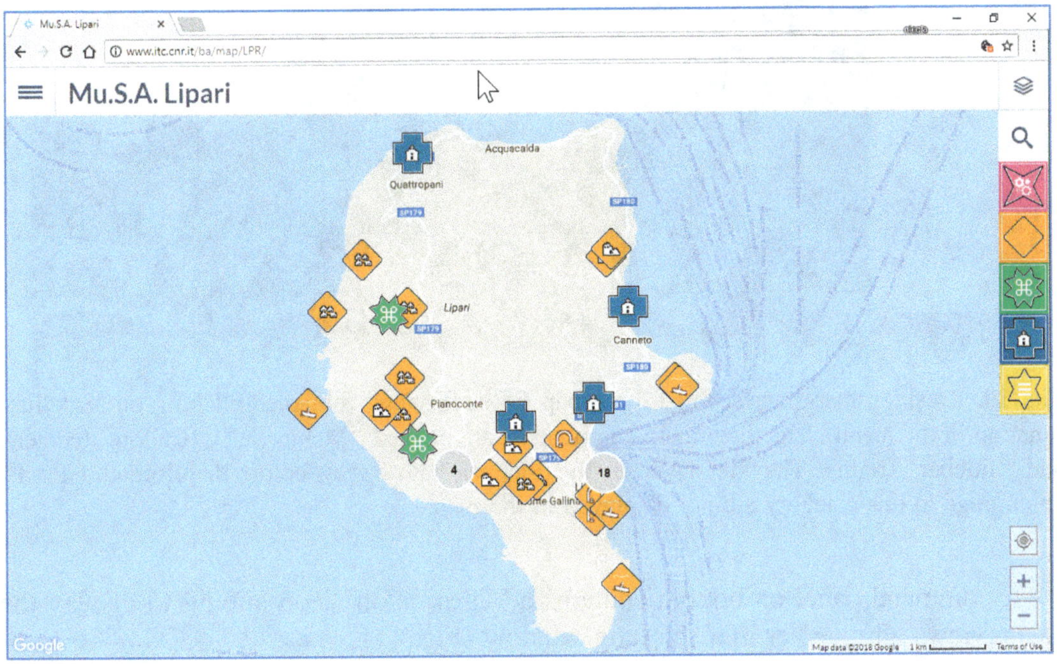

Fig. 9. Desktop map interface of Lipari island (http://www.itc.cnr.it/ba/map/LPR). It has three main components ('Men', 'Callout', and 'Sidebar'), which are closed in the default status. P.o.I.s are visualized on the map through markers with unambiguous colors. (Color figure online)

Menu. This component opens a list of functions applied to the map in two ways. With mouse over the 'Menu' symbol, the list displays only 'self-describing' symbol; clicking on the 'Menu' symbol, the list shows/hides symbols and functions names (Fig. 10, left):

- 'Best site', locating on the map the most interesting site.
- 'Satellite', switching on/off the map to earth view.
- 'Slideshow', opening a window with a moving set of thumbnails (characteristic square image of each P.o.I., used also in the callout and in the sidebar).
  Clicking on a thumbnail, the map centers itself on the P.o.I. which the image belongs, opening its callout—this function is useful for totem installation because attracts the public attention.
- 'Time slider', updating geographic distribution of markers according to the construction century selected by the user in the timeline graphic through a handle control.
  'Folder', displaying the preview of multimedia items (belonging to all the P.o.I.s in the project) item by item in a dynamic resizing window.

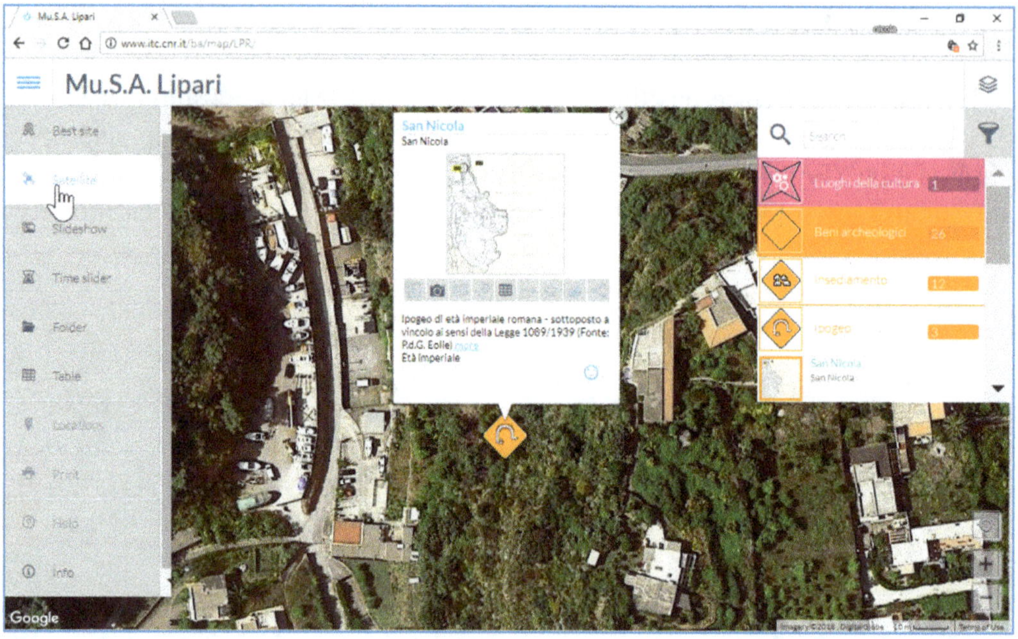

Fig. 10. Desktop map interface of Lipari map in 'earth view' (obtained clicking on 'Satellite' function in the menu). The three main components are opened: 'Menu' (left), 'Callout' (center), and 'Sidebar' (right). The first layer in the Sidebar has a grey color, therefore the P.o.I.s belongings to this category are not displayed in the map.

A command panel on bottom contains a 'Tiles on/off' icon aiming to display the previews all together in a scrolling window (Fig. 11).

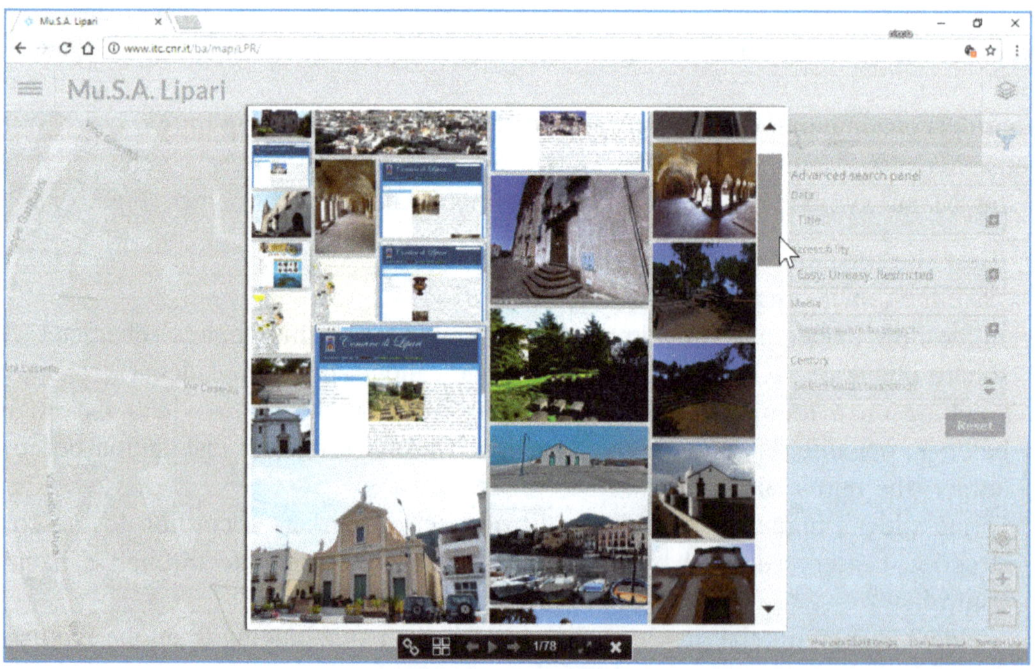

Fig. 11. Multimedia preview in a scrolling window ('Tile') opened in 'Folder' from 'Menu'.

The user is allowed: (a) to locate the respective P.o.I., by clicking on the preview; (b) to view the multimedia, which the preview refers to—as the virtual tour for the Norman Cloister and the Diana's Park, available in the Internet, developed using only one 360-degree panorama (Fig. 12).

Fig. 12. Virtual tour for the Norman Cloister (left) and the Diana's Park (right), available in the Internet, developed using only one 360-degree panorama.

- 'Table', listing the media items, here belonging to all the sites in the project, using a panel with columns (Item, Site, Source, Date, Media Type, and Content) alphabetically ordered.
  A 'Search' function allows finding multimedia according to the letters typed in the textbox. The user is allowed to see the multimedia content by clicking on an item.

Callout. This component is a window—opened by clicking on a P.o.I. box in the sidebar or on a P.o.I. marker on the map—showing:

- Two-line header (name and address).
- P.o.I. characteristic square image, used also in the slideshow and in the sidebar);
- Function icons, allowing user to have a preview of multimedia contents belonging to the selected P.o.I. ('text', 'image', 'video', and '3D') or their list ('Table')—other functions are in development.
- A short description (expandable clicking on 'more').
- The building age (used by the 'time slider' function).
- An accessibility status icon, showing three kind of image according to the physical accessibility of the P.o.I.—easy (accessible to all, at all times), uneasy or restricted. This kind of information has an additional cost because requests on-site survey, but it is fundamental. People using a wheelchair may have no difficulty at home in

finding information about P.o.I.s but, when they get to their destination, they may find that they cannot reach it because of—for example—the presence of staircases at the entrance.

Sidebar. This component is a two-side window showing the symbols of search and layer. Clicking on the 'Sidebar' symbol the application shows/hides the first window (Fig. 10 on the right) having the search box, the filter symbol and the dynamic legend, organized in three levels:

- The first level depicts the main layers, using markers according to the P.o.I.s categories. If the category is divided in types, its marker in the 'Sidebar' has no images/text inside, as for 'Archeological Site' category.
- The second level depicts the sub-layers according to the P.o.I.s types (if any) for the selected category, as 'Village', 'Hypogeum', 'Wreck', and 'Remains' for 'Archeological Sites' category.
- The third level shows P.o.I. info boxes for the selected category (and type), displaying square picture, name, and address, as 'San Nicola' (Fig. 10).

Each box at the first and second level shows the number of the P.o.I. included, according to the search results and status of selections in the filter panel.

The user, according to its interest, could turn off/on each layer or each sub-layer, disabling/enabling the respective point's visualization, thus enhancing the map view.

Clicking on the 'Filter' symbol shows/hides the second window substituting the dynamic legend with the filter panel, allowing the user to set:

- 'Data for search' (Title, Address, and Comment—default: title).
- 'Accessibility level' (Easy, Uneasy, and Restricted—default: all).
- 'Multimedia type' (Sheet, Image, Video, and 3D—default: all).
- 'Building Century' (according to P.o.I. data—default: all).

5 Conclusions

This paper presents the design and implementation of a multimedia map loaded in a single HTML page having multiple features and functions, as distinct from other maps, to support users in searching for cultural heritage information according to their needs.

Future work will focus on the completion of functions provided in the callout ('Destination', 'Favorite', 'Like', and 'Share') for the desktop map interface and the improvement of the 'Language' tab in order to give users to load a whole set of labels corresponding to those utilized in the desktop map interface.

The multimedia demonstration map developed has the potential to help foster greater knowledge about, and resulting awareness of, the natural and cultural heritage objects.

Author Contributions. Maiellaro, N.: project and testing (§ 1, 4); Lerario, A.: case study (§ 2); Varasano, A.: system architecture and software development (§ 3).

References

1. Travel and Tourism Competitiveness Report 2015. http://www3.weforum.org/docs/TT15/WEF_Global_Travel&Tourism_Report_2015.pdf. Accessed 03 Mar 2018
2. Guggenheim, J., Kremser, S., Jhunjhunwala, P., McCaleb, T., Garcia-Mon, A., McCabe, L.: Travel goes mobile. http://img-stg.bcg.com/Travel_Goes_Mobile_Jun_2014_tcm9-84752.pdf. Accessed 03 Mar 2018
3. Peterson, M.P.: Hypermedia maps and the internet. In: Stefanakis, E., Peterson, M.P., Armenakis, C., Delis, V. (eds.) Geographic Hypermedia. Lecture Notes in Geoinformation and Cartography, pp. 121–136. Springer, Heidelberg (2006). https://doi.org/10.1007/978-3-540-34238-0_7
4. Cartwright, W.E., Hunter, G.J.: Towards a methodology for the evaluation of multimedia geographical information products. GeoInformatica **5**(3), 291–315 (2001)
5. Hu, S.: Multimedia mapping on the internet using commercial APIs. In: Peterson, M.P. (ed.) Online Maps with APIs and WebServices. Lecture Notes in Geoinformation and Cartography, pp. 61–71. Springer, Heidelberg (2012). https://doi.org/10.1007/978-3-642-27485-5_5
6. Southern Illinois University Edwardsville – Maps & Directions. http://www.siue.edu/maps/index2.shtml. Accessed 05 Apr 2018
7. Cacia, C.: The activity of UNESCO regarding the element of recovery of the cultural identity: the example of Aeolian Islands. In: Claval, P., Pagnini, M.P., Scaini, M. (eds.) The Cultural Turn in Geography: Proceedings of the Conference, pp. 347–354, 18–20 September 2003, Gorizia Campus (2003)
8. Anzidei, M., et al.: Impact of the relative sea level rise on archaeological and cultural heritage sites of Lipari island (Italy), between the Roman period and 2100 AD. Geophysical Research Abstracts, vol. 20, EGU2018-12015-1, 2018 EGU General Assembly (2018)
9. Ruggieri, G., Calderon Vazquez, F.J.: Tourism development in UNESCO natural heritage sites—the case of sicilian volcanic sites: Mount Etna and Aeolian Islands. Chin. Bus. Rev. **16**(11), 544–554 (2017). https://doi.org/10.17265/1537-1506/2017.11.002
10. Geremia, F., Massoli-Novelli, R.: Coastal geomorphosites of the isles of Lipari and Stromboli (Aeolian Islands, Italy): new potential for geo-tourism. Il Quaternario - Italian J. Quat. Sci. **18**(1), 231–242 (2005). Volume Speciale
11. Bui, H.T., Le, T.A., Nguyen, C.H.: UNESCO world heritage designation. In: Tourism and Opportunities for Economic Development in Asia, January 2017. https://doi.org/10.4018/978-1-5225-2078-8.ch015
12. Caust, J., Vecco, M.: Is UNESCO world heritage recognition a blessing or burden? Evidence from developing Asian countries. J. Cult. Herit. **27**, 1–9 (2017). https://doi.org/10.1016/j.culher.2017.02.004
13. Di Matteo, D.: Tourism performances, government effectiveness and local growth. The Italian cultural heritage perspective. In: Gursoy, D., Nunkoo, R. (eds.) Routledge Handbook of Tourism Impacts: A Theoretical Perspective. Routledge, London (2019)
14. Patuelli, R., Mussoni, M., Candela, G.: The effects of world heritage sites on domestic tourism: a spatial interaction model for Italy. J. Geograph. Syst. **15**, 369–402 (2013)
15. Lo Piccolo, F., Leone, D., Pizzuto, P.: The (controversial) role of the UNESCO WHL management plans in promoting sustainable tourism development. J. Policy Res. Tour. Leisure Events **4**(3), 249–276 (2012). Tourism and Spatial Planning
16. VanBarclom, B.L.: Assessing the economic impact of a UNESCO World Heritage designation. J. Herit. Tour. **6**(2), 143–164 (2011)

17. Cuccia, T., Rizzo, I.: Seasonal tourism flows in UNESCO sites: the case of Sicily. In: Kaminski, J., Benson, A.M., Arnold, D. (eds.) Contemporary Issues in Cultural Heritage Tourism, pp. 179–199. Routledge, London (2014)
18. Cellini, R., Cuccia, T.: UNESCO sites as public goods: comparative experiences in Italy. Revista de Economia Contemporânea **20**(3), 553–569 (2016)
19. Places Mirabilia Network of Unesco Sites. http://www.mirabilianetwork.eu/en/places-mirabilia-network-of-unesco-sites. Accessed 05 Apr 2018
20. Ministry of Heritage and Cultural Activities and Tourism of Italy. www.catalogo.beniculturali.it/sigecSSU_FE/mappaRegione.action?regione=19&r=sicilia&T=1521820871495. Accessed 03 Mar 2018
21. Department of Cultural Heritage and Sicilian Identity. http://www.regione.sicilia.it/beniculturali/dirbenicult/database/museogeo/Site_Locator.asp?zoom=8. Accessed 03 Mar 2018
22. Official website of Lipari. http://www.comunelipari.gov.it/lipari/zf/index.php/servizi-aggiuntivi/index/index/idtesto/73. Accessed 03 Mar 2018
23. Aeolian Islands UNESCO Management Plan - Cartographic attachments. http://unescosicilia.it/wp/wp-content/uploads/2014/09/2-Allegati-Cartografici.pdf. Accessed 03 Mar 2018
24. What is an Entity Relationship Diagram - Entity-relationship model. https://www.lucidchart.com/pages/er-diagrams. Accessed 04 Apr 2018
25. Proceedings of the combined volumes of International Congress (IntCongress 2014) held at Holiday Inn Silom, Bangkok, Kingdom of Thailand between 19th November, 2014 and 21st November, 2014
26. Datatable - A plug-in for the jQuery Javascript library. https://datatables.net/. Accessed 04 Apr 2018
27. Scott Jr., E.A.: SPA Design and Architecture: The Communication Process, November 2015. ISBN 9781617292439. http://freecontent.manning.com/wp-content/uploads/spa-design-and-architecture-the-communication-process.pdf. Accessed 04 Apr 2018
28. Single-page-application Vs multiple-page-application. https://medium.com/@NeotericEU/single-page-application-vs-multiple-page-application-2591588efe58. Accessed 04 Apr 2018
29. RESTful Service Best Practices. http://www.restapitutorial.com/media/RESTful_Best_Practices-v1_1.pdf. Accessed 04 Apr 2018
30. AJAX, Asynchronous JavaScript And XML. https://developer.mozilla.org/en-US/docs/Web/Guide/AJAX. Accessed 13 May 2018
31. Hatami, S.: The Automatic Development of SEO-Friendly Single Page Applications Based on HIJAX Approach, October 2017. https://doi.org/10.1007/978-3-319-68786-5_15, https://www.researchgate.net/publication/320184470_The_Automatic_Development_of_SEO-Friendly_Single_Page_Applications_Based_on_HIJAX_Approach. Accessed 13 May 2018
32. Google Search console, Googlebot crawler support. https://support.google.com/webmasters/answer/6066468. Accessed 13 May 2018
33. Schwartz, B.: Google will stop using the old AJAX crawling scheme in Q2 2018. Search Engine Land, December 2017. https://searchengineland.com/google-will-stop-crawling-old-ajax-crawling-scheme-q2-2018-287653. Accessed 13 May 2018
34. Jenny, B., Kelso, N.V.: Color Design for the Color Vision Impaired in Mapping: Methods Tips. Cartographic perspectives, no. 57, pp. 61–67, Spring 2007. http://colororacle.org/resources/2007_JennyKelso_ColorDesign_hires.pdf. Accessed 03 Mar 2018

Virtual Assistants for the Cultural Heritage Domain

Aleš Tavčar(✉), Jernej Zupančič, and Matjaž Gams

Jozef Stefan Institute, Ljubljana, Slovenia
ales.tavcar@ijs.si

Abstract. Virtual assistants and similar software tools are gaining importance among phone and computer users. The most well-known assistants (Siri, Cortana, Google, etc.) provide general information to users and cannot be adapted to specific needs. Custom implementations usually cover specific domains and are specialized to provide a comprehensive set of information or functionalities from that area. Currently, there is a lack of general applications for cultural heritage, since most implementations are specialized virtual guides for museums or exhibitions. We present an overview of virtual assistants that we developed and are applied to the area of cultural and natural heritage, where we try to improve the current shortage of tools. The presented prototypes provide various functionalities to users and can help them to discover, learn and plan visits to cultural sights.

Keywords: Virtual assistants · Natural language processing · Web services

1 Introductions

In recent years, virtual assistants (VA) have become a popular tool that helps users find information faster and in a more accurate manner. They are web-based services that serve as a human-computer interface to deliver information from a specific domain that the user is interested in or to interact with an information system. Companies like Google, Microsoft or Apple developed general assistants for mobile devices that help users find restaurants or shops close to their location, manage their phone or provide computer-aided support for software packages.

The main advantages of virtual assistants are their ability to understand, to a certain extent, natural language and present the answers in an enriched format (additional links, multimedia presentation, etc.). This way, users can provide questions and queries in natural language, which makes virtual assistants well-suited for less skilled or handicapped users. In addition, virtual assistants can implement speech-to-text and/or text-to-speech systems to further improve the user experience.

Nowadays, assistants are being developed for a wide variety of domains and applications and they thrive due to the increasing publicly available data on the internet, both structured and in free-form. In addition, web based services that offer API access can be integrated into the assistants to provide a comprehensive user experience (for example, booking of flights, transportations, events, tours, medical visits, hair-dressers, etc.). In addition, modern third party services that provide advanced

M. Duguleană et al. (Eds.): VRTCH 2018, CCIS 904, pp. 234–244, 2019.
https://doi.org/10.1007/978-3-030-05819-7_18

functionalities that can also be managed through APIs (for example, messaging, text mining, recommendations, path planning, etc.) can also be exploited by assistants.

Applications of virtual assistants in the cultural heritage domain are not as widespread as one would expect. There is a notable lack of applications for the interested public, providing general information and covering non-specific domains, since most applications are custom solutions intended as virtual guides for museums and exhibitions. The introduction of more generic applications and virtual assistants would help popularize and spread the appreciation for cultural heritage also among youngsters.

In this paper we provide an overview of the various virtual assistants developed at our institutions for the domain of cultural heritage and sightseeing. Virtual assistants integrate several advanced functionalities. Text mining and Natural Language Understanding (NLU) to identify the intent of the users and extract important entities from text. Next, they implement API calls to third party services in order to provide trip planning functionalities and data fusion. All presented assistants are available online and can be modified and thus applied to new domains or different languages.

2 Related Work

Virtual assistant in the domain of cultural heritage have been already applied to virtual visits of cultural sites. They are deployed in real or virtual environments as virtual guides to engage the visitors and deliver a comprehensive learning experience [1]. Other implementations also provide mechanisms, such as multimedia, storytelling, and enriched content to entertain the user during the learning process [5, 6]. All these agents must be flexible, responsive, and provide natural interaction in order to be seen as a social partner by visitors.

Several applications were developed that deliver a personalized museum guide. Mathias et al. [2] proposed a new method for personalized museum tour recommendations. Their research tackles the problem of optimizing museum visits according to visitor's preferences and artwork importance. Huang et al. [3] developed a museum guide system that uses association rule mining to discover recommendations from both collective and individual visiting behaviors. Pechenizkiy and Calders [4] presented a simple user-focused framework for personalizing museum tours that is focused on efficient learning since the system should be able to quickly provide relevant suggestions only after a small set of user preferences.

Other general applications of virtual assistants are in the area of education for instructions and learning [8], delivering information from large data sets like encyclopedias in libraries [9], for informational purposes in e-commerce [10], merging heterogeneous data using multi-agent conversational agents [11], tourism [12], and several others.

3 Overview of Deployed Virtual Assistants

3.1 Platform for VA Creation

We developed a cloud-based platform Asistent [2, 7] for the creation of virtual assistants and during a national project we created and integrated several VAs for web pages of municipalities in Slovenia. The developed web platform supports the creation, management and integration of virtual assistants to an arbitrary web page. It was developed as a Software as a Service (SaaS), where clients access the service via a web browser, which eliminates the need for software and hardware maintenance. Since the software runs in the cloud all future upgrades are applied centrally and are available to all clients instantaneously.

The knowledge base of the deployed VAs for the municipalities was constructed manually and contains the information that municipalities deemed the most important. It covers the general information regarding the municipality, their acts and regulations, instructions and news for residents, natural and cultural heritage and touristic information.

Figure 1 shows an example of a VA developed for the Jozef Stefan Institute. The VA runs on the web pages of the institute and delivers related content to its visitors. In addition, the VA is enriched with specific applications that can be accessed through the Applications bar (see Fig. 1). They are an extension or addition of the basic functionality, since they offer the use of external services. For example, ticket booking for museums and payment of various fees. Moreover, applications can be defined as categories that set the context and focus the search of the assistant to some specific content. For example, users might want to search for answers regarding squares or buildings only in the tourism category. Each provider can define his own set of applications that are displayed in the virtual assistant.

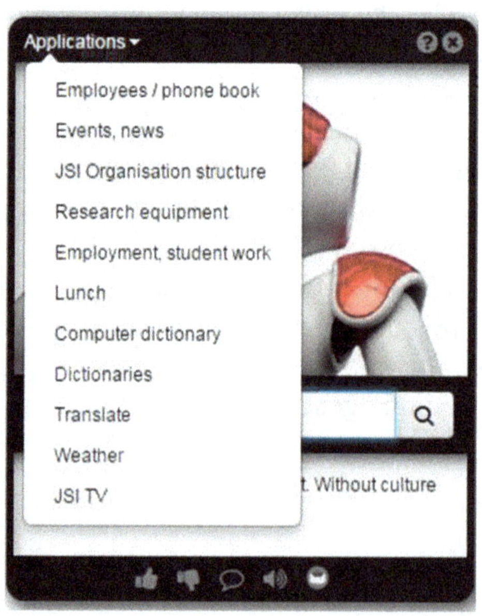

Fig. 1. One instance of the VA with the application tab enabled.

3.2 Virtual Museum Guide

Museums offer to its visitors a wide selection of artwork at their premises. The vast amount of exhibitions is often overwhelming for the visitors and most of them might not be of interest to them. This might cause to miss artwork or entire exhibitions that are best suited to their personal preferences. The growth of the Semantic Web in recent years and the availability of more and more content in the digital and linked data format available on the internet supports the creation and reuse of services of a higher added value. One of such is the virtual assistant for museums that offers virtual tours of institutions covered in the Google Arts & Culture project (Google Street View). At the time of writing this paper, more than 3400 museums and sights are included in the Google Arts & Culture project. To deliver a simple proof-of-concept we mapped into the virtual assistant content from three museums (British museum, Art Institute of Chicago, and National Gallery of Australia).

The application provides a natural language interface using a virtual assistant created through the Asistent platform. The users can input questions or requests and the VA takes care of identifying the correct answer and displays the corresponding feed from Google Street View. In addition, a simple recommender system is integrated in the web service that provides suggestions regarding exhibits targeted for a specific user. Since the recommender does not get implicit rating for items from users, we had to design a recommendation system that learns user preferences based on implicit data (queries, time spent on each answer, motion, etc.) and item features. The algorithm implements a content-based filtering mechanism that is well-suited for this kind of domains. To generate a recommendation, the recommender does not use data from other users but the similarity between items in the dataset and the history of previously searched items to predict ratings for user-item pairs not present in the dataset. We showed that in the limited domain, with a small number of learning examples and user-item pairs the recommender works well, even with new users.

The virtual assistant can deliver information about specific exhibit rooms in the museum (for example, Egypt room), groups of similar objects (for example, Chinese weapons), or important exhibits (for example, the Rosetta stone). The virtual assistant contains the most relevant items and groups from the three museums, but it does not provide a comprehensive overview of the museum, since the mapping and creation of the knowledge base was performed manually, which is relatively time consuming.

The virtual assistant displays a description in the text area (bottom part of the assistant window in Fig. 2) and shows the related feed from Google Street View in the background page. The user can move around at his discretion and explore the presented exhibit. The user can also select the context in which the answer should be presented. For example, he might want to see the Egypt pottery exhibition in the British Museum, not from the other two mapped museums. In this case, the user selects the appropriate museum from the Application dropdown (the top left part of the virtual assistant in Fig. 2). This gives the user the ability to focus the search and obtain more relevant results.

Fig. 2. A query about the Rosetta stone in the British Museum.

3.3 Slovenian Cultural Heritage Database

The developed virtual assistant was created with the aim to deliver a wide range of information to users regarding cultural, natural heritage, and visiting sites in Slovenia. Due to the large amount of data and information that needs to be provided, the mechanism for content delivery was designed in such way to remove the need for manually inputting and editing database entries. This is a crucial step to enable a comprehensive delivery of content for all sights in a specific country. We implemented a web crawler that parsed several web pages related to cultural heritage and touristic information in Slovenia (for example, www.slovenia.info). The crawler was able to classify the type of information that a page has and the type of the attraction (castle, lake, museum, etc.), extract metadata (location, region, descriptions, photos, related web page), and store the obtained information in a structured way. In addition, the crawler tried to obtain additional content also from external links that were included in the provided web pages. All the extracted content was stored in a relational database and the text in the main fields were indexed using Whoosh [3], a python library for indexing free-form or structured text and quickly find matching results based on simple or complex search criteria. Since the text in the database fields is in free-form, Whoosh provides an ideal solution to search within the text and at the same time obtain a relevance score that can be used to sort the search results.

The entire search mechanism in the virtual assistant is composed of four parts. First, the NLU module is used to obtain the intent of the user. The intent can be regarded as the type of the question. The user might want to search for a specific sight or obtain a list or related items. Second, entities are extracted from the query. They are linked to the information extracted with the web crawler. For example, the type of the sight (museum, castle, lake, churches, etc.) and the region or location where the sight is. Next, the obtained values for entities are matched against the records in the database and a set of results is obtained based on the search criteria. Finally, the answer to be displayed in the virtual assistant is generated. A short description is provided if the user searched for a specific sight, or a list of matched items if the query return multiple hits.

The VA prototype supports the following types of questions by a user:

- Show me some lakes in the Dolenjska region.
- List the castles near Kranj.
- Show me some info regarding the Ljubljana castle.
- Museums in Ljubljana.

All the answers are provided in text form, with additional formatting when providing the description of a sight – a short description in the text are below the virtual assistant (see Fig. 3), an url link to the detailed description, category and a location of a sight, and the related web page displayed in the background.

Fig. 3. The virtual assistant provides information regarding the Predjama castle.

In Fig. 3 the user searched for a specific sight (the Predjama castle). The assistant identified the adequate entity and obtained the stored entry in the indexed database, based on the title field of the sight. A short description is provided in the text area of the virtual assistant and the related web page is displayed in the background.

The results of a different query are presented in Fig. 4. In this case, the user searched for lakes in the Gorenjska region of Slovenia. The NLU component identified two entities in the query. First, it classified the type of the query as a list of items. Next, the type of the sight as lakes and the region as Gorenjska. The virtual assistant then searched for all items in the database that matched the identified entities (the region field as Gorenjska and sight type as lakes). Since the query type is a list of items, the module returns the first ten results with the highest relevance score. The list is presented in the text area of the assistant and each element is a hyperlink to the related sight that is shown in the same text area, with the corresponding web page displayed in the background.

The developed assistant and the search mechanism can be applied to different domain and languages.

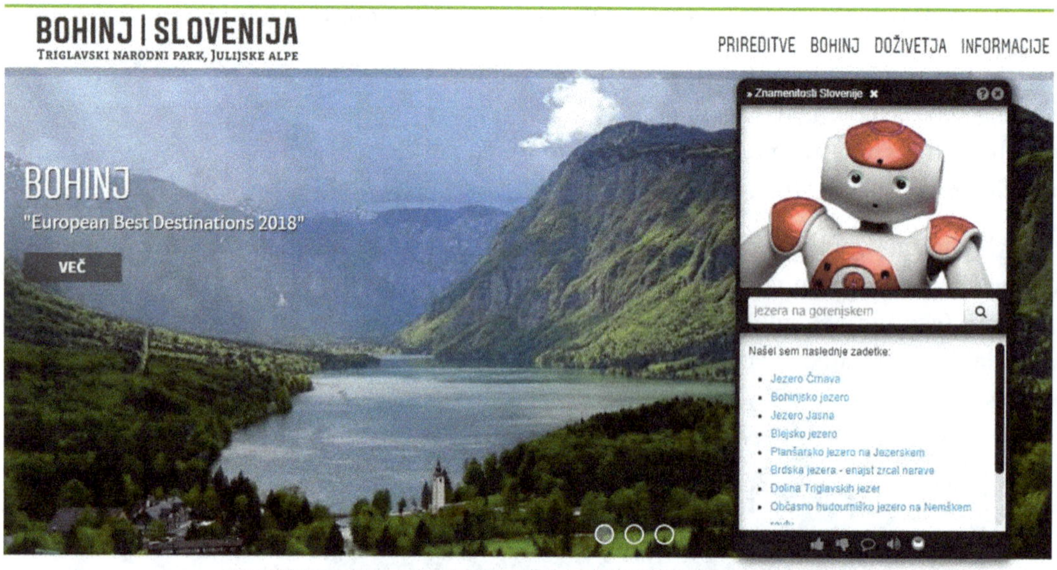

Fig. 4. The virtual assistant showing a list of lakes in the Gorenjska region.

3.4 Virtual Assistant for Sightseeing

Tourism is a domain that can support the introduction of virtual assistants and they can provide significant added value to tourists. Companies that organize trips, tourist centers in cities and others can use the functionalities of a virtual assistant as additional services that they offer. Virtual assistants can deliver information from an area or regarding specific sights, provide content in a segmented, appealing, and entertaining format, they can help users to book tickets for events, sights, and urban transportation, create personalized city tours, and more.

We are currently developing a comprehensive platform that provides all the listed functionalities to enable smart tourism. The system uses several external services to improve the tourist's user experience during trip planning and provides guidance amid the actual trip. The platform integrates: (i) Rocket.Chat, a chat platform where users can communicate; (ii) Interface with Messenger; (iii) eTurist [4], a tour planner based on a recommendation system; (iv) Asistent, a rule based question-answering toolkit; (v) Dialogflow, a natural language understanding toolkit.

The prototype version of the platform supports various kinds of interactions and queries during the communication with the user. The classification of user intents is performed by the specialized virtual assistant that can understand queries and commands from the following categories: general information about a sight, sights near a specific place, similar sights near a specific place or region, adding sights to the preference list, generate path to a sight, recommendation of sights. In addition, the virtual assistant is able to recognize an important word or sequence of words in the query. These words are from the following categories: sight name, sight type, place, and region.

Based on the recognized inputs from the user, the NLU module constructs the appropriate commands, methods, and API calls. The webhook functionality then retrieves the needed data from third party services, if required.

In Fig. 5 part of the conversation between a user and the virtual assistant is presented. The user asks the assistant to recommend something from the Gorenjska region. The search mechanism of the assistant works similarly to the one presented in Subsect. 3.3. The intent of the user is identified and the appropriate entities are extracted from the query. In the presented example, the intent is to get a recommendation and the entity region is Gorenjska. The assistant responds with two lists, the first is a list of potentially interesting places and the second is a list of sights that might be of interest to the user. The user can select one of the presented options by clicking on the interactive buttons or write a new query. The system provides a short description of the selected sight and again lists all possible actions linked to the sight. As before, the user can click

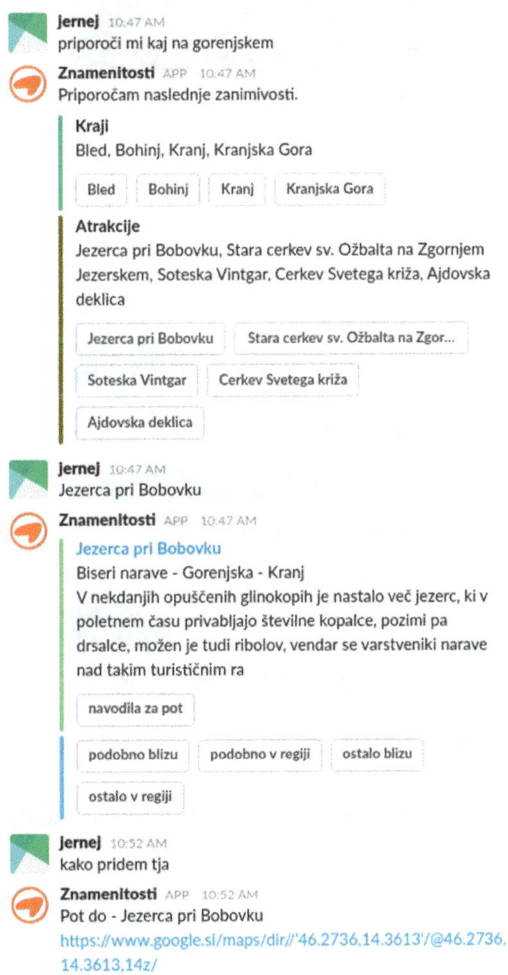

Fig. 5. Part of the communication flow with the virtual assistant.

on one of the buttons or write a new query. In the provided example, the path to the sight is computed and presented in the form of a link to Google Maps.

Figure 6 presents an example of a conversation in the Messenger interface. The user searched for the Tromostovje sight (a bridge in Ljubljana). He then wants the system to add the sight to his bookmarks. Next, the user wants the system to list all his bookmarks. Finally, he instructs the system to plan a trip based on the sights present in the list. The system collects the items and sends a request to the external service eTurist (tour planner) through the API. eTurist computes the shortest path between all items, considering all limitations (transportation method, time, lunch, budget, etc.), recommends and includes new sight along the way that might be of interest to the user, and send back the response in a JSON object that is used to construct an answer by the virtual assistant. Part of the response is also a graphical representation of the computed path in Google Maps, with marked locations and a short description for each sight.

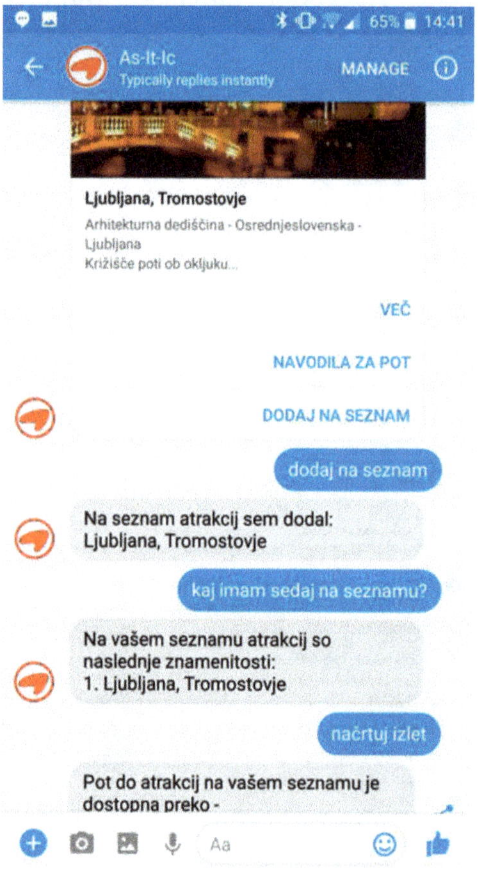

Fig. 6. The virtual assistant interface in the Messenger client.

4 Conclusions

This paper presents an overview of the various virtual assistants developed at our institutions for the domain of cultural heritage and sightseeing. We presented a service for the creation of virtual assistants, an advanced tool for virtual interfaces and three prototypes of virtual assistants providing functionalities and content for different domains. First, a web based virtual guide for museums that delivers information about specific items, groups of exhibits, and rooms inside the British museum, Art Institute of Chicago, and National Gallery of Australia. The assistant shows a short description for each query and displays the pertinent feed inside the museums from Google Street View. Second, a virtual assistant for delivering information about sights, cultural and natural heritage in Slovenia. The assistant implements an intelligent mechanism for the identification of intent and extraction of entities from the user query. This way it is possible to deliver specific and correct information to the user. Finally, we presented a comprehensive platform for smart tourism and sightseeing. The platform integrates chat functionalities in several interfaces, a NLU module, a virtual assistant to understand the requests of the user and deliver enriched answers, and is able to use several third party services to obtain specific information and create personalized trips.

All services and prototypes are available online and can be applied to other, different domains and languages.

References

1. Bickmore, T., Pfeifer, L., Schulman, D.: Relational agents improve engagement and learning in science museum visitors. In: Vilhjálmsson, H.H., Kopp, S., Marsella, S., Thórisson, K.R. (eds.) IVA 2011. LNCS (LNAI), vol. 6895, pp. 55–67. Springer, Heidelberg (2011). https://doi.org/10.1007/978-3-642-23974-8_7
2. Mathias, M., Moussa, A., Zhou, F., Torres-Moreno, et al.: Optimisation using natural language processing: personalized tour recommendation for museums. In: Proceedings of the 2014 Federated Conference on Computer Science and Information Systems, pp. 439–446 (2014)
3. Huang, M.Y., Liu, C.H., Lee, C.Y., Huang, Y.M.: Designing a personalized guide recommendation system to mitigate information overload in museum learning. Educ. Technol. Soc. **15**(4), 150–166 (2011)
4. Pechenizkiy, M., Calders, T.: A framework for guiding the museum tours personalization. In: Proceedings UM 2007 International Workshop on Personalization Enhanced Access to Cultural Heritage (CHIP) (2007)
5. Cimiano, P., Kopp, S.: Accessing the web of data through embodied virtual characters. Semant. Web **1**(1), 83–88 (2010)
6. Doswell, J.T.: PECA: pedagogical embodied conversational agents in mixed reality learning environments. In: AIED, p. 957 (2005)
7. Kuznar, D., Tavcar, A., Zupancic, J., Duguleana, M.: Virtual assistant platform. Informatica **40**(3), 285–290 (2016)
8. Graesser, A.C., et al.: AutoTutor: a tutor with dialogue in natural language. Behav. Res. Methods **36**(2), 180–192 (2004)

9. Rubin, V.L., Chen, Y., Thorimbert, L.M.: Artificially intelligent conversational agents in libraries. Libr. Hi Tech **28**(4), 496–522 (2010)
10. Xu, B., Pan, Z.G., Yang, H.W.: Agent-based model for intelligent shopping assistant and its application. In: The first Conference on Affective Computing and Intelligent Interaction, Beijing, Citeseer, pp. 306–311 (2003)
11. Eisman, E.M., Navarro, M., Castro, J.L.: A multi-agent conversational system with heterogeneous data sources access. Expert Syst. Appl. **53**, 172–191 (2016)
12. Čereković, Aleksandra, et al.: Implementing a multi-user tour guide system with an embodied conversational agent. In: Liu, J., Wu, J., Yao, Y., Nishida, T. (eds.) AMT 2009. LNCS, vol. 5820, pp. 7–18. Springer, Heidelberg (2009). https://doi.org/10.1007/978-3-642-04875-3_7
13. Project Asistent - virtual assistant for municipalities. http://www.projekt-asistent.si/. Accessed 26 Apr 2018
14. The Whoosh Library. http://whoosh.readthedocs.io/en/latest/intro.html. Accessed 26 Apr 2018
15. Cvetkovic, B., et al.: e-turist: an intelligent personalised trip guide. Informatica **40**(4), 447 (2016)

Author Index

www.ingramcontent.com/pod-product-compliance
Lightning Source LLC
LaVergne TN
LVHW082152200926
848484LV00008B/2146